Towards a Critical Multicultural Literacy

Studies in the
Postmodern Theory of Education

Joe L. Kincheloe and Shirley R. Steinberg
General Editors

Vol. 50

PETER LANG
New York • Washington, D.C./Baltimore • Boston
Bern • Frankfurt am Main • Berlin • Vienna • Paris

Danny K. Weil

Towards a Critical Multicultural Literacy

Theory and Practice for Education for Liberation

PETER LANG

New York • Washington, D.C./Baltimore • Boston
Bern • Frankfurt am Main • Berlin • Vienna • Paris

Library of Congress Cataloging-in-Publication Data

Weil, Danny K.
Towards a critical multicultural literacy: theory and practice
for education for liberation / Danny K. Weil.
p. cm. — (Counterpoints; v. 50)
Includes bibliographical references.
1. Multicultural education—United States. 2. Critical thinking—Study
and teaching—United States. 3. Multiculturalism—United States.
4. Critical pedagogy—United States. I. Title. II. Series: Counterpoints
(New York, N.Y.); vol. 50.
LC1099.3.W44   370.117—dc21   97-5192
ISBN 0-8204-3731-X
ISSN 1058-1634

Die Deutsche Bibliothek-CIP-Einheitsaufnahme

Weil, Danny K.:
Towards a critical multicultural literacy: theory and practice for education for
liberation / Danny K. Weil. -New York; Washington, D.C./Baltimore; Boston;
Bern; Frankfurt am Main; Berlin; Vienna; Paris: Lang.
(Counterpoints; Vol. 50)
ISBN 0-8204-3731-X

Cover design by Andy Ruggirello.

The paper in this book meets the guidelines for permanence and durability
of the Committee on Production Guidelines for Book Longevity
of the Council of Library Resources.

© 1998 Peter Lang Publishing, Inc., New York

Printed in the United States of America.

Table of Contents

Acknowledgments

This book represents a milestone in the development of my thinking but is in no way definitive, for that would be violating the spirit of critical thought. It is the culmination of ruminations and struggles waged throughout the last twenty-five years of my life. I could never have accomplished this work without the help and love of my friend and wife, Holly Anderson. She both tolerated its creation and participated in its final development.

I would like to thank my editor for polishing and refining this work and making it intelligible to both myself and those wishing to read it. I would also like to thank the Union Institute and especially Dr. Leland Hall Sr. who aided, guided and encouraged me through the initial stages of the development of this book.

I could not proceed with any further acknowledgments without thanking the people of Latin America and especially the people of Nicaragua for contributing to the person that I have become today. From the struggles of the Nicaraguan people I learned a valuable lesson—that humility and courage can combine with vision and wisdom to form a struggle for humanity that knows no boundaries and recognizes no limitations. This tiny nation of three million people stands as a testimony to all of us concerned with social justice and freedom as to what love, hope and compassionate struggle can acquire and has inspired me to understand within my lifetime, that revolutionary fervor must be forged within a realistic vision of hope and possibility for the human being; a vision and hope for a new humanity and a new human being equipped with the critical capacities, passions and sensibilities to further the journey of liberation.

And finally, no book could have been conceived or written without the ideas and lives of my second grade students at 122nd Street Elementary School in Los Angeles, California. They showed me that imagination and inquiry wedded to compassion and a search for authenticity can transform the world and those in it. For this, I am forever grateful; for they taught me what it means to be a human being and by so doing, taught me the greatest lesson anyone could ever learn.

PART 1

Introduction

Reasoning Multiculturally

The paradox of education is precisely this—that as one begins to become conscious one begins to examine the society in which he is being educated. The purpose of education, finally, is to create in a person the ability to look at the world for himself; to make his own decisions, to say to himself this is black or this is white, to decide for himself whether there is a God in heaven or not. To ask questions of the universe, and even to learn to live with those questions, is the way he achieves his own identity. But no society is really anxious to have that sort of person around. What societies really, ideally, want is a citizenry which will simply obey the rules of society. If a society succeeds in this, it is about to perish. The obligation of anyone who thinks of himself as responsible is to examine society and try to change it and fight it—no matter at what risk. This is the only hope society has. This is the only way societies change.

—James Baldwin
"A Talk to Teachers," (1988)

Making healthy personal and political choices within a complex world leads to a productive and happy democratic life, and our ability to make healthy choices requires a reconceptualizing of life in ways that promote social and self empowerment through independent thought, reflection, and self-examination. This intellectual and emotional empowerment allows us to authorize and validate our lives precisely because our decisions become the product of our own critical thinking. To be knowledgeable, fair-minded, and democratic citizens in tomorrow's world, students must understand the conceptions of various culturally informed points of view within both American and global society. They must understand, as well, the logic of thinking that fuels these culturally informed points of view: the purposes for their reasoning, the questions or problems they must confront, the empirical dimension of their thought, the concepts they use, the assumptions upon which their inferences rest, the consequences of their thought, and their frames of reference.

Students and teachers must, in short, expose and then rupture the structure of oppression and domination evident throughout daily life in the interest of embracing a common humanity. Furthermore, students must engage in a critical historical and contemporary analysis and evaluation of culturally informed points of view, understanding that they too have a culturally informed logic to their thinking. Understanding the logic of their own thinking relative to the logic of other points of view helps students engage in transformative metacognition, placing them in a position to become active agents in the construction of knowledge, and thoughtful consumers of social, economic, political, historical and personal life. For Brazilian educator Paulo Freire (1985), transformative metacognition is a primary disposition of mind achievable only through an earnest commitment and responsibility to rational self-criticism:

> The crux here, I believe, is that I must be constantly open to criticism and sustain my curiosity, always ready for revision based on the results of my future experience and that of others. And in turn, those who put my experience into practice must strive to recreate it and also rethink my thinking (p.11).

It becomes essential to define the concept of "culture" which is a task reasoning minds would respectfully approach differently. As Amin (1989) noted,

> There is no generally accepted definition of the domain of culture, for the definition depends on the underlying theory of social dynamics that one adopts. For this reason, depending on whether the goal is to discover the common dynamics of the social evolution of all peoples, or whether, on the contrary, this search is abandoned, the emphasis will be placed either on the characteristics that are analogous and common to the various cultures, or on the particular and the specific (p. 6).

Simple recognition that distinct cultures exist in the world really constitutes only an ontological statement that brings one no closer to capturing the common and diverse ethos of humanity, or answering and posing questions that can coalesce a common unity in the preservation of diverse humanity. My own hypothesis is that culture must be defined much more broadly than the fragmented singularity that pervades much educational and social theory. Singular definitions of culture invite over-generalizations, oversimplifications, and dangerous opportunities for stereotyping and prejudice. For example as Amin asked rhetorically,

Is it possible to speak today of a European culture encompassing the West as a whole, in spite of linguistic differences? If the answer is yes should the European culture also include Eastern Europe, in spite of its different political and social regime; Latin America, in spite of its underdevelopment; or Japan, in spite of its non-European historical roots? Is it possible to think of a single culture encompassing the Arab or Arab-Islamic world, or Sub-Saharan Africa, or India? Or must these broad categories be abandoned in favor of observing the specificities of their component sub-groups? But then where does one draw the line in the unending divisions and subdivisions of provincial singularity? And what is the pertinence of the differences observed; what capacity do they have for explaining social change? (p. 7).

Amin asks the questions that fail to appear in much of the discourse on culture. By asking what capacity our understanding of cultural differences has to enhance and explain social change, Amin builds on his earlier statement that it depends on the interest of the inquirer and the goal of the social theory one adopts. If we are to concentrate on cultural differences at the expense of human commonality, our definitions of culture will be singular. If, however, our interest in diversity is motivated by and relative to the common characteristics we hold as human beings—the subtle dialectical conditions of people in and with the world—our definition will be broad and committed to an understanding and respect for diversity in light of common humanity.

This search for definition by no means requires an attempt at transcending cultural difference; rather it requires a serious striving at contextualizing difference historically. Explaining the motor of social development—explaining the relationship between actions, decisions, and behaviors of community members—requires an understanding of the historical social production and reproduction of diverse societies. Culture must be understood in communication with the specific set of economic relations that form a given society at a given time in history. Culture is evolutionary and reflects forces both within and beyond its control.

For purposes of theoretical inquiry, I define culture broadly, in the interest of diversity and humanity, as the unique historical manner by which diverse groups of human beings organize and actualize their physical and mental lives in dialectical confrontation with biological survival, oppression, power, resistance, and the struggle for human dignity, self-determination and fulfillment. This definition necessarily includes discourses and narratives regarding gender, race, age, sexual preference, and socio-economic class, or what I refer to here as "disenfranchised narratives." Giroux (1988) has defined culture similarly:

We are using the term "culture" as the distinctive ways in which a social group
lives out and makes sense of its "given" circumstances and conditions of life
(p. 132).

This broad definition does not, however, ignore the notion of "the
dominant culture," the peculiar and specific sets of cultural relationships distinctive to modern capitalist society. On the contrary, in agree-
ment with the Frankfurt School and its theoretical adherents, I acknowledge dominant culture as a central site for the production and
transformation of historical experience. Yet unlike traditional Marxist
theory, which established culture as a mere reflex of economic productive relations and forces and reduced issues of subjectivity, gender,
sexuality, race, and gender preference to the deterministic logic of
scientific economics, the definition of dominant culture I use here recognizes that modern capitalist society has developed both technical
capabilities and more complex ideological vehicles of administration,
socialization, and control that perpetuates its influence throughout a
host of cultural institutions including churches, schools, family, play,
and mass media. Control, power, and the ideological supremacy of
those who exercise authority no longer require the brute physical force
imposed by the State (although the utilitarianism of force remains widely
acknowledged); rather this supremacy finds ideological expression and
hegemony within all cultural spheres both private and public.

In fact, within modern capitalist society, culture itself has been reified
and commodified. For the Frankfurt School this commodification meant
the negation of critical thought itself, as covetous consumerism became the *raison d'etre* of modern capitalist life. Yet although the culture of modern consumerism now penetrates everyday life in ways not
heretofore experienced by citizens of capitalist economies, it must be
understood as a terrain for both power and conflict—that is, a dialectical struggle between dominant culture and secondary or disenfranchised narratives, or what Giroux (1985) called "subordinate cultures"
(p. 163). Social relationships themselves suffer a peculiar debasement
owing to this commodification as they become increasingly mediated
by dominant ideology, defined needs, and manufactured wants and
desires. The cultural realm has been annexed to the prevailing modes
of economic production. According to Adorno and Horkheimer (1972),

Amusement under late capitalism is the prolongation of work. It is sought
after as an escape from the mechanized work process, and to recruit strength
in order to be able to cope with it again. But at the same time mechanization
has such power over a man's leisure and happiness and so profoundly deter-

mines the manufacture of amusement goods, that his experiences are after-images of the work process itself. The ostensible content is merely a faded background; what sinks in is an automatic succession of standardized operations. (p. 56)

The Frankfurt School's analysis and insight are essential to any understanding of the role of schooling, the character of texts and their dominant discourse, and the need to repatriate critical social discourse. For this reason, I use "culture" broadly to describe both the unique historical manner by which human beings make sense of their lives, and particularly and specifically to describe the dominant prevailing market ideology that attempts to reduce to currency the material and psychological life of both the public and private sphere.

Cultural encapsulation and ethnocentricity (the belief in the inherent superiority of one's own group or culture) bar the achievement of intellectual character or human freedom in our growing pluralistic society precisely because they limit our ability to critique our own thinking. Much of what we learn to believe uncritically derives from social structures or the culture of power—television, movies, popular culture, parents, friends, teachers, and the myriad socio-political institutions that govern our lives. This "associational" (or borrowed) thinking generally escapes action, yet it frequently governs what we decide to believe and what we do. As associational thinking substitutes for critical reflective thinking, the uncritical mind looks for stereotypes and simplistic categories in which to file people, places, and concepts. This unquestioned "associational thinking" lends itself to self-delusion, propagandistic appeals, and authoritarian manipulation as uncritical associational thinkers customarily fall prey to political and social demagoguery (Reich, 1946; Milgram, 1974). Without the benefit of critical reasoning within and about diverse cultural points of view, the human mind accepts internalized cultural stereotypes, falsehoods, prejudices, and biases, and becomes disinclined to help transform the world lived in and with others. Unable to experience itself in tune with reality, the undiscriminating human mind is incapable of critical analysis and metacognition. Choices fall away as the world perspective narrows, as does an ability to arrive at reasoned judgment about what to choose, what to do, or what to believe. Devoid of this ability, the uncritical human mind cannot participate fully and wisely in personal and democratic life and can unwittingly encourage illegitimate cultural domination and oppression. For this reason it is important to keep in mind the sentiment Freire (1985) advanced:

> The learners must discover the reasons behind many of their attitudes toward
> cultural reality and thus confront cultural reality in a new way (p. 54).

This "new way" must incorporate a recognition of the value of critical transformative metacognition accomplished through a committed rational cultural critique. Simultaneously, a faith in and enthusiasm for engaging in critical fair-minded reasoning within multiple perspectives regarding complicated personal and social issues must take hold.

As we prepare to enter into the next century equipped with countless technological achievements, innovations, and gadgets, the "social space" that separates us continues to widen. The technological prowess so assiduously acquired and applauded in this century pales when juxtaposed to the social, cultural, and economic deprivations most world citizens face. Cultural, racial, and sexual intolerance builds at alarming rates with dire political and social consequences. Cultural conflicts and tensions open social, political, and religious chasms between Serbs and Croats in Yugoslavia recalling the recursors of the genocide in Hitler's Germany. They have caused nationalistic disintegration in the former Soviet Union; increased and legitimized racial hatred and violence among right-wing hate groups in Germany (Lawday 1991); contributed to a growing cultural intolerance and sociocentric chauvinism that infect French politics; and provided a forum for racism, homophobia, and sexism here at home.

A glance at prosperous Western Germany reveals the country attracted 2.5 million immigrants between 1988 and 1990, absorbing them at twice the per capita pace that the United States did during the heyday of Ellis Island in the early 1900s. The recent epidemic of reactionary parties and such fascist elements as "skin heads" and associated crimes against foreigners there, suggests the dangers in correlating education with the capital and goods of the *free market* as opposed to the emotional and intellectual requirements of humanity. While western capitalist economies herald Germany's manufacturing and industrial recovery and power and the apparent rapport between its managerial and working classes, they often fail to denounce the atrocious stage of German social relations.

Germany, France, Britain, and Italy received a million asylum-seekers between 1989 and1991 (Lawday 1992). Yet, although the notorious Berlin wall tumbled before political, economic, and social demands for freedom and equality, new walls of hate and prejudice now rise. The economically and politically oppressed, from Romania to Sri Lanka, move through Europe in masses, meeting as they go with the messengers of hatred and bigotry. Recent opinion polls among German, French, and Italian voters suggest that one out of three agrees with the xenophobic and ethnocentric rhetoric of the new nationalism and its "war on immigration" (Lawday et al. 1992).

The neo-Nazi racists attacks tend, of course, to single out the poor and often war-weary asylum seekers from Africa, Asia, and Eastern Europe. According to Norman Birnbaum (1993),

> There were 1500 acts of right-wing violence in 1991 and more than 2200 in 1992—with seventeen dead, ten of them German. Among the German dead were a person who was lynched after declaring that Hitler was a criminal, five homeless men, and a handicapped person. No comment was made on the last incident by the German judge who, shortly before, had ruled that vacationers were entitled to refunds for having to endure the sight of handicapped people at their seaside hotel. Nazi ideas of "life unfit for life," one gathers, are still around (p. 441).

The reaction of Europe governments has been alarming. Instead of combatting this sociocentrism and racism with critical reason and political fortitude, the smug and the sluggish political parties prefer to restrain the constitutional rights of asylum seekers, thereby capitulating to the demands of the neo-fascists and their sociocentric agenda. In fact, Helmut Kohl, the Chancellor of Germany himself, commented in face of the quickening violence that "the increasing flood of asylum seekers is the most important domestic issue next to monetary stability" (Lawday et al. 1992). *Ordnung muss sein*: Order must be restored. Rather than publicly condemn the actions of virulent skinheads and xenophobic neo-nazi thugs who burn hostels and kill immigrants and instead encourage a political debate within the country, the political leadership of post-Cold War Germany has embarked on its familiar path of capitulation and deference.

France, like Germany, worries about losing its "French heritage" to increasing immigration. France now has four million registered immigrants, some 20 percent fewer than Germany. But the majority comes from Muslim North Africa. Thus they are easily discernible people of color. A 1991 *Le Figaro* poll found that 52 percent of the French people opposed new immigration and 77 percent favored expelling illegal immigrants. These racist response appear to be buoyed by so-called socialists like Prime minister Edith Cresson, who proposed contracting airplanes to return illegals to Africa (Lawday et al. 1992). Italy, too, adopts racist ideology as Albanian refugees and Africans enter in increasing numbers.

The immigration trends of the 1980s have left a significant imprint on the social fabric of American life as well. Our recently arriving immigrants continue to be mainly Asian or Latin American, many displaced by the secret and dirty wars of the 1960s, '70s, and '80s, others by poverty or political subjugation. They are disproportionately young, poor, and ill-prepared for school (Kellog 1988). Many suffer life in refugee camps before attempting the transition to a new culture (Olsen, 1988). They often face discrimination, physical and psychological hostility, and unjust governmental practices here in America. Many of the young find themselves distinct from their classmates, their experiences, language, and cultural framework grounded in non-Western ideology and values.

Unfortunately, the personal and material reality of American life includes a great deal of cultural intolerance. A glimpse at our own American social fabric reveals evidence of heightened racism and sociocentricity or "group thinking," as we witness incidents like the Bensonhurst killings in New York, the Rodney King beating, the senseless homophobic beating and killing of a homosexual sailor, racist reactions to the Los Angeles rebellion, the rise in church and synagogue desecrations, appeals to "America First" manifested in increased attacks on immigrants, the rabid anti-feminism of the "new right," the political legitimacy of fascism in the legitimization of David Duke, and the countless daily examples of socio-centric and racist ideology that stain the American social, political, and intellectual tapestry.

All of these crimes and incivilities exemplify the challenges to be faced and the hostility to be overcome if we are to unite, cast off the straightjacket of oppression, and live harmoniously in a pluralistic society as diverse human beings. While we witness the world tumble through continual transformations, a postmodern generation grows up in this society unprepared to engage in rational production but more important, unprepared for the rigorous requirements of citizenship, the demands of democracy, the exigencies of family responsibilities, and the personal and social need for competent and rational decision making. As much as this specter poses a dreadful crisis for American education, it signifies a greater crisis for American postmodern life.

The new pluralism of the 1990s coupled with the past struggles of the 1960s requires us to reconstruct pedagogical demands to meet the needs of diverse populations while encouraging reasoning within multiple perspectives in the interest of metacognition; personal, cultural, social development; and the struggle against oppression and discrimination. We can do this only if we include within the curriculum those economic and subjective points of view, both historical and contemporary, that represent values and ideals concerning life different and distinct from traditional Western values. Far from undermining Western values, as some fear, this broadening perspective complements them with others in the service of rational cultural critique so as to create opportunities for critical dialogue and relevant dialectical reasoning in the interest of transformation and human liberation.

This book proposes what I call a "critical multicultural literacy"—a commitment to a pedagogy of liberation and human reason. A critical multicultural literacy implies a pledge to recognize the relationship between theory and practice in pedagogy aimed at constructively creating a praxis that promotes dialoguing, analyzing, evaluating, and synthesizing issues of relevant historical and contemporary multicultural concerns. One should think of critical multicultural literacy as citizenship or character education, precisely because it concerns itself with issues of power, domination, authoritarianism, and the diversity of human beings and their decisions about how to act, think, and behave with others. These concerns are important components of democratic life and unquestionably a pluralistic democracy cannot survive without critically analyzing and evaluating them.

Although diversity appreciation has been promoted by such think tanks as the Hudson Institute and its publication *Work 2000*, as well as in the works of management seminar consultant and author R. Roosevelt Thomas, who see's diversity as strategic in the training of "human capital" and productivity, labor placement and productivity make poor motivators for addressing issues of diversity, domination, the hidden curriculum within the schools, educational equity, and multiculturalism. The needs of humanity, how we behave toward and with each other in the accomplishment of human life, are essential projects that go beyond the organizational structures we implement. Issues of diversity cannot be reduced to instrumentalist requirements of the corporate world. For this reason, I see a critical multicultural literacy wedded to the necessities of the human being, not to the exigencies of the so-called free market. W. E. B. Du Bois' 1930 comment that "the object of education is not to make men carpenters, but carpenters men" applies today as we attempt critically to construct a curriculum in the service of humanity.

A critical multicultural literacy argues that in a pluralistic society education should affirm and encourage the quest for self-examination through social transformation by creating relevant problem-posing activities that allow students to confront in their reasoning the challenges the diversity of everyday life offer. According to Banks (1991),

> Citizenship education in a multicultural society must have as an important goal helping all students, including white mainstream students, to develop the knowledge, attitudes, and skills needed not only to participate in, but also to help transform and reconstruct society. Problems such as racism, sexism, poverty, and inequality are widespread within U.S. society and permeate many of the nation's institutions, such as the workforce, the courts, and the schools. To educate future citizens to fit into and not to transform society will result in the perpetuation and escalation of these problems, including the widening gap between the rich and the poor, racial conflict and tension, and the growing number of people who are victims of poverty and homelessness (pp. 32–35).

Without ample opportunities for students of all colors, genders, social classes, and races to participate in a meaningful environment of inquiry and critical thinking, these citizenship skills will languish. This threat explains why the subjects Banks addressed—homelessness, poverty, and racism, and I would add physical disability, gender inequality, homophobia, and social class—should constitute the object of education.

Without an understanding of the material and psychological constraints, problems, or questions at issue we face as diverse human beings, we can expect no lessening of cultural intolerance or opportunities for personal and social transformation. Furthermore, students need critical opportunities to see their own cultures as others see them, thereby allowing them to reflect on their own cultural beliefs, decisions, and actions. This reflection tends to reduce uncritical allegiance to one cultural group or another, and to encourage insightful reasoning that extends beyond narrowly defined self-interests. Understanding diversity is to understand diversity of thought, action, and conditions so as to challenge social and institutional power structures. It is to understand the logic of thinking, from the point of view of gender groups, gays and lesbians, the aged, the disabled, newly arriving immigrants, people of color, and economically disadvantaged social classes.

Furthermore, by understanding the logic of oppression and domination, students can move beyond the perpetuation and reproduction of these social forms of domination to engage in fair-minded critical thinking with the goal of personal and social freedom. By engaging in self-critical cultural examination and analysis, students can free themselves from unexamined cultural biases and prejudices and become transformative individuals, while at the same time significantly enhancing and expanding their abilities to think and act fair-mindedly and critically about and respond to other culturally diverse viewpoints on historical and contemporary reality. Confronting contemporary and historical reality critically arouses in students an interest in examining various cultural assumptions that inform their own beliefs relative to the cultural assumptions that inform beliefs from diverse cultural backgrounds. Furthermore, the reflective mind can reason out the origins and nature of its uncritical thought and thus more fully and wisely participate in and transform a world shared with others. With increased appreciation and knowledge of diversity, students have an opportunity to become not just in the world but with the world.

For this reason, I suggest that reasoning multiculturally is a dialectical process of becoming human. It is to gain an insight into one's self and others through historical and cultural understanding, while at the same time developing an insight into history and culture through subjective self. The development of critical consciousness on the part of our students promises opportunities for social praxis and transformation that challenge the social structures from which many, internalized associational assumptions and myths derive their origins. Pronounced and defined in these terms, a multicultural literacy is a literacy in the interest of personal and social sovereignty and, as such, remains education for all (Parekh, 1986).

Chapter 1

Constructing a Critical Multicultural Curriculum

> That we have a separate personal consciousness is not denied, but it is not humanity. The human consciousness is collective . . . We are not separate creatures at all.
>
> —Charlotte Gilman

Consider these compelling questions that underlie the construction of a pedagogy that confronts cultural intolerance, prejudice, domination, authority, and oppression: How do we foster a critical multicultural education that transcends the limited parameters of current educational theory and practice? and How do we make it critical in such a way that it is relevant and reflective so as to make it liberatory and transformative, both objectively in social reality and subjectively in the life of the mind? To address these issues, we must examine critically that which poses as multicultural education, that which portends to stand in opposition to multicultural education, and the various critical pedagogical theories and critical thinking theories of education. Or in other words, we must analyze both voices of emancipation and voices of tradition. In this way, the language of critique enhances the possibility of promise.

Multiculturalism

The roots of what is currently termed the "multicultural movement" in education originated in the radical challenges put forth by progressive forces in the 1960s and 1970s. The movement toward a multicultural curriculum originated largely from such of America's culturally subjugated and marginalized, as African-Americans, Mexican-Americans, Native-Americans, and women. These groups have historically taken the lead in pursuing the inclusion of ethnic studies programs at the university and K-12 levels. In the 1960s, multicultural proponents criticized schooling for its restrictive admission practices regarding people of color; they condemned the academic establishment for its subservience to business interests; they reprimanded schooling for its racist, sexist, and culturally biased curriculum; they deplored hiring practices for women and minorities; they exposed the pernicious practice of tracking; they attacked the stodgy condescending curriculum with its weak numbers of neutrality; and they labored to achieve such beneficial entitlement programs as bilingual education and Title VII-mandated educational programs.

These educational movements and struggles of the 1960s and 70s produced a new language of pedagogical critique. With these critiques of schooling came a call for the abolition of inequality in school financing and for a commitment to federal funding for educational programs. Multiculturalists have also traditionally argued that a lack of understanding and acceptance of racial difference is a problem for both teachers and students (Stent, 1973), and the multicultural educational community demanded that classrooms add the issues of prejudice and discrimination to the curriculum. Multicultural theorists advise that rather than seeking to melt away cultural differences within our pluralistic society, schools should celebrate these differences in an atmosphere of inquiry. Accordingly, schools should focus on the cultural enrichment of all students though programs aimed at the preservation and extension of cultural pluralism. They see cultural diversity as a valuable resource to be recognized, preserved, and extended, and they suggest that only by confronting racism and prejudice can we convey an understanding of and appreciation for human dignity.

Perhaps one of the chief problems with the traditional view of multicultural education has been its overemphasis on and concern with issues of assimilation and separatism as they relate to racial diversity. Only recently has a new sociology of multicultural education argued that multicultural diversity appreciation should be extended to issues of sexual preference, sexism, social class, and physical handicaps. Another problem associated with some theoretical practices of multicultural education is a propensity to glorify and romanticize a particular culture or point of view, while uncritically wedding frames of reference to cultural allegiances and self-serving sociocentric thinking at the expense of reflective self-criticism. Any multicultural approach that advocates a "centric approach" to the study of contemporary or historical reality keeps students from gaining insights into their often sociocentric thinking about issues of diversity. Multicultural approaches to education that encourage self-examination, self-awareness, cultural critiques, and personal growth through an identification with and an understanding of one's own culture or heritage represent an authentic pedagogical movement toward egalitarianism and human fair-mindedness in educational discourse and action. On the other hand, inculcating a view of the world from only one cultural point of view promotes sophistical narrow-minded thinking and is pedagogically dishonest. To understand one's history and narrative "broadly and fair-mindedly" in the context of human reality is clearly an advantage; to do so "narrowly and sophistically" at the expense of assuming similar or disparate cultural points of view is just as clearly a disadvantage.

The Entrepreneurial Eurocentric and Male-dominated Curriculum

Conservative apologists for entrepreneurial and conformist Eurocentric and andocentric curricula argue that multiculturalism poses a threat to American democracy, American values, and the American economic system. They equate multiculturalism with separatism and preferential treatment and accuse many multicultural proponents of cultural imperialism. They argue that the values of Western society, conveniently enough including its economic "free market" values, should be taught to all students regardless of cultural background. DeSouza (1991) goes so far as to complain that

> Unfortunately the basic ingredients of what E. D. Hirsch terms "cultural literacy" are by no means uniformly transmitted in American high schools, nor are regular intellectual habits of concentration and discipline (pp. 232–233).

Traditionally, this school of thought views knowledge as analogous to a transmittable infectious disease. They welcome the continuation of power relations and domination as they appear in majoritarian renderings of historical and contemporary reality. They espouse universal principles of education rooted in instrumentalism, power, and the ethos of technocratic rationality supported by entrepreneurial Western values. For them, schooling is simply a means to an end. For them, ideal schooling takes place at vast instructional sites where students receive training in the dominant reified modes of discourse, ideology, and power relations designed to meet the regimented necessities of market forces. Knowledge is less an accumulation of insight generated by human minds than reified wisdom passed on in ritual form from generation to generation. Unearthing ideas of multiculturalism or diversity would threaten the very ethos of this rationality and interfere with the ideological reproduction of daily market-driven life.

When a curriculum is centered within the narrative of the dominant perspective, it serves to promote one historical and contemporary view of the world at the expense of subordinated renderings, or what I call "disenfranchised narratives". Such a curriculum is disingenuous and does nothing to challenge the internalized cultural myths children often absorb as they carry on their daily lives. One of the implications of this Eurocentric colonization of thought is reinforced sociocentricity, or the belief in the superiority of one's culture at the expense of another. As a result, the Eurocentric point of view becomes the ideological protector of the material conditions of cultural intolerance and domination. It also promotes the idea of the significant us and the in significant others, which has so viciously and revisionistically corrupted contemporary life and history by painting an idealistic portrait of the conquerors at the expense of the conquered.

The New School of Radical Pedagogical Theory

A new debate now flourishes among a new school of radical pedagogical theory and practice seeking to interpret schooling as more than the familiar site of instruction. These theorists in general agree that educational sites are part of the philosophical contrivance designed to ensure that the capitalist system sustains itself. Yet these new school proponents focus more on the role of schooling in community life and culture, correctly arguing that schooling and education within society amounts to a struggle among differentially empowered cultural and economic groups. Others, most notably Paulo Freire and Henry Giroux, while generally agreeing with radical philosophies of education, argue that both traditional and radical positions fail to provide an adequate basis for the development of an authentic radical pedagogy that seeks to develop such fundamental classifications as subjectivity and the role of self, mediation between objective reality and subjective life, class, struggle, and personal and social emancipation (Giroux 1988). Furthermore, these critical pedagogues contend that neo-Marxist notions of education have been either too idealistic or too structuralistic—clinging to the metaphor of schooling sites as prisons, or factories, or Tayloristic assembly lines for the construction of false consciousness in the interests of capital domination and the perpetuation of inequality. For them, the result is alienating and disabling pessimism revealing itself materially in a rejection of pedagogical struggle and praxis and a capitulation to despair. Furthermore, for educators like Freire and Giroux, an examination of how domination extends into everyday life and the development of a language of pedagogical possibility that can confront the socialization of domination and the domination of socialization advance of a liberatory notion of pedagogical theory and praxis.

The Critical Thinking Movement

Beside these traditional and radical discourses of pedagogy travels a recent tendency among many educators to call for a shift from the current theory and practice within schooling based on rote memorization and regurgitation of material, to a critically reflective practice based on Socratic learning. Within this movement they suggest, rationality and empathetic reasoning become essential for global development both socially and economically. Furthermore, adherents to this "critical thinking movement" argue that a new conception of self-identity, both individually and collectively, as well as a new practical sense of the value of self-disciplined open-minded thought, is crucial to strengthening and maintaining democratic life (Paul 1990). The pedagogical premise of the critical thinking movement holds that irrational human reasoning is responsible for the deprivations of daily life and the human condition. The movement advocates the development of critical thinking curricula with clearly enunciated practical pedagogical principles and strategies that include both cognitive and affective domains, and it urges the inclusion or "infusion" of these strategies and principles within the curriculum and classroom life.

Developing a New Theory of Education for Liberation

In this book, I suggest that all these positions are somewhat remiss in providing an adequate basis for developing an emancipatory theory of pedagogy that confronts issues of sociocentricity, power, domination, prejudice, oppression, diversity, and the common struggle for human dignity. Traditional theory fails because as radical proponents of pedagogy argue, by virtue of its pathology, it ignores or misunderstands the role of education and its relationship to the larger society. Furthermore, it is mired in entrepreneurial Eurocentric and andocentric notions of historical and contemporary reality and can, therefore, do little to encourage fair-minded critical thinking.

New school or radical pedagogical theorists, while providing a unique and critical understanding of the role of schooling, have been less than helpful in devising actual practical pedagogical strategies one can adapt to classroom life (The exception is Paulo Freire, who developed a radical pedagogical method when working with illiterate peasants in South and Central America). The theoretical tractates have provided improvements over theoretical traditions, but by and large they fail to elucidate examples of an actual pedagogy constructed by teachers for purposes of interrogating material and psychological reality—that is, a practical hands-on pedagogy that confronts domination, authority, and the historical struggle for freedom within the objective and subjective life of students. This is especially true as it pertains to elementary and middle schools. Despite the new-school insistence on the struggle for social emancipation and personal freedom, one looks in vain for answers to such essential questions as these five:

(1) How does one construct a critical problem-posing pedagogy in first grade?
(2) What materials, resources, and themes should constitute the curriculum?
(3) How can teachers of young children provide critical reasoning opportunities using principles and strategies that help elucidate and abolish forms of oppression and racism?
(4) Should the dominant disciplines continue to guide the theory and practice of critical discourse?
(5) If not, how can we continue to teach students the "skills" they need while at the same time herald critical discourse and reflection?

Ignoring nuts-and-bolts questions like these, critical pedagogues have yet to provide a guiding praxis for education.

Critical thinking pedagogues, by contrast, have developed a useful compendium of principles and strategies for constructing a critical thinking curriculum. They have been less successful in understanding education vis-à-vis issues of domination, authority, power, oppression, multiculturalism, and liberation. Their silence on what critical examination and discourse should entail serves to perpetuate the notion that education is a politically neutral act. In neglecting to confront issues of power, domination, oppression, and common forms of human struggle for dignity and sovereignty, critical thinking pedagogues fail to challenge unjust social practices. Nor have many critical thinking proponents confronted issues of educational equity and the pernicious denial of critical thinking opportunities for many students as a result of their race, class, gender, or physical limitations.

Moreover, they infrequently concern themselves with such issues as parent involvement, teacher attitudes, the politics of teacher organizations and unions, lack of adequate school funding, work-place democracy and school restructuring, overcrowded classes, deteriorating school structures, lack of educational resources, authoritarianism and administrative practices, or multilingualism. If critical thinking activities are to flourish at local school sites, we should begin to address more than just the subjective aspects of schooling, but the material conditions of schooling that forge the parameters for subjective thought. The process of articulating, promulgating, and assuring that critical thinking environments and opportunities exist for all students requires an active commitment to confronting actual material inequities.

Finally, many critical thinking educators actually deny that culture plays a role in developing a frame of reference or point of view, or simplistically reduce culture to mere racial differences. This is a sadly reductionist approach and represents an elementary attempt to transcend the concept of culture without critically understanding its logic. Furthermore, adopting this position avoids the need to identify and resist the limitations imposed by the current material conditions of educational production and consumption. Advocates of this position fail to confront the educational needs of the traditionally voiceless among our students who have largely been denied the skills, knowledge, and modes of inquiry that would allow them critically to examine their own subjectivity and the role society has played in the development of this subjectivity. For what I refer to as the "disenfranchised narratives" of working-class students, women, African-Americans, and other minorities who seek to affirm their own particular history and ennoble the cultural experiences that form the stories of their daily lives, this oversight amounts to indurate dismissal. Such a rejection allows no pedagogical basis or opportunity to examine cultural beliefs in light of diversity or the historical and contemporary logic of human oppression and domination; thus, it is non-transformative, non-liberatory, and unedifying.

Citizenship, conscious life in a democratic society, requires individuals willing and able to engage in self-conscious critiques aimed at achieving personal and social transformation. Expanded personal, cultural, and historical understanding spurs the development of fair-minded intelligence—as opposed to narrow-minded intelligence—and personal, and social transformation—in contrast to unconscious affirmation and intellectual stagnation. The ability to exercise reciprocity (imaginatively to place oneself in the "shoes" of others of diverse thought, to consider strengths and weaknesses of opposing cultural and political points of view, and to overcome egocentric tendencies to wed oneself uncritically to one belief or another without the benefit of self-examination and critical analysis) is to confront prejudice and discrimination fair-mindedly and critically. Thus, willing and capable individuals must become more than just loyalists or patriots; they must become fair-minded critical thinkers and conscious actors in personal and social transformation. They must become protagonists of the negation in the interest of possibility.

This project, however, demands both attitudinal changes, or shifts in the values and dispositions of the mind, and cognitive changes, in the adoption and use of critical analysis. The values and dispositions of the reasoning mind require active involvement in emancipation through confrontation, while the principles and strategies of critical thinking continually refine and hone intellectual abilities in the service of these values and dispositions. If, as Maxine Greene (1988) stated, "To be a citizen of the free world means having the capacity to choose" (p. 19), then we must ask ourselves how we arrived at our conclusions and choices, on what assumptions we based our inferences, what evidence we have to support our beliefs, and what other points of view inform the bank of data and evidence we used to support our assumptions and consequent decisions and actions. These essential questions of humanity should take a prominent place in our personal and public dialogue. If we are to struggle against prejudicial dispositions and live together as diverse human beings, we must actively engage in dialogue about diversity, with an interest in developing fair-minded reasoning in the search for personal, social, and political transformation.

I argue here for a new notion of critical pedagogy, one that seeks to link the best features of multiculturalism, critical pedagogy, and critical thinking in the service of a "critical multicultural literacy." I intend to translate the insights and practical necessities of multiculturalism and critical pedagogy within curriculum and classroom life by embracing many of the principles and strategies the critical thinking movement has developed in the service of inquiry. I harness this inquiry to the search for a critical historical analysis and understanding of the connection between the economic organization and life of society, the material and subjective development of the individual, and transformations in the realm of the culture of power.

In short, I have set out to make critical pedagogy more educationally pragmatic and critical thinking more pedagogically political. The dialectical interfacing of multiculturalism, radical pedagogy, and critical pedagogy can produce an educational theory that challenges domination and oppression while providing practical political and pedagogical insights for educators and students of all grades. In offering a defensible idea of a critical multicultural literacy based on multiculturalism, critical pedagogy, and critical thinking, I will need to examine the critical thinking and critical pedagogy movements, respectively, and to analyze and examine traditionalist conservative Eurocentric and andocentric theories of schooling and education, as well as various well-intentioned yet ill conceived approaches to multicultural education that currently find voice in the politics of classroom life. This analysis and examination also requires a comparison of disparate points of view regarding the issue of multiculturalism.

Chapter 2

Critical Pedagogy

Let me say, with the risk of appearing ridiculous, that the true revolutionary is guided by strong feelings of love. It is impossible to think of an authentic revolutionary without this quality.

—Che Guevara
The Complete Bolivia Daries of
Che Guevara (1968)

Introduction

Throughout the 1970s and 1980s, the new critical pedagogy movement began to explore the relationship between culture and power, specifically as it translates into the everyday life of pedagogical theory and practice. Most notable in this movement have been Paulo Freire, Henry A. Giroux, Peter McClaren, Michelle Fine, Walter Feinberg, Philip Wexler, Herbert Gintis, Samuel Bowles, Stanley Aronowitz, bell hooks, Ira Schor, Peter Leonard, Donald Macedo, Tomaz Tadeu Da Silva, Cornel West, Carlos Alberto Torres, Colin Lankshear, Theresa Perry, James W. Fraser, and Michael Apple. These radical educational theorists managed to articulate a theory and practice of education that transcended the ideology of traditional educational theory and practice, and they provided a critique of traditional radical pedagogy whose adherents, they argued, remained trapped within the theoretical confines of domination that perceived schooling solely as a site for producing servile laborers and ideological apologists in the service of monopoly capitalism. For the "new school" of radical educators, this position offered only capitulation to despair and promised no pragmatic approaches to a positive restructuring schooling, curriculum, and classroom life. As Giroux (1989) noted

In spite of its insightful theoretical and political analyses of schooling, radical educational theory suffered from some serious flaws, the most significant being its failure to move beyond the language of critique and domination (p. 130).

These new-school radicals provide a language of schooling that goes beyond the critique of domination to one that encompasses possibility, hope, and compassionate liberation. They correctly believe that education should be a transformative activity aimed at self-production through an understanding of inequitable power and social relations, and they have articulated a defensible notion of schooling that intellectually captures and understands the relationship between politics and pedagogy in the service of transformative education. Challenging the myth that schools are units of democracy and social mobility, these theorists concluded that schools reproduce the logic of capital through material and psychological forms and ideologies of privilege and dependence that operate to define the lives of students from various class, ethnic, gender, and racial groups.

In their critique of traditional social theory, new-school radical theorists argue that traditional pedagogical theory fails to take the political nature of public schooling into account. They point to the suppression of critical dialogue surrounding domination, power, and knowledge. Freire (1985) commented on the implications of conceiving pedagogical practices as devoid of political implications:

> To think of education independent from the power that constitutes it, divorced from the concrete world where it is forged, leads us either to reduce it to a world of abstract values and ideals (which the pedagogue constructs inside his consciousness without even understanding the conditioning that makes him think this way), or to convert it to a repertoire of behavioral techniques, or to perceive it as a springboard for changing reality (p. 170).

This dialogue on domination finds suppression in the service of the capitalist relations of production, the socialization of dominant ideologies, and the interest of popular culture. Some perceive schooling, then, as an efficient method for social control and a site for social indoctrination and production.

In response to this reality, new-school social theorists propound the idea of the "hidden curriculum," arguing that school knowledge and practice are specific representations of the ascendant order that, far from politically and economically neutral, thrust their ideology upon students and teachers alike through a specific set of social relations performed within the classroom and aided by the instruments of multinational corporations and their dominant and self-serving textual representations of knowledge. For advocates of a critical pedagogy, a knowledge of the patterns and methods of behavior currently encouraged and rewarded in the classroom is essential for understanding how the social relations of production are perpetuated in the process of subjective development. They argue, too, that school confers privilege and status on specific students from the dominant culture and, by doing so, relegates to a subtle murmur the histories, aspirations, and goals of disenfranchised cultures or subordinate groups within society. Current didactic pedagogy, then, is really a set of appearances conjured up in the interest of the dominant relations that exist outside of schooling and peddled and personified in uncritical texts that seek less to engage the human mind than to discourage liberatory thought.

In the discourse of new-school educational theorists, the ideological representations within school life operate to disseminate and legitimate larger corporate and political social practices. Thus, educational sites operate as disbursement centers for dominant ideology, values, and practices that support a market civilization and a market morality. Traditional social theorists consider these private interests identical with the public interest and therefore warranted as the bases of commonality and democracy. New-school social theorists agree with little if any of this thought. They see, instead, dominant ideologies that serve to reinforce the inequality evidenced in the social tapestry of contemporary society and fail to reflect the needs of the majority of students they purport to serve—needs that find expression in authentic character development, independent thinking, moral development, and critical interrogation into everyday life. The radical pedagogues suggest that without critical explorations into this legitimizing ideology of schooling, teachers easily fall prey to a form of pedagogical alienation as they fail to come to understand their role as agents of either social conformity or social change and the role played by texts and curriculum as objects of political and economic interests warranting close scrutiny and critical analysis. Thus, a classroom motivated by inquiry assumes the responsibility of confronting issues of authority, both theoretically and practically. But we will see, this is not the current norm in classroom life.

New-school radical educational theorists agree that because schooling as it is currently structured treats knowledge as a commodity (a set of skills and attitudes to be consumed in a not-so-free market of ideas), the roles of schools, teachers, administrators, and students become nightmarishly synonymous with the alienated roles characteristic of the "free market life" of the factory. The regimented classroom becomes the metaphorical equivalent of the tyranny of the assembly line. Students and their subjective lives are carried, often "kicking and screaming," along a pedagogical conveyor belt where teacher-workers consciously or unconsciously bent on inculcating dominant and authoritarian societal culture, attitudes, and skills, labor piecemeal with fragmented curriculums. Step back from this scene and observe the way both the product and the worker become alienated from the entire process of material, mental, and social production.

Meanwhile, the school principal becomes the equivalent of the "on-line-production-manager," assuring through pedagogical "time-and-motion-studies" (in the form of orchestrated seven-step "lesson plans"), that the "worker" and the "product" conform to quality control standards adopted by still another layer of educationally divorced administrative bureaucracy. This "quality control" in pedagogical life expresses nothing more than raw authoritarian power accomplished through culture-dominant standardized teaching, normative individualistic testing of rote memorization, teacher evaluations, and the consequent levels of achievement claims, implications, assumptions, and conclusions. Efficiency and production, or the coverage of greater and greater content, become the dynamic engine perniciously driving schooling further and further away from human values, self-dignity, and conscious individuality. Workbooks and page numbers comprise student assignments as the factory-classroom grows in size owing to its lack of societal commitment to democratic educational ideals, producing classroom managerial problems that often run roughshod over even the most enthusiastic and critically conscious educator. The material limitations of the forces and relations of classroom production become an obstacle to critical and creative thinking opportunities.

Radical pedagogy argues that the commodification of knowledge projects the illusion that students are producers and consumers of their own ideas when in reality they are neither. In this state of pre-alienation, students learn that school lacks living reality and that their relationship to knowledge production promises little creativity and personal resonance. They learn that schools provide few opportunities for learners to discover their public lives and private selves. In fact, school functions more as a staging area for the alienation of consumptive life precisely because it teaches the *need to be taught* rather than the *need to learn*. It promotes dependent thinking rather than independent thought. As such, it turns out dependent people with dependent lives, alienated from the quest for emancipation and liberation and prone uncritically and irrationally to accept authoritarian manipulations and distortions. Schooling, as we know it, is, then, diametrically opposed to human liberation and emancipation precisely because it subordinates the "actor" to a mere spectacle in the fabrication of social distortion. It offers only to prepare students to exist insofar as "exist" connotes survival. A liberatory pedagogy, on the other hand, conceives of a praxis that helps students learn how to "live" a word that implies a deeper discovery of what it means to be critically and actively involved in the process of becoming.

New-school radical theorists illuminate yet another problem: For typical modern thinkers the tragedy is the impossibility of attaching any historical significance and meaning to everyday life. They understand and live the present as if it had no connection with the historical social relations that helped customize it. It is as Karl Marx (1932) saw: "There has been history, but there is no longer any" (p. 102). The problem of the present is difficult for the majority to see as an historical problem, one that can be understood only by its relation to the past. The impossibility, then, lies in attempting to understand ourselves without understanding our past. It would be inconceivable for us to dismiss the empirical dimension of our past in attempting to make sense of why and how we act. Yet this inability to frame personal and political events of the present as part of world history and the evolution of human beings, blocks a true understanding of the personal and social problems of the present..

These new-school pedagogues talk about the importance of providing students with critical opportunities to understand historical reasoning, the abstract-deductive process, and history as an element of understanding self and others if we want our students to achieve insights into the principles and strategies of the critical method and approach. Furthermore, those with a lack of historical understanding can understand questions at issue, including the pedagogical ones, within the framework of the system responsible for dialectically producing them, while that system itself (in this case the system of education) evades critical evaluation. The situation invites patchwork efforts guided by fragmented thinking about education crises. The holistic view is missing, the interdisciplinary interconnections are lacking, and the problem goes ill-defined and alienated from the larger systems of social production.

Because educators are responsible for any changes we wish to see in education, as well as implicated in the reproduction of daily life as conveyed ideology, we must undergo a critical attitudinal shift—the only approach intellectually possible, responsible, and morally significant. We must begin to adopt the language of critique in the interest of possibility. Radical educators, then, urge teachers to examine their roles as historically cultivated and capable of historical transformation and to see themselves as historical beings in the process of being. Identity then becomes in the words of Herbert Marcuse (1941), "the continuous negation of inadequate existence" (p. viii).

An examination of the role of schools at the beginning of this century illustrates a system designed to be a site where students acquired such basic skills as reading and writing. More and more today, schools must perform not simply as sites for inculcating basic skills, but as job-preparatory sites for the new century. Accordingly, students have become instruments of the market, human capital. For critical pedagogues this is an intolerable response to changes in production, for it makes of schooling a mere conveyor belt into the world of capitalism rather than an introduction into self and society.

Moreover as technocracy and technocratic intellectuals dominate, humanistic intellectuals play a less significant part in academic and school life. We hear considerable dialogue over the role of the schools in equipping America for the new millennium of capitalism while we hear little about creating sites for authentic self-production and reflective action and thought. We hear our schools berated for being "one step behind" technology with the need to "catch up" to the new world order. The job of reinforcing dominant ideologies is enlarged to encompass the job of redefining these dominant ideologies for the new "service and knowledge needs" of capitalism. As Feinberg (1989) observed, in the interest of the new, yet traditional educational ideology of competitiveness, the educational establishment busily issues its own self-serving narratives that impugn public education and student attainment. The argument as articulated from the side of education that whimpers about the current sorry state of American productivity pursues the premise that America has somehow lost its competitive ability, its technological superiority, and its supremacy in mathematics and science. The recipe for recapturing this dominance is to raise standards in the schools. These merchants of competitive despair begin with assessment, continually describing how American test scores are lower than those in equivalent countries see, for example (*A Nation at Risk,* 1983). Lower test scores somehow lead to the importing of more foreign goods, German and Japanese cars, and Sony television sets, as confirmation of diminished U.S. productivity and inferior products. The answer lies in hoisting test scores and recrafting assessment. They point to Japan and Germany much as the 1950's doomsayer pointed to Sputnik as evidence of Soviet superiority and then insisted on inflexible assessments and rigorous teacher standards. The naiveté of the argument is transparent. If children would just perform better on standardized tests they too could produce desirable cars, well-engineered computers, and mechanically sound VCRs. Therefore, schooling should be enlisted in helping students develop the skills necessary to compete productively. This myopic approach to standards and assessment offers a "quick fix" for a complex educational problem. As Art Costa (1993) observed,

> Schools, being a reflection of society, will achieve higher, world class standards only when American society imposes higher world class standards on itself. Achieving higher standards requires the devotion of the greatest share of our resources to the development of each person's fullest potential (p. 51).

An Explanation and Critique of Traditional Radical Pedagogical Theory and Practice

The new school of pedagogical social theory seeks to link education to the imperatives of democracy as opposed to the narrow limitations of the so-called free market. It correctly presumes that the struggle for critical thinking should be removed from the battlefield of pedagogical neutrality, and must be desired for its political importance in helping to create opportunities for critical thinking and rational social action aimed at defeating unjust social structures and practices. Education should be valued and assessed for its ability to encourage critical thought, denounce unjust social structures, challenge biased ego and sociocentrically invested assumptions, invite critical disquisition within a climate of investigation, and help students author their own reasoned judgments. From this point of view the notion of democracy itself is more than simply a political conception but a critical habit of thought and reflection among the people democracy purports to serve. Without the development of critical democratic thinking, democracy itself is reduced to hollow rhetoric and unattainable fantasy.

In articulating their vision of education, new-educational theorists acknowledge that radical critics correctly emphasize the political nature of schooling. Characterized by a particular categorization and legitimization of social relations, modes of thinking and reasoning, and specific language configurations, schooling has countenanced or adopted discriminatory practices, marginalization, and exclusion, so as to cancel the lived histories, aspirations, and contemporary lives of disenfranchised groups. Yet as Giroux (1989) has argued, the traditional radical theoretical and political analysis of schooling has failed to go beyond the language of critique and domination. Giroux offered a critique of the critique, which is helpful if we are to move beyond the constraints of our own self-imposed limitations. By arguing for a "language of possibility," Giroux pointed out that radical theorists of education often suffocate in their own critique, failing to view schooling as a site for struggle and conflict offering possibilities for forged coalitions among parents, teachers, and students. For this reason many teachers, students, and community members have felt silenced by a pedagogy that blocks a vision of hope and future and thus fail to see possibilities for critical transformation. For new-school social theorists like Giroux, a language of possibility means helping those who have been excluded from public discourse to be heard. This project involves encouraging understanding and reasoning within multiple perspectives and points of view as represented by those outside, and often subjugated by, the dominant ideology. It means using the concept of authority as a focal point for launching educational lessons that show how authority gains representation and attestation within all spheres of public and personal life. Reminding teachers of the possibility of hope and the danger of capitulation to pedagogical despair, Freire (1985) said this about teaching:

> To undertake such work, it is necessary to have faith in the people, solidarity with them. It is necessary to be utopian, in the sense in which we have used the word (p. 63).

Furthermore, it means understanding how differences between peoples are composed, sorted out, explicated, and constructed, in the power relations of American society. By understanding the *politics of difference*, teachers and students can become aware of the *politics of solidarity*. Once achieved, this awareness poses the challenge of entertaining within the practice of educational discourse a struggle for including diverse narratives within the school curriculum. As Giroux (1989) remarked,

A pedagogy of and for difference does not merely illuminate the welter of conflicting ideologies and social relations that operate within the public and private spheres of students' lives; it also attempts to have students engage their experiences through "political, theoretical, self-analyzing practice by which the relations of the subject in social reality can be rearticulated from the historical experience of women [or from the historical experiences of Blacks, Latinos, poor working class males, and so forth]" (p. 143).

From the point of view of critical pedagogy, students are encouraged to bring the legacies and narratives of their past and present inside the classroom for critical interrogation. They seek not simply clarification or to wallow in their own subjectivity and the subjectivity of others. Instead, subjective clarification gives way to subjective articulation and enunciation, as students congenially strive to examine their thinking from the point of view of diverse narratives of contemporary and historical reality. Giroux (1989) spoke of bringing the logic of critical interrogation into diversity:

The knowledge of the other is engaged in not simply to celebrate its presence, but also because it must be interrogated critically with respect to the ideologies it contains, the means of representation it utilizes, and the underlying social practices it confirms (p. 106).

New-school radical social theory takes up issues of authority as these issues relate to the legitimization of wider community and society, the ethical and political basis of schooling, and relationships between domination and power. Giroux labeled this notion of authority "emancipatory authority," as opposed to the dominant view of authority, which considers teachers as technicians or public servants. This is a dialectical understanding of authority that sees it both as a negative and positive, emancipatory and oppressive. For Giroux, this category of emancipatory authority is the terrain of the transformative intellectual; dominant or oppressive authority is the terrain of the didactic pedagogue, or teacher as technician.

Giroux's formulation has important consequences for adherents to new-social theory approaches to education. Teachers become more than simply intellectuals motivated and concerned with academic excellence and student classroom performance, but professionals concerned with the concept of active engagement and transformation and eager to see the attitudes and cognitive abilities students develop unleashed for purposes of social transformation. The idea of transformative intellectual applies to students as well as teachers. As transformative intellectuals, both teachers and students interest themselves in oppression and the common struggle for human dignity in a political and moral life, institutional forms of production and reproduction, and forms of knowledge, attitudes, and cognitive abilities. With an inclination to learn how to learn comes the realization that one's assumptions are always subject to critical reflection and analysis and people so disposed acknowledge that their perspectives can always be challenged and changed. This idea of truth that Giroux speaks of is comparable to the Hegelian notion of reason, which presupposed freedom and the power to act in accordance with the knowledge of truth. This is a commitment to shape reality in accordance with its potentialities. For Hegel, freedom itself presumes reason in much the way that, for new-social theorists, critical social discourse presupposes liberation.

By embracing authority as emancipatory, a hopeful terrain of pedagogical struggle, educators can devise classroom strategies that inquire into the historical and contemporary reality of community, society, and individuality; the role of schooling as a sight of reproduction, and its moral and political basis; and the relationship between oppression, power, and the common struggle for human dignity.

For new-school pedagogues, then, the objective and subjective conditions of education can be critically imagined only through historical and socio-economic recitations that particularize schooling's wider purpose and interconnectedness within and with a variety of institutional conformations—structures with particular economic, gender, cultural, and socio-political foundations. This perspective is of critical significance to teachers as cultural workers, for we can conceive of the subjective lives of our students and the objective tools of our practice only as relating to the broader forces outside of schooling, including economic equity, social justice, teacher recruitment and training and attitudes, parent and community involvement, bilingual education, relevance, and personalized learning. Educational process and its institutions—its curriculum and political comportment, its implications for classroom life, and the role of its consumers and producers—cannot stand in isolation, nor can we explain or iterate them by developing specific disciplines or by using the disciplines we have. Instead they must be understood relative to the material conditions of life that give rise to their particular agendas. In this way we come to understand that schooling and its objective sites are ideological harbingers of a larger societal program tied to the manner and methods of material production and the social relations that define it. At a certain stage in education, the prevailing ideology and the larger social agenda become antagonistic. The possibility for a paradigm shift can arise at this point, and we have seen it happen in educational restructuring attempts. For this reason the idea of critical pedagogical struggle and conflict can help us become active proponents and manufacturers of a "new pedagogy of liberation."

A critical pedagogy relying on principles and strategies of critical thinking and knowledge acquisition within a wider socio-economic perspective recognizes that schooling relates dialectically to the outside structural forces that shape its objective and subjective ideological conditions. Specifically, any critical analysis of the workplace of educational production, the curriculum, the textbook content and the companies responsible for their production must be understood against the backdrop of social relations, within and beyond schooling itself. It is impossible, for example, to talk about implementing a rich, global, critical notion of pedagogy within a curriculum that enhances classroom life, critical thought, and knowledge acquisition without addressing the wider issues of equity, class, race, gender, culture, and power. If students and teachers suffer inadequate funding, overcrowded classes, discrimination, watered-down teacher-training programs, inauthentic assessment, fraudulent tracking practices, the disdain and disrespect of administrators, union-busting, condescending in-service programs, and a general disconnection from the wider community and broader narratives of public life (themselves laboring under the weight of economic and social neglect), then the social relations of production in which teachers and students labor demand critical examination and analyses.

New-school social theorists see our schools as in crisis not because students are disobedient or test scores are low, but because they fail to prepare citizens with the intellectual commitment and diverse perspectives to reflect on the choices and decisions they must make in the process of becoming. Schooling should help equip students with the critical thinking abilities that allow them to participate wisely and fully in democratic life.

At this juncture in our reflections on schooling we must confront the responsibility of education as a human endeavor, instead of fixating on the imperatives of the free market that favor math, science, and vocational development at the expense of critical thought. Accordingly, educators must put forth a vision of education as a transformative activity aimed at self-production and a critical understanding of inequitable social power relations. By working within our educational organizations and uniting our efforts and struggles with larger emancipatory movements, we teachers can become more critical concerning the process of social and personal transformation, while simultaneously struggling for lower class sizes, increased control, democratic forms of decision making, and curricula aimed at visualizing and institutionalizing critical thinking in the service of humanity. Students, for their part, can recognize and benefit by their teacher struggles, and can themselves begin to see the possibility of social change and to understand that humanity and its insights come after authentic personal and social struggle.

Thus, for the critical educator, making the case for a qualitatively better world is crucial both in action and words. Utilizing critical dialogue, dialectical reasoning, Socratic questioning, and principles and strategies of critical thinking promotes a curriculum aimed at emancipating students from irrational thought and undisciplined thinking. Reflection and action require visualizing a relevant, problem-posing curricula that addresses the endeavors and hopes of diversity within the context of human commonality. Thus a utopian vision of education becomes the ideological point of departure for the teacher at work within the paradigm of possibility. In the face of unbridled greed and individualism coupled with heightened sociocentricity and ethnocentricity, new-school radical social theorists like Giroux have issued a challenge to the dominant modes of schooling and have redefined what it means to be an educator and student in today's world.

Unfortunately, the challenge has gone unaccompanied by practical curriculum suggestions that address the task of critiquing domination while providing opportunities for dialectical and historical reasoning. This gap discomforts precisely because it is historical-dialectical reasoning we want to engage and promote within the critical thinking classroom. Questions regarding Socratic discussions, critical cognitive abilities, the affective domain of education, collaborative learning, the criteria for judging thought, the differences between reasoning and subjective reaction, and thinking through the logic of viewpoints remain relatively unnoticed. It does little good to ask students to embark on the path of critique if both students and teachers lack the analytical and affective dimensions and abilities required to engage critique—that is, if they cannot distinguish good reasoning from bad reasoning, or if they lack the values and dispositions to engage in fair-minded critical thinking. The praxis of pedagogy must incorporate an identification with and recognition of the special nature and significance of controversial issues and how they can be accommodated in the curriculum. Encouraging dialectical reasoning and dialogical discourse imposes the need to encourage open minds and fair-minded critical thinking.

As teachers, after all, we cannot expect our students to arrive with open, fair-minded, critical minds eager for the business of decoding reality. On the contrary, most students come to us as egocentric individuals tied to irrational, self-justifying belief systems that are far too often associational. Most students have little or no experience reasoning empathetically from diverse points of view and are often committed, consciously or unconsciously, to the perpetuation of oppressive reality. Learning how to think critically and reason well must first become crucial goals for the dialectical classroom of inquiry. Students need opportunities to practice critical thinking, to talk about principles and strategies of reasoning that form the foundation for these abilities, to critique and assess their own and others' thinking, and to use these strategies and principles.

Carefully imagined and designed, critical pedagogical instruction should encourage students to learn the principles and strategies of effective reasoning within the discourse and context of authority, domination, and cultural inquiry. Student reasoning should be concerned as early as kindergarten with these issues as they arise in everyday life, stories, narratives, films, and popular culture. Critical thinking about these issues is more than just developmentally appropriate, it is a developmental necessity. For this reason we must ask ourselves a series of questions like these:

What do I want my students to reason about and why?
How can I help students reason more effectively about this or that issue?
How can I help my students develop values and dispositions that will aid their reasoning? What might those values and dispositions be?
How can I help my students understand the deeper logic of what they are studying?
How can I help my students identify historical and contemporary assumptions?
How can I help them interrogate those assumptions Socratically?

How can I help my students develop criteria for successful and effective reasoning?

How can I help my students develop fair-minded critical thinking within multiple perspectives?

These questions rarely appear in discussions about designing a critical pedagogical curriculum. Yet without answers to these questions, one can hardly expect to design artful instruction aimed at eradicating forms of oppression and embracing critical cultural inquiry. Radical educators want to avoid the trap of ineffective didactic instruction no matter how well intentioned. Nor do they want to encourage subjectivism as opposed to reasoned judgment. Engaging in mother-robin feeding (Paul, 1990), no matter how kindly done, will hardly contribute to fruitful critical inquiry and, given the absence of reasoning opportunities, will actually perpetuate and reinforce lower-order learning.

I should also mention here that some outstanding examples of practical critical pedagogy currently exist. Most exceptional is undoubtedly *ReThinking Schools*. Consisting of classroom teachers and educators in the Milwaukee area, this collective publishes a newsletter for all teachers concerned with issues of education. Dedicated to helping parents, teachers, and students solve problems that exist within the public school system, the journal promotes discussion and debate on issues of educational concerns. Educators can find reflective curriculum examples for primary, middle, and high school classrooms. The collective and its publication are devoted to helping parents, teachers, and students empower themselves within the educational environment. Their inquiry encompasses issues that include democratic decision making and curriculum design and implementation. Especially sensitive to the plight of newly arriving immigrants, gender inequality, people of color, and students of lower socio-economic class, *ReThinking Schools* places a high premium on empowering students within both the classroom and the community to combat pestiferous inequalities that promote inefficient and unequal learning and living. The articles feature intellectuals and educators many of whom advance the notion of empathetic, fair-minded critical thinking. In a recent interview in *ReThinking Schools* (1992) the noted historian Howard Zinn, observed that

It's a good idea also to do something which isn't done anywhere so far as I know in the histories in any country, and that is tell the story of the war from the standpoint of the other side, of the "enemy." To tell the story of the

Mexican War from the standpoint of the Mexicans means to ask: How did
they feel about having 40 percent of their territory taken away from them as
a result of war? How did they view the incident that President Polk used as a
reason for the beginning of the war? Did it look real or manufactured to them?
You'd also have to talk about the people in the United States who protested
against the war. That would be the time to bring up Henry Thoreau and his
essay "Civil Disobedience" (p. 6).

Not all that *ReThinking Schools* prints, however, advances a pedagogy designed to promote opportunities for critical thinking and critical reflection on issues of domination. One occasionally senses the
spirit of indoctrination lurking within various approaches to what some
incorrectly advance as critical thinking. If we assume that critical thinking is reasoning, and that teaching for reasoning involves helping students develop their own critical perspective on issues of a dialectical
nature, then the next example is troubling.

In *ReThinking Schools* (1992), educator Leonore Gordon recounts
her experience with her fifth grade class in a small private school in
Brooklyn. She described the class as racially mixed with an even number of girls and boys. The socio-economic backgrounds of the students ranged from lower to upper class. Targeting as the week's lesson the issue of toys and the political implications of their packaging,
Gordon began by reading an excerpt from Liv Ullman's book *Changing,* to help students think about the issue of sexism. She read the
passage in which Ullman recounts her birth, noting that the nurse
apologetically whispers to Ullman's mother that she is sorry she has
delivered a girl and asks if the mother wishes to inform her husband
herself. Gordon described the questions she asked her students after
reading that passage:

Why might some fathers not want girls? Why might some mothers want girls?
If you're a boy what kinds of presents have you gotten on holidays? What do
people expect you to be like? What have girls gotten as presents? What are
they expected to be like? How many girls have wanted trucks? How many
boys have wanted dolls? Tell me about the TV commercials you've seen. What
kinds of kids are they about? (p. 19).

Then she defined "*classism*" with her students by discussing what
makes toy packaging classist. The students apparently generated a
criterion that Gordon posed in the form of a question:, "Was the toy
expensive and unaffordable to working class children?" Evidently if it
was, it was deemed to be classist. From here the students proceeded
to discuss the manipulations of toy corporations in inducing consumers to think they need a product they can do without. At this point

students and teacher planned a field trip to Toys-R-Us where they made notes of the toys they saw that were sexist, classist, and racist, and jotted down the addresses of the toy manufacturers. Back in the classroom following the trip, the students discussed why the packaging was racist or sexist, or why the toys were classist in accordance with their criterion. They reported on various toys both orally and in written reports. Here are some of their comments:

> Students reported on a Super Deluxe Tool Kit showing "a white boy making a racing car. It was racist and sexist. A girl was just holding on helping him."

> Another of the many examples was the Bake and Decorate, with the "fake blue icing, all white sugar things, two little nicely dressed white girls, and a boy. The boy didn't help, he was just ready to eat, and all the parts weren't even included."

> One boy commented, "You don't hardly see Blacks [but you see] plenty of whites . . . like the Barbie dolls. It makes a lot of Blacks feel like they're put down."

> One boy informed us, "We found a really cheaply made thing—a white little boy with stereotyped Indian headdress, not sturdy, and racist and sexist" (p. 19).

The project culminated with a student-generated letter-writing complaint campaign to the corporations responsible for the sexist, racist, and classist toys and their advertising.

As teachers, we should understand that before we can help students reason well, we and they must understand what reasoning is and value the process of "figuring things out for yourself." What Gordon accomplished in her classroom had less to do with encouraging reasoning than with creating opportunities where children might develop the morality Gordon felt they had to develop. No matter how well-intentioned or politically correct, educators must realize that in dignifying and respecting the autonomy of the student (an idea critical pedagogy embraces, at least in theory), teachers must allow students to develop their own moral perspectives. As Freire (1990) remarked,

> The revolutionary leaders must realize that their own conviction of the necessity for struggle (an indispensable dimension of revolutionary wisdom) was not given to them by anyone else—if it is authentic. This conviction cannot be packaged and sold; it is reached, rather, by means of a totality of reflection and action (p. 54).

This realization leads to allowing students to reason through multiple perspectives—scrutinizing, analyzing, and comparing various points of view. In this way, they develop dialectical reasoning and reasoned judgment. This pedagogy can hardly mean subtly compelling or gently coercing students into a particular perspective by constructing the educational game so they must arrive at the solutions, conclusions, or decisions educators intend beforehand. Such an educationally dishonest intention would replicate current didactic approaches to socialization and indoctrination. Unfortunately, this is precisely what Gordon accomplished. For example, asking children why some fathers might not want daughters tells them that some fathers do not want daughters. Similarly, asking students why some mothers might want girls tells them that some mothers might want girls.

Socratic questioning aimed at encouraging student reasoning would have adduced from students whether they thought some fathers did not want daughters and if they thought some mothers might want girls and why, thus creating opportunities for students to posit their assumptions, develop perspectives, and marshal evidence for what they believe in light of what others believe. Similarly, asking students what makes toy packaging classist tells them that toy packaging is classist instead of providing them Socratic opportunities to arrive at reasoned judgment about what they think the concept of classism might be, whether they thought a toy classist, and if so, why.

Gordon repeated her fundamental misunderstanding of reasoning and critical thinking when she *told* the students that manufacturers engage in classist manufacturing rather than allowing them critically to examine, analyze, and explore the issue themselves in the interest of autonomous reasoned judgment. This pedagogical error helps one understand the simplicity of the criteria her students supposedly generated to define "classism." Is classism defined by the cost of a commodity or the unique position one finds oneself in relative to the means of production? Where were the questions that would help students develop criteria for the evaluation of a classist toy? One needs such questions as, "What does the word "classism" mean? What are we evaluating and why? Can you name or describe some toys that are not classist? Why are some toys classist and why are other toys not classist? What are the differences? Given these reasons and differences, can we generalize and list criteria for what is classist? Can we describe what to look for when judging this toy or that toy? What features does a classist

toy need to have and why? How do you know? The problem reap-
peared when the students were told that corporations use advertising
to encourage people to buy what they do not need or believe what
they do not want to believe or what is not in their best interests. A
more critical teacher would begin by asking students if they thought
television ads were manipulative and why; and if they thought they
were being manipulated by television ads, why, and in what ways.
With Socratic questioning, the teacher might also help students reason from the point of view of the television advertisers to capture the
logic of their thinking so as to understand an industry run for profit.

Finally, the reports generated by students that ended the project
were simply subjective assertions and represented no apparent reasoned judgment. Are we to infer that a girl helping a boy, ipso facto, is
sexist? If so, why? Or with regard to the bake and decorate advertisement, does the depiction of two girls mean that the advertisement
promotes sexual stereotypes? If so, why? How do we know? What is
a stereotype? The student asserts that the boy did not want to help
the girls. How does he or she know this? Does the student have evidence for this inference? What was he or she assuming? If a white boy
with a stereotypical Indian headdress is an example of racist advertising, why is it such an example? Would it provide the same example if
the boy were Afro-American? Why or why not? We never see the
students' reasoning on these issues precisely because the teacher has
already done the reasoning for them. They are simply being asked to
"fill in the blanks" of the teacher's reasoning. The lesson becomes
more an example of dogmatic moralizing on the part of the teacher
than indicative of critical thinking on the part of students. The danger
with benevolent didactic instruction is that students begin to
overgeneralize and oversimplify—precisely what critical thinkers hope
to help students eradicate. Again, remember Freire's (1985) exhorta-
tion to socialist educators when he commented on the dangers of indoctrination of any persuasion:

> With the exception of at least Cuba and China, one of the tragic mistakes of
> some socialist societies is their failure to transcend in a profound sense the
> domesticating character of bourgeoisie education, an inheritance that amounts
> to Stalinism. Thus, socialist education is usually confused with the reduction
> of Marxist thinking, a thinking that in itself cannot be "confined" within "tab-
> lets" to be "prescribed." Accordingly, socialist educators fall into the same
> "nutritionist" practices that characterize domesticating education (p. 105).

Certainly the concept of how advertisers and toy manufacturers use racist, sexist, and classist advertising to promote sales is worthy of student inquiry; but bringing this kind of reasoning within the classroom entails more than simply didactically telling students that manufacturers engage in racist, sexist, and classist advertising and then asking them how. I am by no means claiming that Gordon's instruction represents pedagogical Stalinism. But, I think it is valuable to keep Freire's comments in mind to guard against vanguardism within our own pedagogical practice. Teachers should continually search for opportunities to elicit their students' reasoning, encouraging them critically to think their way through issues and concepts and not doing their reasoning for them. As Freire (1990) later noted, teachers who are critically interested in issues of morality do not want to become "preachers in the sand" (p. 44). Instead, we must search for ways students can reason their way toward one position or another, not parrot the thoughts and feelings of the teacher. Unfortunately, teachers like Gordon fall into the trap of benevolent didactic instruction, failing to understand how to promote dialectical reasoning in the interest of reasoned judgment. They instead remain intent upon promoting their own agendas, as admirable as they may be. The result is the perpetuation of propagandized instruction in the service of benevolent indoctrination—a pedagogy that does injustice to the students, fails critically to confront the irrational logic of racism, sexism, and classism, and consequently is non-transformative. Furthermore, it is academically indefensible and open to attacks by parents, administrators, and teachers as demagoguery and propagandistic manipulation.

While progressive educators are embarked on expanding multicultural education to include a recognition of diversity and the development of effective programs that fight bias, prejudice, and inequality, offering a view of education that stresses the importance of reasoning within multiple perspectives on issues of classism, racism, and sexism is far more rational than evangelizing or exhorting one point of view at the expense of another. The recent controversy surrounding the Rainbow Curriculum in the New York City schools points to the issues progressive educators must confront if we are to go beyond the food festivals, arts and crafts, and superficial celebrations of holidays and heroes that limit effectual multicultural education. A rational and defensible approach to educating for an awareness of classism, sexism, and racism hardly rises on a foundation of proselytizing one point of view at the expense of another but is constructed on an interest in creating effective opportunities for students to reason within and about these issues. A critical-thinking approach to the same questions and the same subject of inquiry, by virtue of the fact that it promotes reasoning in the service of thinking and the development of one's own perspective, is defensible academically among both parents and administrative personnel.

Finally, the benevolent didactic approach fails to help students gain an insight into the cognitive and affective dimensions of reasoning and, as such, serves to stunt their intellectual growth rather than help them develop their critical capacities in the interest of self-production. Reason, traditionally anathema to injustice, contains the dialectical seeds of liberation and human freedom. As Amin (1989) noted,

> Undoubtedly, the aspiration for rationality and universalism is not the product of the common world. Not only has rationality always accompanied human actions, but the universal concept of the human being, transcending the limits of his or her collective membership (in a race, a people, a gender, a social class) had already been produced by the great tributary ideologies (p. 72).

Essential to human liberation, democracy, and human freedom must be the capacity to reason well. In the words of Herbert Marcuse (1941),

> Reason as the developing and applied knowledge of man—as "free thought"— was instrumental in creating the world we live in. It was also instrumental in sustaining injustice, toil, and suffering. But Reason, and Reason alone, contains its own corrective (p. xiii).

Marx (1932) himself differentiated the rational human being from the instinctual constraints of animals and insects when he noted that

> We presuppose labor in the form that stamps it as exclusively human. A spider conducts operations that resemble those of a weaver, and a bee puts to shame many an architect in the construction of her cells. But what distinguishes the worst architect from the best of bees is this, that the architect raises his structure in imagination before erecting it in reality (p. 198).

The ability to raise into consciousness and imagination the subject and object of human reality explains our ability to go beyond the mere instantaneous, instinctive responses of the spider to the self-reflective, reasoned judgment of the human being. This is the defining feature of the human. How well we engage in the process of becoming human is to a great degree predicated on how effectively we can reason. Anaïs Nin formulated the relationship between human beings and reason metaphorically and incisively this way:

> Human beings cannot duplicate the infinite intricacy of the living architecture of the wheat-stalk. Nature is best capable of its own forms and of the complex inevitabilities which result in such marvelous phenomena. Human beings are such a phenomenon; and the marvelous in us is our creative intelligence which transcends nature and creates out of it un-natural forms (p. 138).

The propensity to preach morality as opposed to reasoning through morality hectors much of the critical pedagogy movement. Critical thinking is much more than embracing moral positions because they are politically correct. It is reasoning one's way to this position or that position as a result of critical inquiry, critical self-reflection, and fair-minded critical thinking, while simultaneously developing the ability to marshal evidence and reasons for one's assumptions and inferences. If we are to infer that specific toys and their manner of advertisement and manufacture are sexist, racist, or classist, then we must be in a position to proffer our assumptions and the evidence to support them, posit reasons for our conclusions, and defend our position in face of often dissimilar points of view. If a critical pedagogy sets as its task the unveiling of oppressive and authoritarian practices, rendering them transparent and making them visible and accessible for purposes of human transformation, then a commitment to helping students reason must be the foundation of inquiry. As Maxine Greene (1972) observed,

> Whatever the variety of schools, I believe the teacher who is sincerely "radical" has the capacity to move students to do their own kind of critical learning—at higher and higher levels of complexity. I think this teacher has an obligation to teach them the use of the cognitive tools they need, to acquaint them with the principles that structure the disciplines, and to offer the disciplines (which are modes of ordering experience, modes of sense-making) to each one as live possibility. I think he also has an obligation to present himself to students (fellow human beings) as a questioning, fallible, searching human being; to break through the secrecy of certain specialties by engaging his students and himself in the most rigorous, open-ended thinking they can do (pp. 135–136).

Chapter 3

The Critical-Thinking Movement

One of the first things I think young people, especially nowadays, should learn is how to see for yourself and listen for yourself and think for yourself. This generation, especially of our people, has a burden, more so than at any other time in history. The most important thing that we can learn to do today is to think for ourselves.

> — Malcolm X
> "Learning to Think for Ourselves" in
> *Malcolm X's Black Nationalism Reconsidered* (p. 59)

The "Good Student"

"There is a critical-thinking movement gaining momentum at all levels of education today," wrote Richard Paul (1990), founder of the Center for Critical Thinking at Sonoma State University. According to Paul

On the social and political fronts, both the developed and underdeveloped nations face complex problems that cannot be solved except with significant conceptual shifts on the part of large masses of people. Such large scale shifts presuppose increased reflective and critical thought about deep-seated problems of environmental damage, human relations, over-population, rising expectations, diminishing resources, global competition, personal goals and ideological conflict (p. 34).

The critical-thinking movement presumes that the value of critical thinking extends beyond its usefulness in academic pursuits (although the success of these pursuits depends more or less on the thinking skills one brings to them), to include the sum total of, personal and social life. Critical thinking is essential for humankind in its potential for assuring a society founded on faith in reason and fair-minded compassionate thinking. For critical-thinking devotees, knowledge, freedom, morality, and rational productivity all interrelate, and require intellectual discipline and fitness of mind. Society then, argue advocates for critical thinking, must create new opportunities within educational institutions for all students to gain insights into what it means to think critically and fair-mindedly.

Rational self-criticism must lead in this quest as a source of transformative metacognition. Teaching and learning as dialectical expressions of humanity must be the subject of critical scrutiny to keep them fathoming and problematizing critical thinking activities within the totality of the curriculum. Because social freedom, progress, and individual identity depend on the critical faculties humans have the capacity to acquire, schooling as a site for the cultivation of the mind must become both an exalted vision and practical, sustainable reality. Furthermore, amid a recognition that living in a democracy with breadth requires us to find our public selves within our private selves, critical thinking must necessarily translate into personal and public activity. The aggregate of experiences outside our immediate circle form this public life, whether consciously or unconsciously. The more critically conscious we are about our public selves—our decisions, our claims to and of authority, and our self-interests—the more knowledge we have of ourselves. Only when we consciously elevate our public and private lives into critical consciousness to conduct a reflective self-inventory can we become generative, transformative actors in our personal and social existence. By making the private misery and joys of everyday life public, and by critically articulating and analyzing the relationship between our private selves and public selves, we can begin to add dimensions of compassion, humility, and empowerment to our existence. Within the framework of our personal and social relations, in the intricate fabric of well-reasoned thought and fair-minded thinking, we can discern personal and social meaning, humility, unity, and a commitment to one another and the natural diversity that outfits the essence of self-generative existence.

For critical thinkers like Paul, the answer lies in part with engendering thinking at ease with reasoning dialogically and dialectically thinking unperturbed by intricate ambiguity, that values critical scrutiny and a commitment to "an examined life," that welcomes accelerating and complex change, that is not ego-invested or irrationally fixated on ideas, and that is hostile to propagandistic supplication and demagogic manipulation. Embracing the awareness that deceived consciousness or the state of self-delusion operates to render reality that which it seems, one unlocks and banishes the ideological. The destruction of one false illusion leads one to scrutinize others; the undertaking of the practical project of thinking critically suggests other points of view or frames of references that reinforce or expand on our thinking, forcing us to rethink our initial assumptions and conclusions. Idea follows idea in such rapid succession that the critical mind becomes its own reflective oracle; the complexity of the world becomes tangible, transparent, and ultimately transformable. For the uncritical mind, however, people, places, and things become what they seem, synonymous with how they appear. Unconventional points of view, or alternative frames of reference intimidate critical backwardness, while a lack of critical inquiry reifies surface ignorance or at best, surface understanding. Thus the absence of critical consciousness—a state that defines the vast quantity and quality of thinking and modes of being—becomes a form of consciousness in and of itself, a consciousness we can call false consciousness or a consciousness in perpetual irrational unconsciousness.

For those in the critical-thinking movement, these realizations compel a new formulation of the educated or literate person in society. No longer can we tolerate the idea of the critically literate person as a mere repository of facts and details. We must look beyond the appearance of intelligence to understand the rationally intelligent person as a repository of techniques, principles, strategies, philosophies, and insights—a person committed to critical social discourse and reflection. Acknowledging that the complex problems we now face are abstruse and have no pat answers, and that their solutions rely on our ability to reason within multiple perspectives in the interest of reasoned judgment, proponents of the critical-thinking movement point to the failure of educational theory and practice in providing meaningful critical occasions for students to develop their aptitude to reason. Arguing that the ability to officiate rationally requires comprehensive and organized practice in critical thinking, critical-thinking adherents contend that critical thinking cannot be presupposed but must be accommodated. Much as we use the gymnasium to maintain or improve the fitness of our bodies, exercising each muscle relative to the whole, critical thinking requires meticulous and disciplined exercise in the development of thinking skills and strategies, and rational dispositions, values, and passions.

For educators like Paul (1990), instructional practices in most institutions throughout the world are based on a "didactic theory" of literacy and knowledge acquisition (p. 35) and are ill-suited for developing critical minds concerned with the conscious and critical process of personal and social production. One can correlate the didactic notion of education with Freire's (1990) "banking conception" of schooling (p. 62) where teachers deposit facts and figures within students as if they were empty accounts. The didactic classroom features a fragmented curriculum that echoes the dominant discourse, by skill-intensive instruction divorced from holistic problem solving, and by lecture, drill, and ritualistic rote memorization and uncritical regurgitation—or what I call "anorexic-bulimic learning." Students receive infrequent encouragement to examine critically what they read or hear. The curriculum offers content characterized by a general conformity and suited to rapid and superficial coverage. The consumption of information at the expense of the development of knowledge resembles fast food restaurants and convenient stores, with an overemphasis on the distribution of mass-produced quantity as opposed to crafted quality. In such an arrangement the "good student" learns the logic of the dominant system, conforms to the institutionalized expectancies, and accepts the rhythmic numbing of regulated learning. Freire (1990) provided a glimpse of this good student laboring within this system:

> Generally speaking, the good student is not one who is restless or intractable, or one who reveals one's doubts or wants to know the reason behind facts, or one who breaks with pre-established models, or one who denounces a mediocre bureaucracy, or one who refuses to be an object. To the contrary, the so-called good student is one who repeats, who renounces critical thinking, who adjusts to models, and who "thinks it pretty to be a rhinoceros" (Freire, p. 118).

John Dewey (1916) understood the implications in Freire's description of the good student when he laconically and metaphorically addressed the alienation of objectified human existence:

> A clue may be found in the fact that the horse does not really share in the social use to which his action is put. Someone else uses the horse to secure a result which is advantageous by making it advantageous to the horse to perform the act—he gets food, etc. But the horse, presumably, does not get any new interest. He remains interested in food, not in the service he is rendering. He is not a partner in shared activity. Were he to become a co-partner, he would, in engaging in the conjoint activity, have the same interest in its accomplishment which others have. He would share their ideas and emotions (p. 16).

Teachers laboring in the didactic classroom rarely question a student's beliefs or thinking, relying instead on pre-packaged formulas, district-mandated skills, and textually provided concepts, all of which make it advantageous for them to perform the act of schooling as opposed to actualizing the process of education. The result is that students are taught what to think as opposed to how to think—how to be taught as opposed to how to learn—a disingenuous educational script that relegates students and teachers to mere spectators in the perpetuation and reproduction of everyday life as opposed to co-partners in the construction of critical human inquiry. Freire (1990) sketched this narrative relationship between student and teacher in detail:

> A careful analysis of the teacher-student relationship at any level, inside or outside the school, reveals its fundamentally narrative character. This relationship involves a narrating subject (the teacher) and patient, listening objects (the students). The contents, whether values of empirical dimensions of reality, tend in the process of being narrated to become lifeless and petrified. Education is suffering from narration sickness.

> The outstanding characteristic of this narrative education, then, is the sonority of words, not their transforming power. "Four times four is sixteen; the capital of Para is Belem." The student records, memorizes, and repeats these phrases without perceiving what four times four really means, or realizing the true significance of "capital" in the affirmation "the capital of Para is Belem," that is, what Belem means for Para and what Para means for Brazil (pp. 57–8).

Among the crucial pedagogical contributions Paul (1990) makes, is his insistence on the distinction between those problems he calls "monological"—problems capable of being settled within one frame of reference with a specific and definitive set of logical moves, problems that are questions of fact—and problems that are "multilogical"— those problems depending on arriving at reasoned judgment through critical thinking among and between alternative points of view (p. 270). By virtue of the fact that they require reasoning within different frames of reference, multilogical problems necessarily require dialectical reasoning. For example, problems concerning the environment, population, diversity, justice, morality, and politics provoke questions and problems with no pat answers that generate many disparate points of view, illustrate issues on which reasonable persons can disagree, and require an ability to reason empathetically within multiple perspectives in the interest of arriving at reasoned judgment about what to believe, decide, or do.

The current problem, according to Paul and other advocates of critical thinking, is that schooling fails to provide opportunities for students to develop abstract dialogical and dialectical reasoning. Although life is beset by problems and questions requiring reasoning within varied perspectives in the interest of reasoned judgment (problems that are multilogical), schooling fails to define, address, or respond to our obvious need for the development of rigorous critical thinking—preferring the horse-and-buggy days of educational theory and practice.

Addressing the issue of dialectical and dialogical thinking central to the critical-thinking movement, Paul (1990) noted that many problems arise when students are asked to divide beliefs or statements into categories of either "fact" or "opinion" (p. 281). Constructing false categories of fact and opinion either reduces questions at issue to scientific, mathematical, technological, or formula-based procedures, moves, and answers, or in the case of opinion, calls for purely subjective reactions leading one down the road to intellectual and moral relativism. Some problems or questions unquestionably call for factual resolution, and we now refer to these questions as monological. Such questions as "How much will I make in a week if I work eight hours a day for five days at $20.00 an hour?" require only simple calculations. Moreover, questions of opinion, or what might be better termed "questions of preference," require only a subjective response. These are questions like "Should I buy a red car or a blue car? Which ice cream is better, vanilla or chocolate?"

For critical-thinking supporters like Paul, however, the most important categorical concerns are questions that require resolution through reasoned judgment, are conspicuously absent. Arguing that the majority of important questions and issues are neither reducible to mere fact or formula nor embraced and resolved by simple subjective response, Paul advanced the importance of dialectical reasoning to confront issues of a multilogical concern. Whom to vote for is not, for example, a question of fact or preference. Responsible voting requires reasoned judgment, as does responsible parenting, studying, working, and deciding what to believe or what to do. A democracy demands that we judge a candidate for political office on something more than the simple *fact* that he or she is running or we are infatuated with his or her manner of dress, speech, or appearance. Moral, political, and personal questions call for our reasoned judgment, which in turn demands the intervention of critical thought. Although people approach problems or controversies with different assumptions, points of view, conceptual understandings, and purposes, deductive analytical skills can help evaluate our claims to truth and help us develop our own perspective.

Thus, dialectical reasoning is exacting reasoning based on comprehensive principles of critical thinking that requires a competence to assemble and deploy evidence for what we believe in light of what others believe. This thinking is diametrically opposed to close mindedness and is, therefore, defeated by ego or sociocentric thinking. It is concerned with adjudication rather than the mere rendering of opinion, and thus is not limited by the confines of ego-invested subjective response. For Paul (1990), dialectical thinking is fair-minded critical thinking defined as

> the intellectually disciplined process of actively and skillfully conceptualizing, applying, analyzing, synthesizing, or evaluating information gathered from, or generated by, observation, experience, reflection, reasoning, or communication as a guide to belief or action (p. 24).

This notion of dialectical thinking is essential for confronting both multilogical and monological problems. Unfortunately, it is often misunderstood with dire consequences for pedagogical theory and practice. For example, in their publication *Dealing with Differences and Conflict Resolution in Our Schools*, the group *Educators for Social Responsibility* (1992) shows how dialectical thinking is falsely construed and consequently abandoned in favor of intellectual relativism. In a discussion of debate versus dialogue, they stated that

> Debate is characterized by confrontation, a contest between right and wrong in which each side believes it's right (p. 5).

They go on to declare that, on the other hand,

> (dialogue) as contrasted with debate, emphasizes seeking common ground rather than polarizing differences (ibid).

The error here is not simply the false definition of terminology, but more important, equating traditional debate with critical debate. Employed in the interest of reasoned judgment, critical debate is founded on principles of dialogue that sanction fair-minded exchange of different points of view in the interest of adjudicating issues and problems of a dialectical nature. It requires the dispositions and values or traits of a reasoning mind, as well as critical listening abilities in the service of empathetic understanding. It contrasts with uncritical or traditional debate long associated with intellectual competitiveness, a sophistic ego-invested blindness, and the absence of reciprocity and empathy. Critical debate hews to the principle that dialectical thinking cannot be compromised by relativism.

Although students certainly need opportunities to reflect critically on alternative frames of reference in an ambiance of fair-minded dialogue, they will also eventually need to adjudicate perspectives in the interest of developing their own point of view on issues requiring resolution, conclusions, and decisions. This adjudication process cannot be accomplished by mechanisms of dialogue exclusively, but must be informed by critical debate and disputation that require students to enunciate and articulate their beliefs and marshal evidence for what they assume—putting forth clear and accurate reasons for their conclusions, claims, and decisions as they critically and empathetically listen to the points of view of others. Lively debate of a critical nature tests the standards of student reasoning and invites students to develop an appreciation for those standards. Entertaining dialogue without a commitment to dialectical reasoning foments sham empathy and hollow tolerance under an umbrella of subjective relativism with no accompanying decisions or opportunities to advance well-developed conclusions and claims. While dialogue characterized by empathy and reciprocity is unquestionably the foundation for reasoning, critically exploring, analyzing, evaluating, and reasoning within multiple perspectives in the interest of developing one's own perspective is also essential. When argumentation and debate are uncritically conceived and implemented, when they are egocentrically invested in the interest of one viewpoint, they lose their critical character and begin to produce obstinacy and self-invested unjustified beliefs. The answer then is not the wholesale rejection and elimination of debate and argumentation, but a commitment to reformulate and enlist these activities critically in the interest of advancing fair-minded reasoning as opposed to conceiving and engaging in these activities uncritically in the service of sophistic obstinacy.

Because critical dialectical reasoning within multiple frames of references of necessity requires dialogue and communication, the didactic classroom is unfit for the evolution of critical minds. Once again Freire (1990) is instructive:

> Without dialogue there is no communication, and without communication there can be no true education.

Finally, true dialogue cannot exist unless the dialoguers engage in critical thinking—thinking which discerns an indivisible solidarity between the world and people and admits of no dichotomy between them—thinking which perceives reality as a process, as transformation, rather than as a static entity—thinking which does not separate itself from action, but constantly immerses itself in temporality without fear of the risks involved. Critical thinking contrasts with naive thinking, which sees historical time as a weight, a stratification of the acquisitions and experiences of the past from which the present should emerge normalized and "well behaved." For the naive thinker, the important thing is accommodation to this normalized "today." For the critical, the important thing is the continuing transformation of reality, in behalf of continuing humanization (p. 81).

If we want citizens capable of reasoning empathetically and paying effective attention to the necessities of basing their assertions on good reasons and evidence in the spirit of collaboration and empathy, then encouraging questioning and reasoning within diverse points of view is essential. This questioning and reasoning can be attained only in an environment that respects the healthy exchange of ideas in an atmosphere of civility and controversy.

Eight Views that the Critical-Thinking Movement and the New-Social Theorists Share

At this point we should note that proponents of the critical-pedagogy movement and those of the critical-thinking movement have much in common and much of it is hopeful. Appropriating the most positive aspects of these two movements and harnessing their insights to the construction of an authentic multicultural literacy requires us to recognize the complementary nature of their strategies and objectives.

First, both would create a classroom environment based on dialogical and fair-minded dialectical reasoning, that rejects the banking notion of teacher lecturing or what Paul referred to as *mother robin feeding.*

Second, both accept the fact that educational sites operate as indoctrination centers for the legitimization and reproduction of dominant-class practices. They also agree that the task of current conservative pedagogical ideology is to obfuscate the fact that certain pedagogical practices are activities authored and performed by people; instead, these practices are composed and designed to appear as natural law in pursuit of "academic excellence," the code phrase for self-actualized acquiescence to the prevailing social ideology of power and inequality. This anaesthetizing approach to knowledge acquisition rationalizes its bankrupt practices with claims to social and political neutrality. This erroneous neutrality survives on the false premise that education is not a form of political expression, but rather generic and value free. The condescending generic curriculum, with its emphasis on superficial and trivial pursuits rather than relevant critical inquiries, fraudulently proclaims a wide appeal among students while shunning controversy, ignoring issues of authority and domination, depersonalizing learning, and trivializing reality. But as we have seen, to advocate one form of pedagogy or another is not simply to advance objectively neutral educational theories and practices, but to advocate a political vision or point of view. As Paul (1990) observed,

> Let us not forget that schools in the United States were established precisely to transmit by inculcation self-evident true beliefs conducive to right conduct and successful "industry."

> When the time in school increased, it was not because of a demand for critical thinking but for better reading and writing skills increasingly necessary in the commercial and industrial activities of the day (pp. 2–3).

Third, both movements understand that the most powerful weapon oppression possesses is its ability to prevent its citizens from discovering the critical capacities we either already have or can develop. This cognizance and discovery of our critical potentialities would obviously open the social doors to political change and personal emancipation while posing an immediate threat to repressive practices. For Freire (1990) this freedom follows upon the critical awareness and comprehension of the logic of oppression:

> Denunciation of a dehumanizing situation today increasingly demands precise scientific understanding of that situation (p. 57).

Moreover,

> At bottom, when the dominated classes reproduce the dominators' style of life, it is because the dominators live "within" the dominated. The dominated can eject the dominators only by getting distance from them and objectifying them. Only then can they recognize them as their antithesis (p. 53).

Fourth, both movements acknowledge that the best advice for the student of human oppression is to view the system as it historically and currently operates on its most dangerous enemies. This critical demystification of history coupled with opportunities actually to construct history is the central aspect of any curriculum aimed at authentic personal and social transformation. Only by consciously making history can we clearly comprehend it.

Fifth, a common understanding exists that although the family may be the conduit of moral teaching and values, the family as an institution in crisis within today's confrontational society (built as it is on a thousand complexities, societal demands, transformations in relations of production that significantly affect women, and revolutions in technology occurring literally by the minute) can hardly function as the sole institution for character and moral development. The family cannot model and teach morality in isolation, divorced from a society in turmoil, but must work with all other institutions in society. All community establishments must embrace and promote the idea of a moral and humane society and echo the values that accompany this vision. Sadly, this is not currently the case. All of our witnessed and experienced societal relationships teach us our social values. We learn our values in many ways—from the avaricious deceit of the Wall Street junk bond traders, from the darkest recesses of government where corruption and naked lies guide public policy, from the ethos of the ruthless competitive consumerism that defines personal egocentric agendas while it parades as public good.

Critical thinkers and pedagogues alike understand we no longer live in an agrarian society where the images of Grant Wood's *American Gothic* and the Norman Rockwell nuclear family announce themselves as the exclusive embodiments of moral existence and tutelage. Exigencies of modern living impose new global actualities and difficulties that require educators to engage their students in relevant and reflective ethical reasoning in the interest of moral judgment. Many students now experience nightmarish Dickensian lives, especially in our major urban centers. Dramatic social transformations in material and psychological reality including drug addiction, unemployment, despair, racism, sexism, dysfunctional families, homophobia, teenage pregnancies, and for some, the status of being "illegals" redefine what it takes to be an educator, a student, and a citizen. Students bring to our classroom legacies of moral aspirations and hope as well as narratives of deprivation and moral degeneration for which they seek and expect critical explorations, empathetic heavings, and evaluation through radical discourse and rigorous analysis. Educational relevance in the interest of ethical reasoning must become the cornerstone of

any meaningful multicultural curriculum concerned with critical thinking. Educators, like Freire (1985), set forth the objective of the educator this way:

> Their objective shouldn't be to describe something that should be memo-
> rized. Quite the contrary, they should problematize situations, present the
> challenge of reality that learners confront each day (p. 22).

Much earlier, Dewey (1916) commented on the need to problematize
situations for students:

> The essentials of method are therefore identical with the essentials of reflec-
> tion. They are first that the pupil have a genuine situation of experience—that
> there be a continuous activity which he is interested in for his own sake;
> secondly, that a genuine problem develop within this situation as a stimulus
> to thought; third, that he possess the information and make the observations
> needed to deal with it; fourth, that suggested solutions occur to him which he
> shall be responsible for developing in an orderly way; fifth, that he have an
> opportunity and occasion to test his ideas by application, to make their mean-
> ing clear and to discover for himself their validity (p. 192).

Unfortunately, most educators approach the requirements of moral,
controversial, or ethical education the same way they approach a host
of other dialectical issues: with either a wholesale rejection of engaging these issues as simply too controversial for academic discourse
and something to be left to the practices of the family, or from an
arrogated posture of proselytizing universal authoritarian moral dic-
tums for students to internalize and actualize.

But the world does not present itself monologically as morally cut
and dried. On the contrary, morally conflicting claims and decisions
are historically situated and require reasoned judgment, moral self-
examination, self-critique, and a commitment to rational decision
making and fair-minded thinking. Social, economic, and cultural conflicts beg for acknowledgment and recognition, providing relevant av-
enues for the development of independent thinking, democratic decision making, and intellectual character development. Unlike the claims
of many popularly advocated though rickety pedagogical positions,
current reality with all its complexities and contradictions should not
be renounced as too controversial or too intimidating for classroom
discourse. As Amin (1989) stated,

> Propositions concerning the cultural dimension of social reality lend them-
> selves to this kind of danger [of becoming involved in false debates where
> vigorous polemics mask a mutual lack of understanding and impede the ad-

vancement of ideas]. There is always the risk of colliding with convictions situated on, for example, the terrain of religious beliefs. If the goal is to advance the project of universalism, this risk must be accepted. It is a right and a duty to analyze texts, whether or not they are considered sacred, and to examine the interpretations that different societies have made of those texts. It is a right and a duty to explore analogies and differences, suggest origins and inspirations, and point out evolutions. I am persuaded that no one's faith will be shaken as a result (p. 103).

Settling on a curriculum without conflict undermines the need to reason about issues of social and personal relevance. It reduces the role of education to that of disempowerment—a pedagogy divorced from the real world. The implications for teachers laboring under this paradigm is that they work "on" students never "with" them. Students become mere objects to be filled like vessels with teacher-generated pre-digested truth. On the other hand, critical-thinking teachers and new-school theorists who understand the role of education and society as a whole, tend to work "with" students, helping them explore the complexities of their personal, moral, and social existence in light of existing social structures. These educators typically provide opportunities for their students to develop the values and dispositions of learning, encouraging them to see the relevance of learning to reason socially, personally, historically, and morally so as to be in a position to transfer educational insights into other domains of life.

Furthermore, and immensely important, educators concerned with relevance see education and learning as political acts, which require reasoning within diverse and often opposing points of view, reflective thought, theory, practice, transformation, interdisciplinary transfer of learning, and both personal and social commitment. For critical-thinking educators and adherents to critical pedagogy, the student and the teacher are not objects but living subjects in the process of critically knowing and learning. Embracing this notion of critical learning and pedagogy, they redefine education, rejecting vertical authoritarian dictates from above, and the alienating obligatory matrimony of necessity that ends in annulment at 18 years of age, and embracing an empowering journey into humanity and the conscious articulation of self through critical social critique. Understanding the human being as creative, thoughtful, and capable of knowing encourages the offering of honest educational opportunities. Critical-thinking advocates and new-social theorists agree that teachers should develop high expectations for all of their students, listen to their personal narratives, enter within their subjective lives, and have confidence in their abilities to develop fair-minded reasoning while simultaneously remembering that they also are, or can be, conscious and productive beings.

Although common sense suggests a philosophy of education based on relevance and critical thinking, the importance of basing moral education on personal, social, and historical pertinence and reasoning as opposed to good-hearted exhortations and didactic preaching rests on an essential insight that still eludes the educational establishment. The popular but ineffectual self-esteem and character programs, especially in the 1980s—accompanied by pre-packaged programs claiming to curb teenage pregnancies, eradicate rampant drug abuse, heighten self-esteem, and confront adolescent violence—all failed miserably precisely because they were simplistic approaches based on an amorphous understanding of ethical decision making—as opposed to an awareness of historical principles and strategies of critical thinking. They occasionally continue, however, to complement hysterical hand-wringing practices or abstract good-hearted attempts to promote moral rectitude and an ill-defined "healthy sense of self" through didactic discourse. In her article, "The Negro Self Concept Reappraised," Grambs (1972) made the critical-thinking argument that a positive self-concept and issues of self-esteem that persist "in vogue" today should rest philosophically on the assumption of the importance of competency, as opposed to just "feeling good." Grambs assumed that the competent mind can deal with a world in crisis and continual change. A lack of competence, she argued, is the sickness that produces the symptom of low self esteem:

> Competence, in turn, depends on how one comes to view the world around one and one's ability to deal with this world (p. 185).

Developing the ability and confidence to reason is the prerequisite for developing the competence of which Grambs spoke. For this reason, critical-thinking advocates insist that any meaningful self-esteem program should rest its theoretical principles and practical applications on issues that help students develop legitimate competence through healthy critical thinking. In the *Los Angeles Times* of September 16, 1991, the noted psychologist Carol Travis made this very point:

> Today, however, self-esteem is a mere shadow of its former self. Once it referred to a fundamental sense of self-worth; today that meaning has narrowed into merely feeling good about oneself. Self esteem used to rest on the daily acts of effort, care and accomplishment that are the bedrock of charac-

ter; now it rests on air, on being instead of doing. Healthy self esteem used to fall between the equally unhealthy states of insecurity and narcissism; now it runs from "low" to "high," with no recognition, in these greedy times, that some feel too good about themselves, for no good reason (p. B5).

Furthermore,

Parents and educators would do better to focus on helping children achieve competence, perseverance, and optimism, the real contents of self worth. They would do better to help children discover or invent their own best possible selves, to expand their visions of what they can become—even if no one of their gender, race, or culture has ever done it before. True self esteem will follow (ibid).

Sixth, both movements require a thorough understanding of the dominant hidden agendas and limitations of the textual representations of narratives and disciplines, especially in social studies and history texts. The conformity imposed on students and teachers by restrictive texts necessitates the adoption of a critical attitude. The historical representations in most texts convey a sociocentric and Eurocentric bias artfully clothed in the apparel of scientific instrumentalism and objectivity. Paul (1990) observed that

I know of no textbook presently used in a large public school system that focuses on the multilogical issues of social studies or highlights the importance of strong sense critical thinking skills. Monological thinking that presupposes a U.S. world view clearly dominates. At the same time, students don't recognize that they are learning, not to think, but to think like "Americans", within one out of many possible points of view (p. 203).

Unfortunately, the imposition of a single world view is not just the province of conservative or liberal thinkers but finds acceptance among well-intentioned curriculum specialists who actually assume they are creating and designing "units" or procuring "resources" requiring dialectical or multilogical reasoning. Paul critically evaluated the writing prompts for state-wide testing programs that represent the uncritical labor of misguided yet dignified and noble sentiments. One such prompt is entitled *"Critical Thinking Writing Prompt History Social Science Directions: Read the conversation below that might have taken place between two United States citizens during the Cuban missile crisis in 1962.*

Speaker 1: These photographs in the newspaper show beyond a doubt that Russians are building missile bases in Cuba. It's time we took some strong action and did something about it. Let's get some bombers down there.

Speaker 2: I agree that there are Russian missiles in Cuba, but I don't agree with the solution you suggest. What would the world think about America dropping bombs on a neighboring small island?

Speaker 1: I think the only way to deal with the threat of force is force. If we do nothing, it's the same as saying let them put missiles there that will threaten the whole hemisphere. Let's eliminate those missiles now with military force.

Speaker 2: The solution you propose will certainly eliminate those bases, but innocent people might be killed, and world opinion might be against us. What if we try talking to the Russians first and then try a blockade of their ships around Cuba, or something like that?

Speaker 1: That kind of weak response won't get us anywhere. Communists only understand force.

Speaker 2: I think we should try other less drastic measures that won't result in loss of life. Then, if they don't work, use military action.

Imagine that you are a concerned citizen in 1962. Based on the information above, write a letter to President Kennedy about the missile crisis. Take a position and explain to President Kennedy what you think should be done about the missiles in Cuba and why. State your position clearly. Use information from the conversation above and from what you know about the missile crisis to support your position (p. 196).

The sociocentric bias inherent in this writing prompt is evident in what is absent—namely, facts, data, or points of view which a Soviet child might rely on in developing an opposing line of reasoning. The world appears in the garb of objectivity, yet the costume presents a one-sided rendition of historical circumstance in and for the interest of American advantage. By fashioning a narrow, rigid argument impenetrable by alternative points of view—with its one-sided representation of reality that fraudulently pretends to be historically objective—the text writers introduce devastating implications for student reasoning. This snapshot of reality committed to text by subjective minds receives acclaim as the genuine objective monopolization of truth deserving of not just applause and appreciation, but of a more insidious obedience and obligation—to be placed on a curriculum pedestal as intellectual justification for rote memorization and conformist regurgitation ideologically visualized and advanced as reality knowledge. The good guys and bad guys are pre-cast in the hidden script or what Giroux (1985) referred to as "the hidden curriculum" (p. 42).

The Russians are assumed to be the bad guys and the assignment expects students to accept this as truth and then on the basis of this associational un-examined assumption infer a conclusion to the crisis. The curriculum is hidden precisely because it conveys a dominant ideological position through subtly crafted self-serving historical censorship of any oppositional or alternative reasoning. Such a curriculum is contrived and concerned (1) with an obfuscation of reality accomplished and rationalized by propagandistic reification and the continuation of sociocentric and egocentric appeals to rigidly defined morality, (2) with governing political discourse, and (3) with erecting a structure manufactured from a vested interest in complicating human experience for self-serving purposes. Presented such sociocentric textual renderings, students come to internalize the myth that their country is above reproach and always justifiable. They come to accept sociocentricity as probity, which inhibits their ability to reason dialogically and dialectically concerning self, and contemporary, historical, and multilogical problems.

Poetically, this uncritical thinking benefits those elite forces with vested interests in propagandizing reality in accordance with their own class-induced and egocentric interests. Nationalism gains respectability by masquerading behind the assumptions that a democracy is something we are and that totalitarianism is something they are. Thus, the world is uncritically divided between the significant us and the insignificant others. Some of us are freedom fighters, others terrorists; some are Islamic fundamentalists, others good Christians; some of us live in democratic countries, others in communist countries. This easy, uncritical thinking opens dangerous opportunities for demagoguery accompanied by the false kindling of racial and ethnic strife, war, cultural conflict, totalitarianism, and carried to extremes, militaristic adventures in genocide.

Partly for this reason, teachers continually look for texts that require augmentation with outside resources in written, visual, auditory, human, or other forms that assure that alternative points of view enter educational discussions. As a teacher, I myself search continually for alternative points of view on multilogical issues precisely because the current texts leave out the voices of disenfranchised and subjugated. In fact, most texts are useless and best consigned to back shelves than placed in the eager hands of students. These multi-million dollar renditions of constructed truth could hardly be distributed by oversight or bad judgment on the part of benevolent corporations and their minions. Rather, as new—social pedagogues and critical-thinking advocates contend, the dominant texts generally embody the altogether conscious manipulations of an ideological manufacturing process concerned with the production of historical and contemporary reality in the service of authority.

Accompanying this insight comes the perception of the multinational character of corporate textual production; one perceives the logic of their promotion, the hypothesis that underlies their pedagogical gimmickry, the assumptions and claims that guide their sales appeals to school boards, and of course, their overriding concern, the profits generated during this mission. In addition to representing reality as one-sided truth in the exercise of self-interest, current texts fail to encourage critical thinking in virtually all domains of inquiry. Most texts and their corporations show more interest in accumulating critical mass than promoting and encouraging critical thinking.

In the quest for supplemental materials that go beyond the rhetoric of traditional texts, I have a lot of company. But teachers seeking to supplement ineffectual textbooks find themselves confronting time constraints, resource accessibility problems, fund shortages, and inadequate administrative support. Personal priorities keep many of us from devoting every waking moment to accomplishing what should be institutionalized resources for teaching critically. For some teachers, the lack of authentic texts and the intellectual bankruptcy of the current materials produce disillusionment with the practice and theory of what now poses as authentic education. For others, this disenchantment converts itself into critical resistance in conjunction with students, colleagues, and parents. Consider, for example, Freire's point that teaching students how to read and write is wholly insufficient in and of itself. Students must do more than simply read phonetically. They must read critically—that is, learn how to reason and how to analyze a text. Noting the failure of texts and the hidden curriculum and ideology inherent within the contrivance of their written pages Freire (1985) adduced one reading text he had seen:

> One of these readers presents among its lessons the following two texts on consecutive pages without relating them. The first is about May 1, the Labor Day Holiday, on which workers commemorate their struggle. It does not say how or where these are commemorated, or what the nature of the historical conflict was. The main theme of the second lesson is holidays. It says that "on these days people ought to go to the beach to swim and sunbathe." Therefore, if May 1 is a holiday, and if on holidays people should go to the beach, the conclusion is that the workers should go swimming on Labor Day, instead of meeting with their unions in public spheres to discuss their problems (p. 47).

Both critical-movement advocates and new-social theorists agree, with Freire, that texts must be read critically, have their logic consistently analyzed, and be evaluated against human reason. When reading a book

> We must analyze the content of the passage, keeping in mind what comes before and after it, in order not to betray the author's total thinking (p. 3).

Similarly, when one studies texts

> This critical attitude is the same as that required in dealing with the world (that is, the real world and life in general), an attitude of inward questioning through which increasingly one begins to see the reasons behind facts (p. 2).

Understanding the logic of an author's thinking is, indeed, crucial if we are to understand what he or she chooses to emphasize, to leave out as extemporaneous, to use to point up similarities and differences, and to avow as worthy or truthful. A critical understanding of inauthenticity—the type that appears, for example, between the covers of traditional texts—requires the deployment of critical faculties in the interest of revealing the assumptions, conclusions, claims, points of view, evidence, reasons, and inferences proclaimed as correctness. The insistence upon "political correctness," so often disparaged by traditional educators as the agenda of neo-liberals and misguided 1960s radical throwbacks, finds its most visual expression and exposition among precisely these same pedagogues. These traditional critics proclaim as objective truth their own specific agendas and points of view on contemporary and historical reality. They are the hypocritical vanguards of the politically correct group—a thinking they so vigorously attack.

One of the most important realizations in commenting on texts is that critically reading, analyzing, evaluating, and synthesizing texts are activities that students can engage in to expose the dominant ideology and sociocentric refuse that all around them finds utterance as truth. For example, the drama critic Nat Hentoff (1966) described a teacher who enlisted his students in the process of critically reflecting and acting upon fraudulent representations of slavery in their texts:

> The children in Mr. Marcus's fifth-grade class, incidentally, have been doing some important questioning. They analyzed a sizable number of social studies textbooks and they found every one to be wanting. Then they wrote letters to the publishers and some of the people in the school system pointed out that certain matters of opinion were being treated as facts: the statement in one book for example, that on the whole, the slaves were happy on the plantations. The children got many replies, and not being satisfied with some, they wrote again (p. 33).

When the teacher responsible for the critical thinking lesson was asked about the reactions by the school system to the children's letters he commented that

> There were inquiries. Nothing was said that was an outright condemnation, but implicit in the questions was: "How could you let this happen? What kinds of lessons are being given in that social studies class? Was the teacher biased? Did you discuss this project with the children? Perhaps there were better textbooks in the catalogue that were not analyzed?" Those are the kinds of questions that keep teachers passive. My answer was that at this point there is no social studies textbook which treats the Negro fairly, and that the children's questions were a true culmination of their research and were an excellent learning experience (p. 33).

This type of critical thinking and critical action aimed at exposing the hidden agenda of texts can empower students as they begin to see the logic of the frames of reference and identifiable interests that permeate these books. Furthermore, by extending their opinions into social action, they come to understand the logic of the rationale that would defend the truth these educational materials advance. Finally, by engaging in critical activity whereby these students actually challenge decisions and actions of administrative personnel, they experience the harsh reality of a system caught up in its own irrational reproduction and incapable of engaging in criticism: a valuable political lesson in and of itself. Such a depiction is important for both teachers and students because it demonstrates that texts are not value free or apolitical but represent a larger discourse that finds voice outside of classroom life. As Giroux (1985) observed,

> At the same time, the discourse of production has to be supplemented with analysis of textual forms. In this case, it is necessary to enlist a discourse that can critically interrogate cultural forms as they are produced and used within specific classrooms. What is significant about this type of discourse is that it provides teachers and students with the critical tools necessary to analyze those socially constructed representations and interests that organize and emphasize particular readings of curricula materials. This is a particularly important mode of analysis because it argues against the idea that the means of representation in texts are merely neutral conveyors of ideas (p. 103).

Another promising use of this idea might involve students as early as primary school in a critical analysis of how traditional texts represent Thanksgiving. Of course, the depictions are monolithic, so the teacher would need resources and materials to supplement the reading and provide other points of view for children to analyze. Through these types of activities students come to learn that historical render-ings are far from objective truths but represent a specific ideological or cultural frame of reference with a unique logic. Giroux considers textual analysis imperative because

> It points to the need for careful systematic analysis of the way in which mate-rials are used and ordered in school curricula and how its "signifiers" register particular ideological pressures and tendencies. At its best, such a discourse allows teachers and students to deconstruct meanings that are silently built into the structuring principles of the various systems of meaning that orga-nize everyday life in schools. In effect, it adds a new theoretical twist to ana-lyzing how the hidden curriculum works in schools (p. 104).

The fundamental realization for teachers and students laboring with inadequate textual materials is that we begin to understand (Paul 1990), that texts dishonor to both students and teachers when

> They imply that the facts speak for themselves and that they (the textbooks) contain the facts, all the facts, and nothing but the facts. There is nothing dialogical about their modes of canvassing the material or in the assignments that accompany the account the student is inevitably led to believe (p. 194).

Yet in the same way Giroux advocates "emancipatory authority" as the educational battleground for possibility and hope, we can come to view ineffectual or misleading texts and censorship itself as a forms of "emancipatory textual misrepresentation." They invite both students and teachers to focus on the clandestine messages imbedded in their pages, and to use them as instruments for critical analysis in the inter-est of understanding their logic and the obstacles to freedom they erect. Freeing ourselves from the victimization of textual dishonesty requires critical collaboration with our students and colleagues and with the whole community of parents, leaders, educational advocates, school boards, and progressive unions in a commitment to examine critically the contemporary and historical portraits commissioned by those in power with a vested interest in posing, proselytizing, and reifying one certain historical narrative as objective truth.

Seventh, both critical-thinking advocates and new-social theorists have a common commitment to autonomy of thought, a point Paul (1990) has made:

> It is essential that we foster a new conception of self-identity, both individu-ally and collectively, and a new practical sense of the value of self-disciplined, open-minded thought. As long as we feel threatened by those who think dif-

ferently from us, we will listen seriously only to those who start from our premises, who validate our prejudices, and end up with our conclusions. We will continue to stereotype, to distort—in order to reject—what the "others," the "outsiders" say. We must learn, in other words, something quite new to us: to identify not with the content of our beliefs but with the process by which we arrived at them. We must come to identify ourselves, and actually respond in everyday contexts, as people who reason their way into, and can be reasoned out of, beliefs. Only then will we feel unthreatened when others question our beliefs, only then will we welcome their questions as a reminder of the need to be ready to test and re-test our beliefs daily at the bar of reason, only then will we learn to think within multiple points of view, with a sense of global perspective (p. xvi).

Inviting a virtual glasnost of the mind promises possibilities for transformative autonomy of thought aimed at combating dependent thinking and the consequent act of uncritical responding. Furthermore, autonomy of thought inevitably leads to autonomy of action.

Eighth, both critical-thinking proponents and new-social theorists look for the resuscitation of a pedagogical theory confident in hope and possibility, rejecting despair in favor of the affirmation of life and the possibilities for growth and freedom. Despair and cynicism too often echo in the discourse and educational practices of teachers, administrators, parents, and students, thereby limiting liberatory practices and discouraging vision. In the face of material rapacity, moral degeneration, a loss of commity, the retreat of working class cultural movements, one-sided discourse, heightened sociocentricity, racist ideology, and the rigid totalitarianism of thought, one often feels diminished hope. But one need not accept it. Sharon Welch (1985) addressed the dialectic of an appreciation for existential hope:

> The sheer weight of the apocalypse obliterates utopia. The catastrophe no longer conjures up images of redemption. Instead it produces cynicism, which is no less ideological. Cynicism is the total embrace of the power of reality as fate, or as a joke, the "unhappy consciousness" of powerlessness. It is the hardened, wizened posture: detached negativity which scarcely allows itself any hope, at most a little irony and self pity (p. 211).

Notice the poignant observance that despair and cynicism represent capitulation to powerlessness—a detached negativity or the existential foible of fools. The "power of reality as fate," represents the reification of subjective reality as truth and a capitulation to history as advanced. Welch saw that the lack of hope and the absence of vision are themselves ideological contrivances that can lead one only into a cul-de-sac of persistent pessimism.

By contrast, Cornel West (1993) spoke of building a community of hope:

> To talk about human hope is to engage in an audacious attempt to galvanize and energize, to inspire and to invigorate world-weary people. Because that is what we are. We are world weary; we are tired. For some of us there are misanthropic skeletons hanging in our closet. And by "misanthropic" I mean the notion that we have given up on the capacity of human beings to do anything right. The capacity of human beings to solve any problem (p. 6).

Yet, as West suggested, we must face this world-weariness as problematic and a challenge, not a foregone conclusion. He challenged us to view history as incomplete, a world not yet finished. For West, to give up on the concept of hope is to sink into sophisticated analysis or sardonic critique and reflection.

Paul (1990) too conceded the importance of maintaining a vision of possibility, although he argued that the task ahead, coping with fundamental changes in education, will be slow and arduous. Nevertheless, he expressed his faith in human reason:

> Only through slow, painful change, with much frustration and circling about, only with multiple misunderstandings and confusion, will we work our way eventually into rational lives in rational societies (p. xvi).

Both camps agree that without a vision of expectation—a vision that assumes the practical possibility of a life founded on reason, rational criticism, moral compassion, and hope—educational practice can offer no possibilities for social or personal emancipation. Anti-utopianism as an ideological reflection of human and moral abandonment finds no comfort in the vision of hope that must inform a pedagogy for and of emancipation.

In the spirit of this dialogue, I recall the liberation theology inherent in the life of Rigoberto Lopez Perez, a young revolutionary who struggled against the Samoza regime in Nicaragua. Having assassinated Samoza, Lopez explained in a letter to his mother his sense of liberation in eliminating the dictator who had unmercifully oppressed the Nicaraguan people for years. Although I do not condone Lopez's act, his sense of liberation based on the idea of the new person forged out of the dignity of duty to humanity and by the implacable critique and negation of oppression and inequality—an idea produced and modeled by the Cuban example and most notably personified by Che Guevara—exemplifies deep-seated expressions of hope founded on what Freire calls the vocation of human beings: humanity. The pressures of accumulating egoism and irrational self-existence fuel a revolutionary commitment inspired by feelings of love for human beings and for the possibility of a future free from irrational hatred, oppression, racism, sexism, and objectification of people.

The 1980s, with their worship of avarice reinforced by political and religious fanaticism, destroyed many forms of dialogical community and public spheres of artistic discourse and culture that offered multiple perspectives on social issues. They also decimated the natural environment while repressing the free expression of ideas and the more radical intellectual traditions. This rampant capitalist dominance has depleted us spiritually, ruptured our bonds as humans, and commodified our historical past and present as trivial episodes—melodramatic docudramas paraded and bandied about for our superficial perusal.

By contrast, the lessons I learned living in the revolutionary society of Nicaragua in the 1980s were clear and straightforward: a concern for unity, a commitment to conscious struggle, an understanding of the logic of oppression and its practical agenda, and a respect for human difference in the service of unity. These lessons, coupled with an appreciation for humility and modesty as values and dispositions, taught me a conception of the revolutionary citizen committed to individual autonomy and social equality as a moral virtue fostered in the interests of fraternity, sincerity, and belief in the possibility of freedom.

This emancipatory "new society" must instill a commitment to the development of self as community, without the need to sacrifice self-generative autonomy to the demands of conformity. This sense of self and society must be a creative conviction committed to artistic visions and rational possibilities: a life capable of creative transcendence precisely because through creativity we go beyond mere representation toward the possible idea—that is, toward the realm of expectation and hope. One need not be an historian of Nicaraguan life and the struggle of its people to appreciate the sentiments of war-torn Nicaraguan mothers, many of whom suffered the loss of one or more children as they brought flowers to the grave of Carlos Fonseca Amador, founder and revolutionary leader of the Sandinistas, murdered by Samoza's National Guard. One mother summed up the feeling of all:

This grave of Carlos Fonseca is also the grave of my son.

The Logic of Fair-minded Critical Thinking:
The Four Directions of Reasoning

Not all advocates of critical thinking accept the idea that dialectical reasoning can solve problems. In fact, much of the work in the field of cognitive psychological problem-solving theory proceeds with an emphasis on technical problems and solutions, which reduce problem solving to categories of algorithmic technical moves. Problem-solving theories have far too often been confined to simplistic scientific models advocating procedural steps that, if ascended in regular order, inevitably lead to critical thinking and the "right" answer. Most technical-based critical thinking is antidialectical precisely because it insists upon solutions within constrained structures. Furthermore, it limits student reasoning to stages. In his book, Howard Gardner (1991) commented on the restrictions of early infancy researchers like Piaget:

> The limitation of the early infancy researchers (including Piaget) lay in an underestimation of what the infant knows—information that can be elicited when the infant is "questioned" more directly and more appropriately about specific bodies of information or knowledge (p. 48).

Brother Eagan Hunter (1991), at the School of Education at St. Edward's University in Austin, Texas, made a similar Piagetian mistake:

> Piaget tells us that the transition from concrete to formal thinking takes place at the beginning of the secondary school age. The expanding faculties of the mind are a challenge to developing persons. When they begin to experience the powers of reflective and internalized thinking, they become fascinated with debating and challenge (pp. 72,76).

On the other hand, philosophically based critical-thinking advocates understand that the reasoning mind is far more complex than reductionist, echelon notions of generative logic would lead one to assume. One of Paul's (1990) most insightful contributions is this essential question:

> What does a mind need to know about itself to reason well? (p. 3)

If we want students to reason effectively about such issues as domination, inequality, social oppression, personal freedom, democracy, and individual responsibility, then what the human mind can accomplish to improve effective reasoning becomes an even more pressing issue confronting a humanity interested in preservation and transcendence.

Furthermore, as teachers, we need to know the art of interrogation, the logic of human thinking, and the principles and strategies of critical thinking. Taking charge of our minds in the interest of social and personal transformation imposes the need to improve the quality of our thinking. A commitment to improve thinking translates into a pledge to live an examined life, with a healthy intolerance of oppression and human objectification.

Critical-thinking advocates all characterize critical thinking as rational thought coupled with the values and dispositions of a reasoning mind. In other words, they acknowledge both an affective dimension and a cognitive dimension to comprehensive and effectual reasoning and refer to this partnership as the key to fair-minded critical thinking. Logical reasoning alone is ineffectual without the values and dispositions that motivate self-authored independent thinking. If one does not value such attitudes as independent thinking, collaborative learning, intellectual integrity, and a commitment to empathy and reciprocity, dialectical thinking that requires entering diverse points of view remains an impossible task. Accordingly, Paul (1990) suggested that reasoning, or the process of figuring things out for oneself, proceeds in four distinct yet complementary directions.

Abilities of the Reasoning Mind

One direction or dimension of reasoning is the recognition of nine abilities of the reasoning mind:

(1) uncovering significant similarities and differences,
(2) refining generalizations and oversimplifications,
(3) clarifying issues, beliefs, and conclusions,
(4) developing criteria for evaluation,
(5) generating and assessing solutions to problems,
(6) analyzing or evaluating actions or policies,
(7) comparing and contrasting ideals with actual practice,
(8) transferring insights into new contexts, and
(9) identifying and exploring concepts, arguments, and theories.

These reasoning abilities and others combine to form larger orchestrations and to become constituent parts in the larger organizations of thinking. How well we can critically understand, internalize, and exercise these abilities in conscious processes requiring critical thought defines our effectiveness in reasoning critically.

Although critical-thinking abilities are essential and comprise one of the four directions of reasoning, much more is involved in our thinking when, for example, we assess a solution, or compare similar or different situations, or evaluate arguments. Paul (1990) noted that we bring certain elements in our reasoning to the activities of thought (p. 391). Whenever we attempt to draw conclusions about people or, circumstances, or decide what to believe or what to do, much more goes on beneath the surface of our thought. I define "reasoning" here as drawing conclusions based on reasons. We find, of course, good reasoning based on justifiable conclusions and evidence and poor reasoning based on lack of evidence or unwarranted and unjustifiable conclusions. That which we "take for granted," unconsciously affirm without the benefit of interrogation, or accept as obvious has bypassed in our thought processes and escaped inquisitive affirmation or negation. These received ideas can impede our ability to reason effectively. Making explicit that which is often implicit in our thinking enhances our critical abilities and elevates our thinking to conscious, committed engagement in the quest for reasoned judgment.

The Elements of Thought

We can now see a logic to figuring something out. This logic is ascertainable by someone with a self-invested interest in the perfections of what Paul (1990) called "the elements of thought"—a noticeable attraction to and appreciation for clarity of thought, precision, accuracy, depth, relevancy, logicalness, and fairness. These elements comprise the second direction of our reasoning, and Paul grouped them into categories.

(1) The purpose or goal of thinking. The human being thinks for a purpose with a goal in mind. Any defects in the definition of that purpose for thinking can disrupt any attempt to accomplish that purpose. Educators should know that students often fail to understand the purposes of instruction: why we study history or contemporary social reality. Without a clear conception of the goal or purpose of thinking about one issue or another, students find it difficult if not impossible to engage subject matter successfully.

(2) The question at issue or problem to be solved. All of our attempts to reason about something requires that we confront at least one question at issue or problem that needs to be solved. If we remain unclear about the question we are attempting to solve, or if that issue is divorced from the purposes of our thinking, we can hardly expect to find a sensible answer to it. Therefore, we must critically identifying with clarity, precision, and accuracy the problem or questions at issue we are attempting to resolve.

(3) The information we have to help think. Our reasoning requires that we have some information about that which we are attempting to decide. We need data to formulate answers to problems and to pose even greater and more insightful questions. Defects and deficiencies in the information we possess can occur when we labor without the benefit of alternative points of view or if we lack information from disparate sources. Thus, attempting to solve problems requires that we distinguish between relevant and irrelevant information in an atmosphere of dialogue. Once again, one can hardly stress the importance of this point too much. Because textual representations of historical reality often fail to provide students with more than the dominant ideology, we teachers must consistently strive to bring subordinate legacies into the classroom.

(4) The conceptual dimension of reasoning. Whenever we reason we use concepts to convey our thinking, and concepts tend to be closely associated with what we take for granted or what we assume. Effective reasoners are clear and precise about the concepts they use, paying particular attention to whether those engaged in dialogue share the same assumptions and definitions. Good reasoners also pay close attention to the concepts others use, seeking clarification and accuracy and looking for hidden assumptions that underlie the use of language. For example, when I lived in Nicaragua, I heard that the freedom fighters were the Sandinistas and the terrorists were the Contras. Back in the U.S. I heard that the freedom fighters were the Contras and the terrorists were the Sandinistas. Miscommunication derives from defects in the use of concepts and a misunderstanding of their assumptive nature. How are concepts and assumption related? In his vitriolic treatise entitled "Listen Little Man," written after the advent of fascism in Germany, Wilhelm Reich (1948) illustrated the assumptive nature of concepts:

"It's all the fault of the Jews," you say. "What's a Jew?" I ask. "People with Jewish blood," you say. "How do you distinguish Jewish blood from other blood?" The question baffles you. You hesitate. Then you say, "I meant the Jewish race." "What's race?" I ask. "Race. That's obvious. Just as there is a Germanic race there is a Jewish race." "What are the characteristics of a Jewish race?" "A Jew has black hair, a long hooked nose, and sharp eyes. The Jews are greedy and capitalistic." "Have you ever seen a southern Frenchman or an Italian side by side with a Jew? Can you distinguish between them?" "No, not really." "Then what's a Jew? His blood picture is the same as everyone else's. His appearance is no different from that of a Frenchman or an Italian. On the other hand, have you ever seen any German Jews?" "They look like Germans." "What's a German?" A German is a member of the Nordic Aryan race." "Are the Indians Aryans?" "Yes." "Are they Nordics?" "No." "Are they blond?" "No." "See? You don't even know what a Jew or a German is." "But Jews do exist!" "Of course Jews exist. So do Christians and Mohammedans." "That's right. I meant the Jewish religion." "Was Roosevelt a Dutchman?" "No." "Why do you call a descendant of David a Jew if you don't call Roosevelt a Dutchman?" "The Jews are different." "What's different?" "I don't know." That's the kind of rubbish you talk, little man. And with such rubbish you set up armed gangs that kill ten million people for being Jews, though you can't even tell me what a Jew is. That's why you're laughed at, why anybody with anything serious to do steers clear of you. That's why you're up to your neck in muck. It makes you feel superior to call someone a Jew. It makes you feel superior because you feel inferior. You feel inferior because you yourself are exactly what you want to kill off in the people you call Jews (pp. 30–31).

For the uncritical fascist mind, "degenerates," "Jews," "communists," "Gypsies," and "Bolsheviks," all conceptually weighed the same, conveyed the same meaning, and were used to describe the same people— which resembles the way contemporary neo-conservatives use such concepts as "feminist," "liberal," "politically correct," "gay," and "socialist" to refer to their political enemies. Helping students explore the conceptual nature of their thought and the thought of others inevitably leads one to consider the underlying assumptions that fuel these concepts.

(4) Assumptions: the starting point for all reasoning. Our thoughtful reasoning must begin somewhere. We base our thoughts either on unsubstantiated suppositions we take for granted or on suppositions that have been substantiated. That assumptions are beliefs on which we base our reasoning is a fundamental insight for critical-thinking advocates. Much of what we learn to believe is irrational, ego-based, unexamined, and outright false. Associational thinking—or thinking that relies on assumptions that have been internalized through uncritical allegiance to institutions of power, authority, culture, friends, family, and media sources—is "borrowed thinking," not reflective thinking. Examining our assumptions in light of the assumptions of others can curb problems in our reasoning. Furthermore, critically engaging dominant assumptions regarding everyday life can lay bare the repressive nature of authoritarian structures. The importance of recognizing the significance of assumptions as the beginning for all reasoning stands out in the thinking of Malcolm X. On the importance of thought Malcolm (1964) stated that

> One of the first things I think young people, especially nowadays, should learn is how to see for yourself, and listen for yourself and think for yourself. This generation, especially of our people, has a burden, more so than any other time in history. The most important thing that we can do today is think for ourselves (p. 59).

Malcolm's personal life became marked by a commitment to thinking and analyzing different assumptions about what to believe, decide, and do. He dedicated himself to self-improvement and radical self-love through a commitment to autonomy of thought. His early assumptions about Elijah Muhammad and the Nation of Islam led him to specific conclusions, decisions, and beliefs in action. Yet Malcolm had the critical ability to examine what he believed in light of the best evidence without fear of suspending commitments that allowed him to change his point of view on vital issues he regarded as important and essential. Malcolm X embraced the fundamental ideal that human beings can transcend whatever differences divide us through critical examination of the assumptions that spark and guide our thoughts and actions. Furthermore, he knew that one reaches this understanding through dialogue with reality, or the confrontation between what is human and what is oppressive. The progressions in Malcolm's thought and his ability to engage in transformative metacognition to achieve self-betterment and social justice—this marked the radicalism the dominant culture associated with his life though it calls attention to the power of understanding the motivating force of assumptions as the launching pad for all thinking. This commitment to radicalism in thought—a devotion to living an examined existence while understanding the frailty of beliefs, the need for evidence, and reasons to support assumptions and conclusions—reduces the deficit of human misunderstanding and disunity. Patricia Hill Collins (1992) noticed Malcolm's ability to test assumptions:

First, Malcolm X's definition of race and his perceptions of the connections among race, color, and political consciousness changed. During most of his time with the Nation of Islam, Malcolm X saw race as a biological reality instead of a socially constructed, historical phenomenon. This assumption of biological essentialism influenced his Black Nationalist philosophy. Relinquishing this biological essentialism in the last years of his life opened the doors for a greatly reformulated Black Nationalism, one encompassing different notions of Black political consciousness and the types of the political coalitions that Blacks might forge with other groups. The importance of being able to distinguish worthwhile political coalitions from dangerous ones becomes increasingly important to an African-American community situated in today's complex multiethnic, multinational political economy (p. 61).

Malcolm himself commented on his prior assumptions, and the process of their reappraisal, and his unwavering systematic appreciation for transformative metacognition through assumptive examination:

That morning [in Cairo] was when I first began to reappraise the "white man." It was when I first began to perceive that "white man" as commonly used, means complexion only secondarily; primarily it describes attitudes and actions. In America, "white man" meant specific attitudes and actions toward the black man, and toward all other non-white men. That morning was the start of a radical alteration in my whole outlook about "white" men (p. 333).

This idea of a vested interest in self-authored examination and change, the personal dedication to recognizing and examining assumptions in light of reality, an important revolutionary attribute of Malcolm X as leader and thinker, and it confirms his fraternity with such great thinkers as Che Guevara. For teachers, questioning students about the origin of their assumptions helps them locate their thinking within the confines of social and political life and places them in a superior position to change both reality and the reality of their thinking.

(5) Marshaling evidence for assumptions. Much of what we assume or take for granted lodges in our minds unsupported by well-founded evidence. If our thinking proceeds on unsubstantiated assumptions or beliefs without benefit of evidence, the rest of our logic becomes irrational or problematic. The goal then is to learn the art of marshaling logical and relevant evidence for what we take for granted, or on the other hand, acquiescing in the fact that we lack the evidence to confirm our belief. Constructing a critical social curriculum that insists upon marshaled evidence remains central to promoting critical social discourse.

(6) Drawing inferences, conclusions, claims, or decisions.
Understanding that our reasoning has origins and proceeds somewhere is another essential insight for critical thinkers. Drawing conclusions and making decisions about what to do or what to believe
occurs by processes or "steps" called inferences. When we infer, are
we considering any reasons we might have for the ensuing conclusion? Clarity and precision about our inferences and the reasons that
inspire them coupled with a sensitivity to conclusions others make
promotes healthy rational thinking. Because our inferences rely heavily
on what we assume or believe, any problem with our assumptions can
lead us toward faulty decisions or inferences.

(7) The implications and consequences of thinking. Because
reasoning is directional, beginning at one point and leading to another, we should understand that all of our reasoning, good or bad,
has consequences or implications. Are we aware of—can we state—the
implications of our thinking? Have we considered the consequences
of believing this or deciding that? Effective reasoners consider these
questions and place a premium on a healthy awareness of the consequences of their thinking and the conclusions they draw. They take
into consideration the road on which their thinking proceeds and where
it might be taking them. For many students, the consequences of thinking and the thinking of others go unexamined in and outside classroom life. Teachers committed to radical interrogation and examination consider helping students perceive the implications of their thinking
and the thinking of others as cardinal.

(8) An awareness of point of view or frame of reference. All
reasoning takes place within a point of view or frame of reference.
Imprecision, narrow-mindedness, egocentric preoccupation, false or
misleading analogies and metaphors—all these may infect reasoning.
Furthermore, we must become and remain conscious of the points of
view of others and clear about their claims, assumptions, points of
reference, and the direction their thinking may be taking them. Understanding that we all have our viewpoints can be difficult yet essential
in determining the effect of one or more views on our thinking. Furthermore, students must be willing to alter their viewpoints in light of
the best evidence. It does little good to ask students to take the path
of dominant critique if they lack the understanding that domination
and subjugation are points of view that claim supremacy over others.
Helping students recognize and critically interrogate points of view
becomes an fundamental exercise if they are to eradicate domination
and oppression.

Discussing the principle of abstraction as a methodological tool, Paul Sweezy (1992) pointed out two questions: (1) What problem is being investigated? and (2) What are its essential elements? (p. 15). In other words, the abstract-deductive method of thinking assumes an ability to recognize the problem or question at issue and those parts or elements of that question that give rise to new sub-questions. Hegel in his introduction to *The Philosophy of History* (1900), observed that when engaging in critical analysis in the

> process of scientific understanding, it is important that the essential be distinguished and brought into relief in contrast with the so-called non-essential. But in order to render this possible we must know what is essential (p. 65).

Thus, the ability to distinguish between relevant and irrelevant information is essential to any coherent approach to scientific inquiry, be it in the personal, sociological, economical, psychological, or monological domain. But how can we tell relevant from irrelevant information? If we had a pat answer, we could reduce the methodological method and its inquiry to pure routine. It is important to formulate assumptions about what seems essentially relevant to the question at issue and then work back and within and between these assumptions to find the clarity and logicality of the inferences or conclusions we draw. This search ushers in the idea of the data of evidence, because without evidence it is impossible to verify the efficacy of any abstraction or assumption. Therefore, Sweezy's (1992) words become salient and helpful:

> If we are to understand the achievement of a particular scientist, we must try to identify his key hypotheses and to see, if possible, where he gets them and how he develops their implications (p.16).   .

In Sweezy's thinking we can see an appreciation for clarity and precision in recognizing the elements of thought within the reasoning of any individual on any given issue. Specifically, Sweezy emphasizes identifying the logic of one's thinking, questioning its origin for the sake of metacognition, and exploring the implications of this thinking on any given issue.

The Values and Dispositions (or "Traits") of Mind

Critical-thinking advocates point to the abilities of thinking and the elements of thought as two of the four directions of *effective reasoning*. Moreover, effective problem solving and critical thinking entail

collaborative or communitive problem solving undertaken in a dialogue that encourages the healthy exchange of ideas and varying points
of view, all of which depend on clear communication. Without this
communication, dialogue and communicative problem solving become
idealistic goals incapable of achievement. To develop effective communicative collaborative problem-solving skills, effective reasoners
focus on more than the elements of their thinking or the abilities they
must exercise in the service of good reasoning. They are particularly
mindful of the values of human thinking or what Paul (1990) referred
to as those "traits of mind" that are essential if we are to work and
communicate collaboratively (p. 392). The values and dispositions of
collaborative problem solving form the third direction of reasoning,
and we can isolate 13 of them:

(1) A commitment to independent thinking as opposed to de-
     pendent thinking;
(2) A commitment to and understanding of intellectual perse-
     verance as a necessary component of effectual reasoning;
(3) A devotion to intellectual empathy or reciprocity in develop-
     ing the value of reasoning within different points of view;
(4) A commitment to intellectual humility or the ability to sus-
     pend judgment until all the evidence is in and all points of
     view have been given an opportunity to be heard;
(5) Faith in the ability to reason as an essential prerequisite for
     being able to address difficult problems as opposed to a com-
     mitment to irrational thought;
(6) Intellectual curiosity or the renewed and continued interest
     in pursuing interest about this or that issue;
(7) Intellectual responsibility or the understanding that the de-
     velopment of one's thinking and commitment to critical learn-
     ing and thinking is the responsibility of the student rather
     than the teacher;
(8) Intellectual discipline or the basic understanding that all
     achievements require commitment, enthusiasm, and hard
     work accomplished through self-actualized disciplined
     thought;
(9) Critical listening or the understanding that collaboration can-
     not take place within a climate of deafness to points of view
     (critical listening is to be distinguished from the act of mere
     listening as critical listeners consistently search for the logic
     of what they and others are entertaining in thought);

(10) Intellectual civility or the requirement that we treat each other and our ideas in ways that convey our interest and faith in human beings rather than simply an ego-invested attack against the person harboring ideas we perhaps are not in accord with;

(11) Fair-minded thinking or the commitment to enter within points of view or frames of reference completely different from what we believe;

(12) Insights into our often ego- and sociocentric thought, which are essential for fair-minded critical thinkers precisely because our ego- and sociocentric investments can act as blinders for how we perceive individuality, the world, and problems and questions that confront the human race; and

(13) Intellectual courage or the ability to take a stand for what we believe in light of the fact that "group thinking" might far outweigh rational decision making.

Without these values and dispositions of the reasoning mind there can be no commitment to or enthusiasm for communitative conscious self-reflection, figuring things out for oneself, entertaining disparate points of view, or decoding the historical intricacies of what it means to be human. Yet far too little emphasis falls on this affective dimension of critical thinking, and students often fail to actualize critical disquisition precisely because ego- or sociocentric beliefs vitiate communitative discourse. Teachers should acknowledge the importance of values and dispositions of reasoning successfully to encourage a robust and critical discourse, and thinking that extends beyond the narrow confines of ego-invested self-interest.

Standards for Reasoning

For Richard Paul, critical reasoning requires still more than a sensitivity to the elements of thinking, the abilities of thinking, and the values and dispositions of the reasoning mind. It must also be mindful of standards for reasoning—standards that have as their goal clarity, specificity, accuracy, consistency, broadness, significance, depth, precision, adequacy for purpose, fairness, and a sense of completeness. Collectively, these standards comprise the fourth direction of good reasoning. We want students to identify their assumptions and the assumptions of others accurately. We look for reasoning to be fair and broad, not unjust and narrow. We want students to use concepts with clarity. We want their thinking to be logical and consistent. Helping students internalize these standards will appreciably increase the quality of their reasoning—that is, help them to reason well. For critical thinkers like Mathew Lipman (1988), good judgment is the characteristic of critical thinking and takes everything into account. Yet, as Lipman noted, this process of taking into account implies criteria for judging one's thinking and the thinking of others:

> A set of criteria is an instrument for judging. Since critical thinking and arriving at reasoned judgment is a skill, and skills cannot be defined without criteria, critical thinking employs criteria and can be assessed by them. Criteria are reasons but a kind of reason: a reliable kind. Therefore citing good reasons for our opinions or decisions differentiates ordinary thinking from critical thinking (p. 40).

These four directions of reasoning encompass the theoretical formulations of critical thinking advanced by Paul and other similar pedagogues. They embody a reasoning arsenal invaluable in helping students critically explore, evaluate, analyze, synthesize, and develop their own perspectives on personally, socially, historically, and educationally relevant problems. Teachers can use this comprehensive arsenal to help their students gain insights into the special task of reasoning. Improving the human mind involves improving, through intellectual exercise, the four directions of effective thinking. The critical-thinking movement has made a valuable contribution in developing these four effective strategies all teachers and students can employ in an environment of inquiry and critical exploration that heralds reasoning about human liberation and oppression, while challenging domination and authoritarian control.

Socratic Questioning

Socratic questioning, always at the heart of critical thinking, is a tactic that fuels students' thought, elicits and probes their thinking, and allows them to develop and evaluate their thinking and the thinking of others by forcing them to make this thinking explicit. Students need opportunities to develop and examine their thinking and the thinking of others in an atmosphere of inquiry that gives them a chance to slow their thinking down, to express it patiently and with clarity, and to put a premium on the process of questioning as opposed to the tyranny of obsessively searching for the "right answer." Furthermore, Socratic questioning helps students elicit the thinking of others, unmask authority and dominion, and herald reflection and critical self-inventory. A requisite for fair-minded and critically constructed Socratic questioning is a serious and deep compassion for and commitment to the students' thinking. Without a commitment to compassionate discourse with students, Socratic questioning becomes pseudo-educational gimmickry.

Socratic questioning is based on the idea that all thinking has a logic the mind can assess. It is specifically concerned with the elements of thought that students bring to disciplines, questions at issue, and discussions of problems. Contrary to a chaotic free-for-all where students assert mindlessly formulated questions and amorphous discussions based on unsystematic thinking, Socratic questioning requires a thoughtful systematic probing of students' thinking and is based on its own logic. Structured Socratic thinking takes student thinking from the ambiguous to the clear. With its commitment to guided questioning, it probes beneath the surface of thought, raises essential issues, helps students arrive at their own well-reasoned judgments and perspectives through conscientious reasoning, and helps them gain an insight into the elements of their thinking and how these elements pertain to the controversies and issues they confront. In short, it is a structure of thinking and questioning that is unequivocally committed to helping students and teachers discover the structure of their own thoughts and the thoughts of others in the interest of transformative metacognition.

Paul (1990) loosely categorized three general forms of Socratic questioning he identified as (1) spontaneous or unplanned Socratic questioning, (2) exploratory questioning, and (3) issue-specific questioning (p. 362). Developing a sensitivity to the types of questions one poses to students is an essential requirement for the teacher committed to comprehensive Socratic questioning. Furthermore, it requires that we listen critically and carefully to what others say; take what they say seriously; recognize and reflect on our assumptions and the assumptions of others; seek explanatory power through requirements of examples, analogies, and objections; distinguish between what one believes and what one actually knows; and be willing to play the role of devil's advocate with the interest of helping students marshal evidence for what they think relative to what others think, while maintaining a healthy sense of skepticism (p. 370).

The following Socratic discussion represents an attempt to get students (in this case workers) to think critically about what they perceive as labor relations and why. It provides an example of the ability of Socratic inquiry to lead people to insights about their thinking and the thinking of others.

In her article "Union Maid" in the *Monthly Review* for February, 1993, Aleine Austin described her assignment for the National Maritime Union as an assistant to the Union's Educational Director, Leo Huberman. Working as the River Ports Education Director giving educational instruction on trade unionism in the major ports along the Mississippi and Ohio Rivers in 1944, Austin had a chance to observe Huberman's philosophy and teaching method. The small exchange that follows illustrates Huberman's understanding of critical thinking and the art of Socratic questioning. Coupling his questioning technique with an understanding of the role of education and politics, Huberman appears to have been an astute educator:

"Don't lecture!" was his lesson number one. "The first thing a good teacher wants to do is get the students involved," he explained. "A lecturer usually is more concerned about teaching the subject matter than he is about teaching people. Lecturing turns a student into a passive recipient. The trick is to stimulate students to become active thinkers."

"How do you do that?" Austin asked. "By involving their experience. Start where they are. Ask them questions that draw on their own knowledge. Do you know Latin?" When she nodded, he broke down the word "education" into its Latin roots and asked her to analyze them. She did:

E-duc-ation

out from—lead—the act of

"You see," he pointed excitedly to her translated syllables. "Lead out from or draw out from—that's the original meaning of 'education.' You draw on what your students know. The seeds of their understanding are in their old experiences. You draw out from them what they already know."

From there they prepared a lesson plan for the first class. Even the topic started with a question: ***Why Unions?*** Here is a sample of the dialogue that took place in Leo's introductory class the next day:

Leo: Who is stronger, you or the employer?
Boatman I: My employer, of course.
Leo: How do you know that?
Boatman I: I have to go to him to get my job.
Leo: What enables him to give you the job?
Boatman I: He owns the boat.

Leo: Why don't you own the boat?

Boatman I: Me? Where would I get that kind of money?

Leo: So you need money, or capital in order to own a boat. The same holds true for a factory, or restaurant, or any kind of enterprise that employs others to make a product or provide a service. But why does that make an employer stronger than a worker? Doesn't he need workers to operate the boat? (He points to another boatman to answer his question.)

Boatman II: Sure, he can't run the boat without us.

Leo: Then you can decide what wages you'll work for, can't you?

Boatman II: I can decide what wages I'd like to work for, but that doesn't mean I'll get them.

Leo: Why not? (Points to another Boatman.)

Boatman III: Because some other bloke can come along and accept less.

Leo: But aren't you free to refuse to work for a wage you feel is too low?

Boatman III: Sure, and I'm free to starve, too. But if I want to eat, I have to take the wage the employer offers, no matter how low because if I don't, someone else will. I'm powerless, that's all.

Leo: Isn't there anything you can do to get some power?

Boatman III: Well, I could try to talk that other bloke out of working for so low a wage.

Leo: (addressing the whole class) Would that work?

Boatman IV: Naw. What good would one other worker do? You'd have to get all the boatmen in the port to refuse to work below a certain rate before the employer would pay any attention.

Boatman V: That wouldn't work. He'd just go to another port and hire his boatmen there.

Boatman VI: Suppose you get all the boatmen in all the ports to refuse to work, say, below $5.00 an hour. Then you'd have some power, wouldn't you?

Boatman II: You'd have a union!

Leo: What do you mean by a union?

Boatman II: You know! A union is when workers unite.

Leo: For what purpose?

Boatman II: To control their wages.

Leo: Control? Can they get any wage they want?

Boatman V: Sure. They're in the driver's seat now.

Boatman II: Yeah. They could drive the employer right out of business by demanding too high wages.

Leo: What would the employer do if the union demanded, say, $10.00 an hour and he felt that he'd lose money or his business would go broke?

Boatman I: Maybe he'd compromise. Maybe he'd offer $7.00 or $8.00.

Leo: You mean he'd start bargaining with the boatmen?

Boatman I: Yeah, I guess that's what you call it.

Leo: Well, didn't you say before you'd have to take what the owner offered or starve? Now you're saying he'd bargain with you. What's different now from before?

Boatman I: Before I was just one person acting alone. I didn't have any bargaining power. Now, with all the other workers united in a union, I've got real bargaining power by joining together with the rest of the boatmen.

Leo: You sound like you're quoting from the Supreme Court. Let me read a section from a decision made in 1937. "Long ago we stated the reason for labor organizations. We said they were organized out of the necessities of the situation: that a single employee was helpless in dealing with an employer, that a union was essential to give laborers an opportunity to deal on *an equality with their employer.*" That's what unions do. They don't make workers stronger than employers; they make workers "more equal" to employers, by giving them a voice in determining their wages and working conditions. Does anybody know what kind of bargaining that is called?

Boatman I: Isn't that called Collective Bargaining?

"Right," Leo affirmed with a broad smile. I smiled, too. "Someday, I will teach like that," I promised myself (pp. 40–43).

The Positive Contributions of the Critical-Thinking Movement

The critical-thinking movement presents pedagogy with a vision and direction for education that draws a completely different portrait of the notion of schooling and addresses the exigencies and potentialities of our current level of educational production—our notion of what it means to be an educated person in today's world. Amid the multitude of beliefs and viewpoints on any subject, from constructing a home to permitting women in combat, most human activities and conclusions require fair-minded thinkers able to enter into viewpoints often diametrically opposed to their own. This ability is fueled by a desire or a value placed on dialectical thinking. Thus for current critical-thinking advocates the question becomes, "What kind of principles, strategies, curriculum designs, issues, student groupings, and teacher training and in-service procedures can promote the creation of a vision of schooling devoted to reasoning?"

Critical-thinking adherents engage the nuts-and-bolts questions of how to set up rational staff development programs that help teachers learn the principles and strategies of critical thinking, how to elicit and sustain administrative support for critical thinking curriculums and classroom attempts, how to get students to take responsibility for their own learning, how to encourage them to find answers for themselves and discover and solve problems collaboratively, how to help students toward an insight into the power of subject matters and find expression for them within their own personal lives, and how to promote civil dialogue among students on issues of controversy and moral dimensions.

These questions are crucial because without a sufficient arsenal of principles and strategies for interrogating students' lives and contemporary and historical reality, dialogue converts into abstract relativism or at worst, didactic proselytizing. If we want students to discover for themselves Eurocentrism as historical monopoly; if we seek their exploration and commitment to the eradication of racism, sexism, and oppression; if we value and want their critical analysis of contemporary events; if we desire their active involvement in critiquing and changing historical reality, then we must become adept at the art of designing instruction to sharpen student thinking on these issues. Dialogical and dialectical treatment of multilogical issues requires more than simply the desire to explore them; it requires an ability to design discussion, questioning, grouping, and collaborative learning to afford generous opportunities for students to reason. An ability to issue a reasoned conclusion about race relations in this country, or immigration, or affordable housing, or gays in the military requires much more preparation than unexamined opinions require.

Paul's four directions of reasoning force us educators to ask ourselves how we might design our instruction so as to engage students in the construction of substantiated assumptions and justifiable conclusions. Because all teachers work with lesson plans of one kind or another, most critical-thinking adherents encourage that critical thinking be infused within the current educational curriculum rather than be "taught on the side" as another "add on program." For teachers who want to abandon the segmented curriculum of isolated disciplines in favor of a holistic, interdisciplinary curriculum designed around dilemmas, problems, and questions at issue, an understanding of the principles and strategies of critical thinking becomes essential. Because we want our students to think critically in all domains or subject areas, Paul suggests basing lesson plan designs or critical-thinking infusions on understanding the current educational practice in a given lesson. Critiquing the lesson constructively and adducing its specific failure to enhance or encourage thinking eventually leads to redesigning the lesson so as to use the principles and strategies of critical thinking.

This practical philosophy of thinking and reasoning depends, of course, on a teacher's ability to think critically. It is impossible to teach for reasoning if we lack a clear conception of what good reasoning is. These insights developed by those in the critical-thinking movement add a practical and positive component to both educational theory and practice. Applying these strategies for reasoning and thinking critically should be the goal of all educators concerned with helping their students explore personal, social, political, and environmental issues that directly affect their personal lives.

The Needs that Face the Critical-Thinking Movement

Equipped with a coherent and transformative principles for encouraging student thinking, the critical-thinking movement must become more sensitive to the problems of inequality, oppression, racism, social and cultural divisions, authoritarianism, and inauthentic renderings of history if it is to become truly liberatory. Critical pedagogy now abetted by critical-thinking strategies has as its task the unmasking of the oppressive and authoritarian activities of pedagogy so they may be recognized and challenged. Critical thinking should then be focused on the experiences of the oppressed, with the understanding that these experiences harbor both positive transformative potentials and the seeds of domination and internalized oppression. Working on these experiences with students to free human potential and reveal the logic of domination should be the function of the critical-thinking teacher. When we speak of "critical thinking," we include the need to work critically with others and to decide collaboratively what kind of world we want to live in. Critical thinking entails much more than thinking; it presumes a commitment to thinking in the interest of changing social reality. We want students to think critically about the social state of reality and the implications of ideology on their daily lives so they may become more thoughtful producers and consumers of personal and social knowledge.

The techniques Paulo Freire developed in his literacy campaigns raised dialectical questions of subjectivity and objectivity worthy of examination. After two months of participating in cultural group discussion activities, a peasant told Freire (1985),

> When we were tenants and the master would call us naive, we would say, "Thank you Master." To us that was a compliment. Now that we're becoming critical, we know what he meant by naive. He was calling us fools. We (the teachers) asked him, "What do you mean by becoming critical?" "To think correctly," he answered, "to see reality as it is" (p. 17).

Studying Freire's case histories, we can see that the peasants held certain associational assumptions about the psychological and material basis of their lives: their relations to production, authority, and personal authorship. These assumptions arose out of the objective reality of their domination, leading them to believe, for example, that the master is superior in all ways to the peasant. The implication of accepting this assumption as reality is the reproduction of domination both subjectively and objectively. We are the subjects of the processes of our beliefs. We can either be conscious and critical subjects, authors of the history of our lives lived with and for others, or mere subjective pawns, uncritical reproducers of unquestioned historical conditions, claims, and subjective reality—our own jailers, so to speak.

Meanwhile, unmasking assumptions by problem posing and Socratic questioning creates the opportunity for critical literacy and transformative metacognition. Helping peasants question the origins of their associational assumptions became essential in uncovering the associational nature of their thinking while exposing the implications of continued domination. Unmasking associational assumptions breathes dialectical life into an understanding of reality as opposing points of view emerge to negate unexamined associational thinking. Questioned assumptions influence lived life and can alter one's acceptance of material conditions. The peasant found the origins of associational thinking within the objective and subjective reality of social and economic relations to the master. These relations had been enforced by the superstructure and popular culture of "the master narrative." The peasants' only evidence was for their assumptions were their unexamined objective and subjective experiences clothed in the reproduction of the dominance of everyday life. This experience shared with others in collective unconsciousness had become the incontrovertible truth the peasants internalized to rationalize patterns of behavior and objective reality. Devoid of opportunities to penetrate the logic of the master narrative both subjectively and objectively, they had memorialized the implications of these unexamined associational assumptions in personal enslavement, and alienation, and they had objectified them historically in the reproduction of the social relations of production that preserved the associational assumptions in the service of personal, social, and political incarceration.

Thus, the vicious cycle of domination, exploitation, and uncritical acceptance of beliefs as a way of life continues as historical de-evolution in thought and practice. Associational thinking or irrational learning is the voiceless reflection of internalized oppression as much as it is the lived expression of domination. The voice of internalized oppression becomes the expression of domination by its very dialectical nature. This dialectic of oppression can be unmasked only by educational opportunities that allow people to gain insights into the logic of domination, subordination, and associational thinking through Socratic questioning and problem posing. So we see that education can never be neutral. True education for liberation must constantly be poised to unmask the fraudulent repression of everyday life. It must be committed in both political and social terms to the absolute negation of irrational thought and action through critical reasoning about the circumstances and realities of oppression and associational thinking. It must be mirrored in affective dimensions of humility and modesty, civility and fair-mindedness, responsibility and discipline, and perseverance and courage. Furthermore it must be modeled in the practice of everyday life. As Karl Marx (1932) noted early in his life,

> If you wish to influence other people, you must be a person who really has a stimulating and encouraging effect upon others. If you love without evoking love in return, i.e., if you are not able, by the manifestation of yourself as a loving person to make yourself a beloved person, then your love is impotent and a misfortune (p. 241).

In the words of Ghandi, "We must become the change we seek."

Storm and Parsons (1982), in their book *Facing History and Ourselves,* quoted a teacher as stating,

> All the elegant teaching strategies in the world are useless without rich content material (p. 4).

Critical thinkers like Paul (1990) hint at this realization but fail concretely to confront and internalize the need to concentrate on rich content dedicated to improving the human condition. Commenting on critical thinking and personal and social production, Paul noted that

> Furthermore, critical thinking, because it involves our working out afresh our own thinking on a subject, and because our own thinking is a unique product of our self-structured experience, ideas, and reasoning, is intrinsically a new "creation," a new "making," a new set of cognitive and affective structures of some kind (p. 9).

Yet our thinking is often not the product of our self-structured experience, but is instead the product of ideological and institutional norms and standards of power and domination, pseudo-culture, prejudice, and false advertising. That is to say our self-structured experience is experience socially structured or related to the material conditions of human existence, not simply our existential or subjective realities. This formulation is not meant to diminish the role of the individual; on the contrary, it is a celebration of true individuality as opposed to unconscious individualism. This "creation," or new "making," then becomes perceived as a political act, an adventure in dialectical reasoning and understanding, a realization of socially structured domination and the wherewithal to challenge it.

Thus, this creative thinking becomes the act of self-production through social transformation. Here is where the ideas of critical thinking and critical pedagogy overlap. If we subject current and past reality to critical examination, reflection, and analysis, then questions of how we reason well and how we help our students reason well become essential. For example, take the question of Columbus's arrival on this continent. To understand the points of view of the Taino Indians, Native Americans, or African-American cultures relative to this event, this question arises: What do we need to do to reason well about these points of view? First we need to identify some question at issue or problems to be solved. How can we help students do this effectively? Then we need some information about these points of view. Do we have the resources? If not, where do we find them and why do we lack them? Do our students know how to locate these narratives? If they are not in our texts, have the students discussed why?

Once students have the appropriate resources, which usually appear outside their texts, how can they critically examine these narratives? What assumptions guide the African-American narratives at the time of Columbus? Are they different or the same as the Native-American assumptions? Why or why not? Did they have evidence for what they believed? What evidence? What conclusions did these points of view arrive at concerning Columbus's arrival? Were they different or the same? In what ways? What were the implications of these conclusions historically?

I would also want my students to reason historically, connecting the past with the present by analyzing the logic of contemporary points of view surrounding Columbus. They would need to engage in the same rigorous analysis when reading these accounts. Finally, they would want to develop their own perspective on the issue either in the form of a group report, individual reports, role-playing, drama, and so forth. Students need to understand standards for good reasoning, sensitivity to evidence, the need for relevant data, and the importance of information in the form of alternative points of view. Ultimately, to engage in this collaborative endeavor of capturing the logic of diverse and disenfranchised historical narratives, students would need to gain an insight into the affective dimension of learning, paying particular attention to critically listening, reading, speaking, questioning, and writing.

As much as critical pedagogy concerns itself with the what of education critical thinking has concerned itself with the how. Linking these two powerful insights while helping students understand the logic of that which they study is essential if they are to learn to reason effectively and capture the subject domain intellectually. Moreover, the subject domain itself must be critically scrutinized for what it represents or fails to represent as an opportunity for acquiring knowledge about oppression, racism, sexism, equality, critical thinking, transformative metacognition, and critical action. Trivial pursuits at this point are discredited pedagogical practices that undermine relevant contemporary, and historical thinking circumventing the benefits of social- and self-production, and self-authored transformation.

As much as proponents of the critical-thinking movement insist on addressing the wider issues of domination, authority, and subjugation, they must also make sure to raise these issues among parents, in the wider community struggles, within teacher organizations, and before political leaders. For this reason, critical-thinking advocates must pay particular attention to issues regarding restructuring education, educational equity, multilingualism, the privatization of schooling, and multiculturalism. Combining the best features of critical pedagogy and critical thinking in the service of developing an educational theory and practice devoted to humanity requires us to use the views and strategies of the critical-thinking movement in the service of eradicating social injustice. We must also exercise a commitment to emphasizing the importance of cross-cultural learning while concentrating on developing the values and dispositions essential for critical thinking. Concentrating educational efforts on wider community issues so as to transform the material conditions of education in favor of higher-order learning must become the political agenda of the critical-thinking movement.

Chapter 4

Discrete and Cosmetic Multiculturalism: Eurocentrism, Androcentrism, Entreprenurialship, Afrocentrism, and the "Heroes and Holidays" Curriculum

The European West is not only the world of material wealth and power, including military might; it is also the site of the triumph of the scientific spirit, rationality, and practical efficiency, just as it is the world of tolerance, diversity of opinions, respect for human rights and democracy, concern for equality—at least the equality of rights and opportunities—and social justice. It is the best of the worlds that have been known up until this time. Consequently, it becomes impossible to contemplate any other future for the world than its progressive Europeanization. For the most optimistic, this Europeanization, which is simply the diffusion of a superior model, functions as a necessary law, imposed by the forces of circumstances. The conquest of the planet by Europe is thus justified, to the extent that it has roused other peoples from their fatal lethargy. For others, non-European peoples have an alternative choice: either they can accept Europeanization and internalize its demands, or, if they decide against it, they will lead themselves to an impasse that inevitably leads to their decline. The progressive Westernization of the world is nothing more than the expression of the triumph of the humanist universalism invented by Europe.

—Samir Amin
Eurocentrism (1989, p. 108)

Disenfranchised Narratives and the Complacent Classroom

Centered within the narrative of the dominant perspective, a curriculum that promotes one historical and contemporary point of view at

the expense of subordinate points of view, or what I call "disenfranchised narratives," is disingenuous and does nothing to challenge the
internalized myths about culture children absorb in their daily lives. In
fact, this monological presentation of the dominant culture as reality
promises forever to silence the culture of the disenfranchised while
advertising as truth a depiction of people and points of view from a
Eurocentric, androcentric, and entrepreneurial frame of reference. The
result of this monopolization of thought is reinforced sociocentricity,
or the belief in the superiority of one cultural posture (its economic,
gender, and social functions) over another.

Classrooms that adopt this philosophy of pedagogy follow routines
that (1) depict only one socio-economic historical point of view on
issues of contemporary and social relevancy; (2) consciously or unconsciously stereotype; (3) fail to acknowledge differences in historical
and contemporary cultural points of view among peoples of color,
newly arriving immigrants, women, and the disabled; and (4) ignores
or disdains perspectives regarding sexual preference. We see these
attitudes displayed in classroom toys, posters, educational materials,
bulletin boards, and of course curriculum content materials. As a result, the Eurocentric point of view becomes the ideological protector
of the material conditions of cultural intolerance and domination. It
functions to propound the revisionist idea of the significant us and the
insignificant others that dishonors contemporary life and history.
Eurocentric education teaches that what is written of history is benign
and benevolent, and what is benign and benevolent, has been the
subject of history. This demands a passive acceptance, an uncritical
affirmation, and a personal and social acquiescence in "fact" as the
appearance of truth, which by the very presentation of its ontological
superiority affirms itself, marginalizes disparate frames of reference,
and obtains without challenge, a monopoly on the claim to truth. This
is an ego and sociocentric truth concerned with and for itself, a truth
borne of a specific set of social and economic relations and developments coupled with a lack of personal and social consciousness and
an allegiance to historically distorted oppression.

Metaphorically speaking, by its sheer dominance of discourse
Eurocentricity expresses and objectifies nothing more than its desire
to slumber—that is, to remain dormant and find recognition as a dream
presented as waking reality. In this somnambulism, Eurocentricity becomes the guardian of sleep and the banisher of those other narratives likelier to achieve real sociocentric truth. Both in form and con-

tent, Eurocentricity becomes the celebratory monologue of the naked image of its self-portrait of power. It is the tyranny of received truth over the democracy of expression, a view of history that reduces to "sin" any deviation that challenges the Euro knowledge base.

When one studies contemporary fascist thought, one notices its similarities to Eurocentrism and the Calvinistic idea that who reaches heaven involves both a fear of the "wrath of God," and God's random choices. In the act of choosing, from the Calvinist point of view, God decides whom to exclude, whom to "damn" to hell—that is to say, Slavs, Gypsies, Jews, Indians, Quakers, non-whites and non-conformists—much the way fascism seeks expressive delineation. Calvinism amounted—still amounts—to a totalitarian alliance of Church and State and the idea that God (too!) predetermines those who gain access to his "kingdom"—"those" being the financially successful, white European men, significant others, and persons with economic and political "standing" in an inherently unequal community. Calvinism, of course, grew into something much more than a Protestant sect—namely, the rationalization of a specific socioeconomic order where acquisition measures goodness.

Enforcing this nonsense required education to play a significant and precise role in presenting a picture of self-serving reality, especially when the issues of power and franchise came up. With the belief that men and women are essentially evil at the core of the Calvinist, the only cleansing could be a life of endless toil and self-denial—a handy requisite for the emerging needs of capitalism. This subservience then needed to be taught and incorporated soundly in educational theory and practice as a sound socialization practice. Considering the plight of the "insignificant others," the peoples of color and diversity doomed to hell with no possibility of reprieve, we can discern an incipient "master race" theory. In *Religion and the Rise of Capitalism*, R. H. Tawney (1954) observed that

> Calvin did for the Bourgeoisie of the sixteenth century what Marx did for the proletariat of the 19th. The doctrine of predestination satisfied the same hunger for an assurance that the forces of the universe are on the side of the select as was to be assuaged in a different age by the theory of historical materialism (p. 99).

Furthermore, Wasserman (1972) noted that

> Puritanism became an endless tribute to a single-minded drive to amass wealth and power, to the unhappiness of man, to a petty community consciousness

and universe limited by a divine and wrathful divine authority, and to a relentless fear of death and what might lie beyond (p. 43).

The Calvinism of the sixteenth century clearly informs Eurocentrism with its claims of truth, goodness, "choices" for preordained sanctity, and apologies for the need to oppress the unchosen. With religion in the service of the imposition of European capitalism came docility to conform with the new demands of social production. Similarly, an ideology of conquest developed during the Renaissance, a period that included the traditional year of European incursion, 1492. The conquest of the Americas developed a sense of heightened sociocentric thought among Europeans who for the first time began to form and then implement an ideology of conquest. As Amin has insightfully stated:

> In a certain way, then, capitalism as a potential world system did not exist until there existed a consciousness of its conquering power (p. 73).

This is to say that the ideological dimensions of the "new social order" marked by private enterprise, market exchange, and free wage labor was dialectically created and rendered indispensable in rationalizing and ordaining egocentric, sociocentric thinking and conquest. Objective reality in this way became ideologically ordained.

We see this European superiority defined and coalescing into what we now know as Eurocentrism, or the arrogance of a theory of world history, a global project, or a "new world order" forged from revolutionary changes in socio-economic reality. I treat Eurocentrism here as the contrivance of a developing capitalistic society and then its greatest ideological defender. Eurocentrism must attribute, as Amin noted, a false sense of universalism to the world, rationalizing the ecumenical superiority of the "free market" order and thus legitimizing the historical record in its own self-interest. It does this by elevating European culture to a lofty level of pseudo-development while imposing on the histories and narratives of other peoples' particular and fragmented traits, rationalizing their accomplishments as aberrations of the universal European norm, primitive in ideological form and material content. In this way, Eurocentrism becomes more than just the ideological protector of a capitalistic mode of production; it also serves as an ideological apologist for oppression, inequality, and authoritarianism. It has become a religion in its own right—a hideous reflection of itself.

Historically, Eurocentrism in this country has expressed its view of reality in outright racist terms for example, Moody (1910) quoted, our most prominent "national entrepreneurial heroes," J.P. Morgan, as saying,

> Niggers are lazy, ignorant, unprogressive; railroad traffic is created only by industrious, intelligent, and ambitious people (p. 188).

Teddy Roosevelt (1916), himself a rabid proponent of a Eurocentric view of the world, urged in his book *Fear God and Take Your Own Part* that we

> . . . insist on the thorough Americanization of the new-comers to our shores, and let us also insist on the thorough Americanization of ourselves (pp. 56–57).

Roosevelt then went off on a diatribe directed at the President of Harvard University, stating in no uncertain terms that

> the futile sentimentalists of the international arbitration type [promote] a flabby timid kind of character which eats away the great fighting qualities of our race (p. 57).

In 1897, according to Wasserman (1972) Roosevelt told the Naval War college that the "great masterful races have been fighting races" (p. 55).

This is the man who, according to Richard Hofstadter (1948), boasted that "I killed a Spaniard with my own hands" and observed that

> I don't go so far as to think that the only good Indians are dead Indians, but I believe nine out of every ten are, and I shouldn't like to inquire to closely into the case of the tenth. The most vicious Cowboy has more principle than the average Indian (p. 212).

This is the man who led this country as a highly revered president. Here is Roosevelt in his book *The Winning of the West* (1905):

> During the past three centuries, the spread of the English speaking peoples over the world's waste spaces has been not only the most striking feature in the world's history, but also the event of all others most far reaching in its effects and its importance. There have been many other races that at one time or another had their great periods of expansion—as distinguished from more conquest—but there has never been another whose expansion has been either so broad or so rapid (pp. 1–4).

Clearly Roosevelt entertained master-race assumptions, and as a spokesman for the United States of America successfully modeled an early version of the Eurocentric and sociocentric superiority so apparent in contemporary reality. In Hofstadter's account, in 1899, before he was elected president, Roosevelt commented that

> In every instance the expansion has taken place because the race was a great race. It was a sign and proof of greatness in the expanding nation, and moreover bear in mind that in each instance it was of incalculable benefit to mankind. When great nations fear to expand, shrink from expansion, it is because their greatness is coming to an end. Are we still in the prime of our lusty youth, still at the beginning of our glorious manhood, to sit down among the outworn people, to take our place with the weak and craven? A thousand times no! (pp. 212–213).

Roosevelt went so far in his xenophobic lust as to encourage American women to bear more children to ensure the dominance of the Anglo-Saxon race, much as Hitler later did in Germany. It is no surprise that he sent "The Great White Fleet" around the world. An ideological tool designed to sustain imperialistic adventures into Cuba, the Philippines, and Nicaragua, racial rhetoric from the likes of Theodore Roosevelt echoed in the halls of education and elsewhere throughout the country. The superiority of the Anglo-Saxon race joined the agenda in nearly every American classroom while at the same time it raised a useful thirst for third world invasion and colonialism. Thus what paraded as education was simply the apologetic pedagogy of Eurocentrism, sociocentrism, and racial superiority. Our students have few opportunities to examine American history of this kind critically. That the frankly racist sentiments expounded by prominent Eurocentric ideologues never appear in American history texts is a conscious strategy. In his book *Beveridge and the Progressive Era*, Bowers (1932) quoted "progressive" Senator Albert Beveridge of Indiana:

> Grant never forgot that we are a conquering race, and that we must obey our blood and occupy new markets, and if necessary, new lands. . . . He had the prophet's seer-like sight which beheld, as a part of the Almighty's infinite plan, the disappearance of debased civilizations and decaying races before the higher civilization of the nobler and more virile types of men. . . . It is God's great purpose made manifest in the instincts of our race, whose present phase is our personal profit, but whose far-off end is the redemption of the world and the christianization of mankind. . . . God has not been preparing the English speaking and Tectonic peoples for a thousand years for nothing but bane and idle self-contemplation. No! He has made us the master organizers of the world to establish system where chaos reigns (pp. 68–76).

In other words, Eurocentrism had as its chore civilizing "the savages."

With this kind of ranting and raving urging on global expansion and imperialism it is no wonder the Eurocentric point of view pervaded the school systems, or that fascist sentiment found—and continues to find—expression in Western Europe and here at home. Eurocentrism has appointed itself the principal apologist for and protectorate of inequality among peoples in the name of profit, avarice, ethnic purity, and egocentric self-vested interests. Senator Beveridge went on to memorialize his own egocentric thinking:

> I walked the floor night after night and I am not ashamed to tell you gentlemen, that I went down on my knees and prayed Almighty God for light and guidance more than one night. And one night it came to me this way—I don't know how it was but it came. . . . There was nothing left for us to do but to take them all, and to educate the Filipinos, and uplift and civilize and Christianize them, and by God's grace do the very best we could by them as our fellow men for whom Christ also died. And then I went to bed, and went to sleep, and slept soundly (pp. 68–76).

Eurocentric thought has a unique and interesting ability to postulate a world defined and governed outside of human experience. Eurocentrism rationalizes itself to the exclusion of human beings; it becomes a spectacle, a universal law that transcends the history of natural diversity and humankind. Its divine ordination allows Eurocentric thinking to impose itself on every form of life, from the natural environment to the diverse human beings who occupy it. It thus becomes instrumentalist both in form and content, defining the parameters and limits of nature, human thought, and human behavior.

We are all taught to view the world as if it were some linear progression beginning with the Greeks, continuing through the Roman hegemony, feudalism and European capitalism, up to today. This view of history ignores the histories of countless millions of peoples on the peripheries of this parade. The Eurocentric view of world history and present reality hardly mentions, let alone respects, the African and Asiatic contributions to knowledge and civilization. Again, Amin Samir (1989) is instructive:

> The product of this Eurocentric vision is the well-known version of "Western" history—a progression from Ancient Greece to Rome to feudal Christian Europe to capitalist Europe—one of the most popular of received ideas. Elementary school books and popular opinion are as or even more important in the creation and diffusion of this construct as the most erudite theses developed to justify the "ancestry" of European culture and civilization (p. 90).

A glance at recent children's literature on Christopher Columbus (Osborne,1987) reveals this inauthentic supremacy of the Eurocentric viewpoint:

> When Christopher Columbus was a child, he always wanted to be like Saint Christopher. He wanted to sail to faraway places and spread the word of Christianity. Columbus marveled at how God had changed everything for the best (p. 3).

Or consider this passage from a still-in-print volume on Columbus (D' Aulaire 1965) suggesting that he began

> to think that the Lord had chosen him to sail west across the seas to find the riches of the East for himself and to carry the Christian faith to the heathens (p. 16).

These two examples of the dominant narrative would propagandize the world in the interest of one point of view—the *non-heathens*, usually white Europeans bent upon spreading the Christian truth. Such passages, far from restricted to studies of Columbus, can be found throughout textbook treatments of historical and contemporary reality. European idealization and mythology routinely divides the world between the "heathens" and the "non-heathens." These texts give children early moral lessons in domination and subjugation. For many, the texts provide their first exposure to the world of military adventurism, foreign policy, action, conquest, and war. Never do these books encourage students to examine, explore, evaluate, synthesize, or capture the logic of, for example, the Taino Indians' narratives at the time of Columbus's landing; nor do they critically examine the narratives of the Caribe Indians or the oral histories of Amerindians, or Black slaves brought to Madeira as a result of Columbus's "discovery." Presenting students with one Eurocentric viewpoint, which promotes the interests of those in control of public discourse, serves to strip classroom life of critical thinking and thus cripple the future. In short, it represents the tyranny of replacing dialogue with monologue in the name of education.

In her indictment of the new Houghton Mifflin series of textbooks that could yield 52.9 million dollars in sales to California school districts alone, Elizabeth Martinez (1992–93), pointed out that

> The world view put forth in these texts rests on defining the United States as "a nation of immigrants." This view sees Native Americans as the "first immi-

grants" based upon their having come across the Bering Strait from Asia (although this theory is rejected by many Indians, a disagreement not mentioned in the series). After Indians come Africans (but weren't they brought here in chains?) and then Mexicans (but wasn't their homeland seized by Anglo force?). Europeans and Asians round out the list of so-called immigrants (p. 10).

Martinez has discovered the hidden curriculum and then discussed the inadequacy of basing a textual account of American history on the immigrant "salad bowl" conception precisely because it leaves out disparate cultural, gender, and economic points of view. She causes one to ask, for example, why the disparate views of Native Americans elude the book and why the Spanish and Mexican domination of Native American land is left out. The point is, all of us need to examine and critique our own cultures. Martinez continued:

> The immigrant model has usually included the "melting pot" metaphor; the Houghton Mifflin series rejects that now tarnished image in favor of the "salad bowl" which allows different peoples to retain their ethnic identity and culture inside one big unified society. But how different is the bowl from the pot? (p. 10).

Excluded from both the salad bowl and melting pot are issues of domination and power that have driven America's socioeconomic development, and world history in general. It is not enough to "season" the Eurocentric salad bowl with accounts of "great waves of immigration." Accurate portrayals of the cultural, racial, and economic diversity of our society demand an understanding of historical events involving power, disempowerment, gender, equality, ethnicity, culture, economic wealth, authority, and capital accumulation. Students should understand that the racial and economic domination and repression they suffered at the hands of Eurocentric domination and capitalist conquest unites many of the "so-called immigrant cultures." As Martinez adduced, Houghton Mifflin uses its third grade social studies text, *From Sea to Shining Sea*, to depict Mexicans for third graders "only as farm workers and even then their historic role in producing great agricultural wealth is not recognized" (p. 10).

Also absent from the accounts of Mexican Americans in the third grade text are their struggles to gain equality and their struggles against a series of economic and social repressions here in the United States. Focusing on the fourth grade edition, *Oh California*, Martinez acknowledged that it offers lots of Latinos, but they are almost all "explorers" and "settlers" and missionaries or upper-class ranchers. Nowhere do we find lower-class Mexicans or those many Mexicans violently repressed, driven off the land, even lynched, from the Gold Rush days to the 1930s. Gone are the massive strikes by Mexican workers in the 1930s, or the deportation of thousands who were actually citizens. Nowhere do the fourth grade children encounter the repressive organizations developed throughout the mid 1800s to the 1930s, that targeted and continue to target Mexicans for exploitation. Conveniently shunned are the organizations for justice and equality Mexican-Americans founded to fight that repression.

Martinez recognized that excised from this revisionistic portrait of history are the people's struggles for self-determination and humanity. Any hint of subjugation or domination has dropped from sight. Without opportunities to understand the logic of oppression, students can hardly develop a critical literacy in the interest of eradicating oppression. By offering up this type of pedagogical pabulum as "multiculturalism," Houghton Mifflin makes sure students see a history unlikely to help them understand their present or infer their future. They give up their heritage and the realization that men and women—in this case, Mexicans—faced racial hatred, socioeconomic exploitation, and dehumanization in this country. Because these attitudes and behaviors persist (similar examples of exploitation and dehumanization occur and can be found throughout social relations between many cultural groups and the American power structure) students lose a chance at a true historical perspective and thereby fail to understand and resist contemporary forces of power and economic exploitation. They become historically disabled, mentally ill-equipped to define life through history and history through life.

Continuing her critique of the presentation of "multiculturalism" in the Houghton Mifflin series, Martinez pointed out that

> The books for Kindergarten, *The World I See*, and Grade 1, *I Know a Place*, lay the foundation for Eurocentrism. Both include a thematic photo with several pupils of color, including a probable Latino, and then the K volume has one story about Mexico. But the drawings in the "Long Ago" pages of the K book are overwhelmingly populated by whites; one image shows 31 persons out of 35 as white, another makes all 20 people white, and so forth (p. 10).

Martinez went on to explain that

> A special form of Eurocentric perspective, Hispanicism, flows through the Houghton Mifflin series. Again and again the "customs" and "culture" and

"traditions" of the Mexican people in the U.S. are described as originating in Spain—a European country. Indian or mestizo roots go unnoticed. This would be laughable (how many people in Madrid eat tortillas and beans?) if it were not so racist (p. 11).

Yet the cultural viewpoints of the mestizo and Indian cultures that heavily influenced Mexican life and culture are insidiously absent from the texts. In explaining Eurocentrism Martinez pointed out that

The Houghton Mifflin authors actually discuss Eurocentrism (Grade 8), defining it as "the notion that Europe is the Center of the world." They then, however, affirm that viewpoint by stating, "And for a long period of time it seemed to be. From the 1500s to the 1900s, European countries controlled a large part of the world (p. 11).

There the explanation ends, still leaving readers with a Eurocentric view of Eurocentricism. The same book tells us that

U.S. citizens . . . tended to look on Mexico as a backward nation, an attitude that has continued to this day (p. 11).

No comment on or criticism of this viewpoint appears. Once again, omitted from discussion are points of view that argue with the Eurocentric explanation and predominance—points of view like those of African Americans, Native Americans, or the Mexicans themselves. Where are the critical-thinking questions among the other "thought-provoking" questions displayed in the colored clusters at the end of the chapters? What is a backward nation? Does it depend on your point of view? Why was Europe seen as the center of the world? Who defined this point of view? Whose purposes did it serve? Who got left out of this assumption? What would a Eurocentric view of history assume? Why? What evidence would it rely on? What would one infer about people and life from this perspective? Why? Are there other points of view that conflict with this one? What are their historical origins? What assumptions form these points of view? Do they have evidence for what they believe? What would be the implications of each point of view?" All such critical-thinking questions are absent from the text.

Martinez addressed the Houghton Mifflin treatment of the Alamo in its fifth grade series:

The Grade 5 teachers edition emphasizes that students should see the Battle of the Alamo as "an important symbol of freedom and liberty" where "heroes" fought for Texas Independence (p. 11).

Where are disparate points of views that suggest the battle at the Alamo involved colonization and land theft? Its heroes, Europeans, believed they had a divine right to take land and then win memorialization for their "courage." We never see the conquest of Texas from the viewpoint of the conquered. Mexicans see the Alamo less as a victory than as a moment of resistance to the colonization and the imposition of authority. Where is this point of view? Martinez set the historical record straight: William Travis was an escaped murderer, James Bowie was a slave runner, and Davy Crockett was found hiding under the floorboards after all the rest had been killed. Somehow these facts escaped the Houghton Mifflin series.

What this strained version of "multiculturalism" shows hardly helps students to reason critically. Without an understanding of power, human struggle, racism, oppression, and the common struggle among diverse people, students lack the information they need to arrive at reasoned historical judgments. They cannot understand how these forces continually reappear in contemporary reality, in popular culture, and in their own lived realities; precisely because of the imposition of Eurocentric thought as truth, students lose opportunities to reason within different historical points of view in the interest of fair-mindedness. Their rational decision making about what to believe and do about other people and themselves loses out to the prerogatives of a Eurocentric ideological curriculum consciously designed to force-feed citizens. When Spike Lee observed (in November of 1992) that all African Americans should take a day off school and see his film *Malcolm X*, he was neither promoting the film nor seeking profits. Lee was merely implying that contemporary education remains Eurocentric and has ignored the legacy and thought of Malcolm and African Americans in general, and that schooling provides little raw material for radical self-help, the development of historical awareness, and rational decision making. Lee was arguing, in short, for diversity of points of view within education. He realized that the current educational agenda continues to exclude the voice of disenfranchised narratives.

Teachers fall victim to this exclusion along with the children they serve. Presented with revisionist and racist history devoid of diverse cultural and economic points of view, teachers find themselves powerless to explore their own histories through acquaintances with alternative perspectives. Accompanying these texts for school districts, in-service training sessions show teachers how to disseminate the Eurocentric propaganda—that is to say, the product of someone else's unexamined thinking. They must become, consciously or unconsciously, classroom megaphones for the revisionist multiculturalism in the texts.

Another dereliction of the Houghton Mifflin series is its reluctance to help students critically and constructively critique all cultural forms of domination, be they Latino, African American, Asian, or European. All cultures are sociocentric in nature and have committed errors to achieve some sociocentric advantage or another. These texts fail to provide the information or outline the issues to allow students to examine all sociocentric cultural beliefs in the interests of rational historical and social criticism.

Just as insidious as these textual presentations of history as the "immigrant model" successfully blended in "the salad bowl," the texts leave out issues of power, domination, and struggle students might hold up to their own lives. They are dominated not only by a Eurocentric perspective but also by a gender and class perspective that presents expansionism, exploitation, inequalities in power relations, and subjugation as natural human behavior. We never find out who owns the salad bowl, how he acquired it, or why. As Martinez observed, those like Murieta who fought the U.S. occupation of Mexican lands in California and the Southwest during the Gold Rush days are demonized as rogues:

> Many Mexican people saw [Murieta] as a resistance hero. But the Holt Rinehardt and Winston book calls the resistance heroes "bandits" (p. 11).

Once again, critical multicultural literacy is limited by the advantageous exclusion of other cultural points of view. We simply lack the logic of the other perspective, the other frame of reference: No questions ever appear about what Murieta might have been thinking that led him to the decisions he made and the actions he took.

Without the ability to reason within different points of view, students can hardly develop fair-minded reasoning or critical literacy. Excluding from the historical record points of view not in keeping with the Eurocentric explanation of human reality deprives students of critical-thinking opportunities and produces uncritical minds and easy prey for domination and authoritarian manipulation. We need the work of Martinez and like-minded scholars if we hope to redesign texts and lessons that help students appreciate different cultural, economic, and ethnic points of view. Teachers have to have the time to work cooperatively to critically understand history themselves and then critically examine and analyze the tools of their trade—those textbooks produced by multinational corporations less interested in fostering critical insight into history and contemporary reality than in gaining allegiance to their economic agendas. We teachers must continually question whether and where students receive exposure to the ideas of African-American, Latino, and Asiatic cultures. When they study individuals from historical or contemporary reality do they study the assumptions and conclusions that fueled their existence or simply memorize facts and details for test-taking purposes? In the primary schools, what books and materials in the curriculum other than folk tales and legends offer opportunities for discovering, exploring, examining, and analyzing the social, ideological, and personal lives of diverse geographic, economic, political, and ethnic cultures?

Allow me one last comment on the Houghton Mifflin social studies texts heralded as the last word in multicultural fashion: The fifth grade text, *America Will Be*, contains a four-page chapter entitled "Struggle for Freedom." On one page appears the picture of and small story about W.E.B. DuBois. He is cast as the "leader of the Black movement for equality" and one of the founders of the NAACP, all of which is true (pp. 512–513). In the meager portrayal of DuBois, however, we never learn that he was the first African-American to receive a Ph.D. in this country, was an active member of the Communist Party with strong views during a rebellious time for American labor, and was eventually driven from this country and forced to live in exile. We can all visualize students asked about DuBois, one of the greatest thinkers of the century, responding on the fill-in-the-blank ditto or rote-recall test: "He was a founder of the NAACP."

While teaching in the Los Angeles Unified School District, I found little within the system on in the school libraries that captured the narratives of the disenfranchised. As teachers we have little at our disposal in the way of literature, art, or history to convey diverse and alternative points of view. It thus becomes tempting for teachers, particularly of primary children, to teach "to the text and to the test"—to rely, that is, on the pre-packaged gimmickry of multinational corporations like Houghton Mifflin or Holt. Said another way, it is difficult for most teachers to engage, especially in the early grades, in any form of cultural critique that challenges the assumptions of Eurocentric ideology. Diverse material has, of course, been written; it simply has yet to become a fit subject for the textbook companies whose wares-for-profit comprise the bulk of our classroom resources. Nor has it become the subject of critical examination and analysis among administrators, curriculum specialists, or boards of education.

Meanwhile, the defenders of sociocentric self-interests and the enemies of multiculturalism translate attacks on Eurocentrism as attacks on America—an America nevertheless dedicated to the mythology of Euro-based knowledge and ideology. Many, defenders of Eurocentrism are Christian fundamentalists forging coalitions throughout the United States to proscribe educational materials and literature and to assure that "traditional family values" inform the curriculum. In an article in ACTION, the California Teaching Association newsletter, Robert Simmonds, the founder of Citizens for Excellence in Education, blames the recent Los Angeles riots on a multicultural emphasis in the schools. He notes that the riots

> Were spawned in our public school classrooms . . . where we have been teaching multiculturalism instead of Americanism for 10 years now, and indoctrinating our children with values clarification and self-esteem (p. 9).

According to Simmonds, multicultural education emphasizes racial differences and fosters prejudice rather than a shared American identity. Part of a Christian fundamentalist movement, Simmonds would "take over" our public schools through vouchers and by gaining control of local school boards.

Another even more prominent apologist for the Eurocentric right is Dinesh D'Souza (1991), author of *Illiberal Education* and a luminary among the traditional conservative educational elite:

> Although university leaders speak of the self-evident virtues of diversity, it is not at all obvious why it is necessary to a first-rate education. Universities such as Brandeis, Notre Dame, and Mount Holyoke, which were founded on principles of religious or gender homogeneity, still manage to provide an excellent education. Similarly, foreign institutions such as Oxford, Cambridge, Bologna, Salamanca, Paris, and Tokyo display considerable cultural singularity, yet they are regarded as among the best in the world (p. 230).

"Best in the world at what?" That is the ultimate question. In training and producing educational cyborgs and apologists in the interest of reproducing Eurocentric tradition and ideology, they are indeed some of the best universities in the world. But against a yardstick of creating unique opportunities for students of all races, socio-economic classes, and genders to achieve an education concerned with human dignity and social justice, their case is somewhat less compelling. In fact, the universities D'Souza applauds are economically inaccessible to most people in this country and certainly people of color and women. For D'Souza and his ilk it matters little that Japan is hostile to cultural difference, highly sociocentric, and prejudiced. All that matters are the interests of capital, the fundamental criterion—that is to say, whether the institutions educating people can reproduce the joy that accompanies capital accumulation:

> The study of cultures can never compensate for a lack of thorough familiarity with the founding principles of one's own culture. Just as it would be embarrassing to encounter an educated Chinese who had never heard of Confucius, however well versed he may be in Jefferson, so also it would be a failure of liberal education to teach Americans about the Far East without immersing them in their own philosophical literary tradition "from Homer to the present." Universal in scope, these works prepare Westerners to experience both their own, as well as other, ideas and civilizations (p. 255).

The fault D'Souza so facilely reveals here is his conviction that one understands oneself first and then proceeds on, so-to-speak, to the more "exotic" awareness—the postulation of a form of linear progression of thought, consciousness, and education that requires us to start with our "own" cultural history as if it were reified above the experience of the world of others. For Dinesh and his colleagues, we discover ourselves first and then others, not ourselves *through others*. His notion of the educated person is someone who has heard of Confucius, not one who can think critically about issues that demand dialogical and dialectical thinking. D'Souza even presumes to portray the thinking of Paul Robeson in the service of his own self-interested attack on multiculturalism when he writes:

> Paul Robeson recalled that his father took him "page by page through Virgil, and Homer, and other classics." As a result, Robeson says, "a love of learning, a ceaseless quest for truth in all its fullness, this my father taught." (p. 256).

D'Souza fails to mention that Robeson belonged to the Communist Party, was well read on issues beyond the parameters of Eurocentrism, and became a victim of Eurocentrism and racism. For Paul Robeson, forced like DuBois into exile for his political views, being resurrected like this as a defender of the universal value of Western literary work would be a cruel joke.

As to "political correctness," the current sloganeering attack by right-wing Eurocentrists is boldly hypocritical. As Troy Duster, a professor at Cal-Berkeley quoted by Beneke (1992) recognized, we have had campaigns for someone's brand of political correctness from the witch hunts in Salem to the McCarthyism of the 1950s (p. 15). The multicultural critics coined the current term "political correctness," thus labeling anything that would challenge current sociocentric thinking as foreign and extreme. The *Utne Reader*, a popular culture magazine, recently republished an article by John Taylor (1991) first published in the *New York* magazine. In his article, Taylor noted that:

> In the past few years, a new sort of demagogic and fanatical fundamentalism has arisen. The new fundamentalists are an eclectic group; they include multiculturalists, feminists, radical homosexuals, and Marxists. What unites them—as firmly as Christian fundamentalists are united in the belief that the Bible is the revealed word of God—is their conviction that Western culture and American society are thoroughly and hopelessly racist, sexist, and oppressive (p. 50).

According to *Time* magazine of April of 1991,

> A troubling number of teachers at all levels regard the bulk of American history and heritage as racist, sexist, and classist and believe their purpose is to bring about social change—or, on many campuses, to enforce social changes already achieved (p. 16).

In the first place, Taylor failed to construct a convincing analogy between his political correctness and religious zealotry. He seems unable to discern that historical evidence for one's beliefs differs from the fundamentalism of theology. Yet the political correctness of the right goes unquestioned when we raise the Gulf War, or poverty, or race, or economics, or eugenics, or abortion, or countless controversial issues. The right has always been "politically correct," and as proof there exists a population of Marxist educators who were summarily fired for their political views in the 1960s and 1970s. The real champions of political correctness fail to mention this uncomfortable fact when they ridicule those who challenge racism, sexism, homophobia, and inequality. In fact, D'Souza's political correctness appears in his observation that the "uninhibited ideological proselytizing" of the movement for social change in education belies the very notion of scholarship. For D'Souza, "If education cannot help to separate truth from falsehood, beauty from vulgarity, right from wrong, then what can it teach us?" (p. 230). D'Souza should ponder his own perfectly valid question. For education should help us learn how to arrive at our own reasoned judgments on what constitutes truth, beauty, and the right. But failing to provide or heed an historical record cripples any search for the answers. For those like D'Souza it is always their truth, their beauty, and their notions of right and wrong.

Although she directed her comment at what she called "ethnically oriented intelligence tests," Jane R. Mercer (1985) imparted a sound idea of multiculturalism in stark opposition to D'Souza's claims:

> [A] multicultural perspective would recognize the integrity and value of differ-
> ent cultural traditions. It would not assume that the Anglo-American culture is
> necessarily superior to other traditions, or that Anglo conformity is impera-
> tive for social cohesion. It would accept the fact that there are multiple cul-
> tural mainstreams in modern America and that individual citizens have the
> right to participate in as many of these mainstreams as they wish. Differences
> in life-styles, language and values would be treated with respect, and persons
> from minority cultures would not be regarded as culturally disadvantaged,
> culturally deprived, or empty vessels (p. 32).

For critics of multiculturalism and critical thinking Mercer's type of reasoning is unacceptable and even un-American.

The Entrepreneurial and Androcentric Classroom

I recently reviewed a widely utilized educational program in public schools for third, fourth, and fifth graders entitled *Homestead*. Put out by the Interact Co., Homestead is a social studies program-kit advertised as "A simulation of establishing a frontier farm and com-munity" (p. 74). The teacher learns in the accompanying manual that this simulation "game"

> . . . is concerned with the daily life of frontier settlers. This simulation gives
> students a better understanding of the kind of lives these rugged frontiers-
> men lived, particularly how their decisions changed the West. By making de-
> cisions concerning what kind of land to settle, what types of crops to raise,
> where to build roads and what persons should run their government, students
> can gain a better understanding of one important period in American history
> (p. 2).

The important period in American history is the post-Civil War settlement of the West. The simulation is designed to be used by "flex-ible creative teachers who desire a participatory classroom" (p. 3). The whole simulation has a soap opera "feel good" sense about it, a "fun game" that promises to involve students in the quest for histori-cal knowledge. Unfortunately, the historical information the kit pro-vides represents the viewpoint of Eurocentric male settlers. Nowhere did I find any reference to Native Americans or their viewpoint on homesteading as a form of invasion and conquest, or the implications of homesteading on former Native American lands and life. Nowhere did I find a discussion about those allowed to homestead and those who were not and why—or about socio-economic necessities, the "alternate" immigrants, women, and people of color. The kit failed to present the struggles of the West in terms of the great Range Wars that took place during the post-Civil War era, the development and growth of both the Black and White Farmers Alliances that enrolled millions of members, and the common struggle of different ethnic groups, feminists, socio-economic classes, and cultures against the newly forming monopolies. When studying U.S. history, Harvey Wasserman (1972) believed students should be able to learn that the Farmers Alliance spread through Texas and over the Southwest culminating in the Grange movement, that by 1890 the Northern alliance of farmers settled in the West had over a million members, that the Southern Alliance claimed as many as three million members and the Colored Farmers Alliance centered in the South had another 1.25 million (p. 70). Moreover, these groups all worked together in a common struggle against the railroads, cattle barons, and land sharks.

All references to "robber barons" disappear when students are asked to consider the impact of the railroad. Instead, students learn that

> the new railroad in your community will mean wealth and prosperity for some, lower prices for others, and possible disaster for a few (p. 4).

By contrast, as quoted in Harvey Wasserman's *The History of the United States*, Milton Smith, president of the Louisville and Nashville Railroad in the late 19th century, explained his conception of humanity this way:

> Society as created was for the purpose of one man's getting what the other fellow has, if he can, and keep out of the penitentiary (p. 47).

I found no chance in the simulation game that I reviewed for a student to examine these opposing historical points of view critically. The simulation game silences the historical voices of the farm labor struggle during this period. The Students Guide declares that

> the unofficial winner is the person who has earned the most money and acquired the most land (p. 4).

In short, whoever becomes the best capitalist, à la Milton Smith, wins. We see here an ideology of inequitable power encouraging rugged, competitive individualism, avarice, egocentric reasoning and behavior, and sophistic thinking—something a "flexible creative teacher who desires a participatory classroom" might want to think twice about.

Obviously, this attractively packaged educational game is really a male Eurocentric representation of revisionist entrepreneurialism in the post-Civil War period. By encouraging students to earn the most money and acquire the most land in the name of heroic "frontiersmanship," they become animated to compete, place their personal interests above community interests, actualize narrow-mindedness to acquire more assets, and compromise their integrity in face of accumulating property and wealth. Even worse if it is possible, they develop no insight into ego or sociocentricity, but rely on sophistic thinking to "get their way" and eventually "win." The kit, of course, has a different idea of what "attitudes" the students will experience. According to its Teacher's Guide, the attitudes students experience include

> (1) appreciation of the dedication of persons who left secure [sic] "civilized" communities to go to live on the perilous frontier and (2) respect for frontier Americans who used democratic processes while trying to solve frontier problems: boundary disputes, representative government, taxes (p. 2).

The student participants begin by taking on family identities throughout the game. A list of these identities appears at page five of the Teacher's Guide. Of 36 families 32 are white, two are Chicano, and two are Black. No Native Americans, Asian Americans, or Latinos beyond the two Chicanos appear. Of the 36 families, only two are immigrants with no citizenship, one an Italian winemaker and the other a German doctor. The other 34 are all U.S. citizens even though the Student Guide says that the West was settled so that "many poor people and immigrants would have a chance to live a better life." (p. 7). Twenty-four of the 36 family possibilities are nuclear with eight identities having no family. I found no overt representation of single women who struggled to survive at this time of history. This "educational game" turned out to be a version of "The Rifleman," the popular 1950s television series that itself painted an idealized picture of one Lucas McCain, a "sodbuster" and homesteader during post-Civil War times. In *The Rifleman*, the badguys homesteaders McCain encountered were the swarthy "banditos," Native Americans, dance hall girls, and petty thieves, never the conniving monopolistic railroad barons, land speculators, New York banking interests, or the many cunning merchants who extorted from the poor, and preyed upon those forced or enticed to move West.

This new pedagogical gimmickry markets the same old racist myths while neglecting to incorporate the viewpoints of Native Americans, or frontier women, or (really) children. The missing feminist, ethnic, diverse economic and cultural frames of reference assure that students will avoid historical insights into the affective dimension of learning— empathy and reciprocity—for they will never be invited to reason within the different points of view struggling for recognition during this time in the West. Denied the information, students can hardly come to realize these viewpoints existed. Nor will they analyze the elements of thought that comprised these various viewpoints. The assumptions that guided cultural, feminist, economic, and ethnic frames of reference and voices of resistance; the purposes of their thinking; the inferences that they drew; and the implications these decisions and actions had in distributing power and wealth in the West—all lost in the interests of marketing a diverting "educational" game. Here we have make-believe education, a make-believe town based on make-believe history, and make-believe entrepreneurial market management, and decision-making aimed at setting up a class system.

For example, the jobs or businesses the student who is "forced to move to town" (a clever and friendly way of indicating the implications of going broke or being driven off the land by monopolistic railroad interests or land speculators) finds include "bankers, general store owner, newspaper publisher, bank clerk, general Store clerk, and newspaper reporter" (p.14). The seamstress, the construction worker, the saloon keeper, the blacksmith, the barmaid, the farmhand—that is, the laboring men and women—are nonentities. The class system is ensconced; merchants, doctors, farmers, bankers, and shopkeepers run the government and town; blue collar workers vanish. In their place, the teacher and students use "spread sheets" to figure out their crop yields, their land values, their income and expenses, and their "running balances." The section on "Leaving the Farm" issues these instructions:

> If you should want to move to town, what will you have to do? You will have to sell or rent your land to a classmate. If no one will buy, the teacher will represent other pioneers and will pay you the market value. You will have to

buy a lot in town for a price listed on the TOWN MAP; you will also have to build a house at a cost of $500. Finally, you will have to find a job or start your own business (p. 13).

We know that by the early 1890s farmers everywhere were losing their farms to corporate business, speculators, and banks. According to Wasserman (1972), 25 percent of the farms in Kansas, Nebraska, Iowa, Missouri, Illinois, Indiana, Ohio, and Pennsylvania rested in the hands of Wall Street and the figure exceeded 50 percent in the South. The farmers who eventually rebelled numbered in the millions and included women, Blacks, and immigrants (p. 71). We also know that 200 dollars, an immense sum at the time, to buy a homestead was economically out of reach to most Americans.

The American Association of University Women's report entitled *Creating a Gender Fair Multicultural Curriculum* (1992) stated that

> A curriculum that focuses exclusively on the experiences and perspectives of a single cultural group is ethnocentric—the exact opposite of a multicultural curriculum. Many countries with ethnically homogenous populations have a standardized national ethnocentric curriculum that is taught in all schools. The United States has no national curriculum; curricula are determined at the state and local levels. But in practice, most American public schools follow a highly uniform curriculum that has been shaped by tradition. This traditional curriculum is essentially Eurocentric; that is, it emphasizes the perspectives, history, and products of certain groups of European Americans. In addition, it still centers on the perspectives and accomplishments of men, largely ignoring women of all races and ethnicities (p. 2).

Here are four examples of this Eurocentric perspective:

(1) Slaves were happy and carefree and slavery was a life style; (2) the forest Indians were hostile savages in need of Christian salvation; (3) the Mexicans were dirty invaders bent upon occupying what is now the West; and (4) the westward expansion brought civilization to the plains Indians. Meanwhile, the railroad barons were the good-willed men who built the country; the bankers were benevolent lenders and community leaders who financed America's expansion; and the friendly merchants and storekeepers were those "community leaders" and small entrepreneurs who provided the material for the needs of the new country.

The AAUW report also noted that

The contributions and experiences of girls and women are still marginalized or ignored in many of the textbooks used in our nation's schools.

Schools, for the most part, provide inadequate education on sexuality and healthy development despite national concern about teen pregnancy, the AIDS crisis, and the increase of sexually transmitted diseases among adolescents.

Incest, rape, and other physical violence severely compromise the lives of girls and women all across the country. These realities are rarely, if ever, discussed in schools (p. 3).

When a curriculum fails to reflect the diversity of students' lives, as the AAUW pointed out, it both delivers an incomplete message about the people and the world in which they live, and it "turns students off" as it fails to address their lived realities. Furthermore, a culture that idealizes sexual exploitation in much the same way it idealizes militaristic colonization and violence, is rarely the focus of study. The AAUW report continued:

[An earlier] 1989 study showed that of the ten books most frequently assigned in public high school English courses only one was written by a woman and none by members of minority groups (p. 5).

Hence, Amin's (1989) conclusion is ultimately compelling:

Eurocentrism is therefore anti-universalist, since it is not interested in seeking possible laws of human evolution. But it does present itself as universalist, for it claims that imitation of the Western model by all peoples is the only solution to the challenges of our time (p. vii).

Finally, the pervasive Eurocentric approach to cultural literacy serves in the classroom to increase intolerance, prejudice, racism, and cultural disappreciation as students internalize a cultural code of oppression and subjugation offered as the norm. Furthermore, a Eurocentric education is essentially dehumanizing and reinforces false notions of power, supremacy, and conquest, at the expense of the disenfranchised and subordinate versions of historical and contemporary reality. For students of diverse backgrounds and women it represents something much worse: a revisionist harrowing of their individual and cultural lives.

The Tourist or "Minority-of-the-Month" Approach to Multiculturalism

Although praiseworthy in its goals and fashionable in today's public schools, a tourist approach to multicultural education rests its pedagogical assumptions regarding multicultural knowledge acquisition on the premise that the mere exposure to other cultures will arrest prejudice development and decrease prejudicial attitudes. In other words, if we just give bigoted students more information about other people they will learn to exercise tolerance and empathy, and abandon any propensities for racism, sexism, and classism (or younger children will never develop these attitudes in the first place). The hope is that sharing "foreign" culinary experiences, artifacts from other countries, folk dances, geographical insights, and international music will arrest prejudice development, erase prejudice attitudes, and increase appreciation for diversity.

Although perhaps an improvement over the Eurocentric notion of education, this tourist approach generally deteriorates into visiting bulletin boards on specified cultural days, hosting once-a-year assemblies to celebrate a minority leader or two, studying ethnic and gender groups during designated months, engaging in "units" on other cultures, and sharing geographical insights into and discussions of natural resources from other countries. This tourist approach really comes down to a well-intentioned but naive grafting of an exposure-driven multicultural program on an already Eurocentrically defined curriculum. For this reason it reinforces Eurocentrism.

One example of a noble but uncritical attempt to increase student awareness of culture is *Sharing Our Diversity Grade 2* (1976) published for teachers by the Sacramento School District. Activity #94, "The Spanish Conquer the Aztecs," asks teachers to

> . . . summarize the events and forces which led up to the Spanish conquest of the Aztecs, assist students comprehension of worksheets followed by the film-strip (p. 189).

Turning to the worksheet provided for students, one finds the sheet divided between "Aztec things the Spanish had never seen before they came to Mexico" and "Spanish things that Aztecs had never seen before they came to Mexico" (p. 252). Black-and-white pictures of cups of hot chocolate, corn, squash, guns, big ships, and pyramids decorate the page. The next sheet provides a three-paragraph story of the Spanish explorers. The Spanish wanted the Aztec gold, silver, and land. Moreover, the Spanish won because (1) at first the Aztecs thought Cortez a God, (2) other Mexican Indians who did not like the Aztecs helped the Spanish fight them, and (3) the Aztecs died from strange Spanish-borne illnesses (p. 253).

Next, students are asked to memorize these materials for future recall questions and then to discuss "A time I felt scared about something that was strange to me." One finds the connection between the fears the children recall and the lesson tenuous at best, unless a teacher manages to emphasize the fear the Aztecs, the Indians, and the Spanish conquistadors no doubt felt. Any second grader able to tell what the Aztecs had never seen, tell what the Spanish had never seen, and explain the causes of Aztec colonization, steps smartly down the road toward eradicating racism and intolerance.

Another new series distributed by Lifetouch National School Studios Inc. (1992) offers a lesson on African-Americans entitled "Harambee: A Celebration of African American History." Here is its goal objective:

> Students will be able to discover the richness of the African-American culture and history, and enhance their research and communication skills (p. 14).

Here is how the lesson plan proceeds:

> (1) Begin by discussing how each ethnic group has helped make the United States the country it is today.
> (2) Discuss the history of African Americans in the United States.
> (3) Discuss the African-American culture. If possible have guest speakers come into the classroom to discuss various aspects of culture. Songs, art, food, dances, and folktales should be covered at this time. Students can write their own stories or try art projects.
> (4) Assign each student a famous African American to research. Be sure to include contemporary as well as historical people. Explain what students will be doing at Harambee. Work on clothing, dialogue, etc. You may wish to have some students be in charge of music or be tour guides at Harambee. They could do research on music or other aspects of African-American culture.
> (5) Have a dress rehearsal for the "living timeline" the day before the presentation.

Celebrate at Harambee with music, food, artwork, and the "living timeline" (p. 15).

Despite the earnest tones, the "tourist" or "heroes-and-holidays" approach fails to accord children the opportunity they need to appreciate themselves in a world with others—namely, a chance to reason about the assumptions and claims that comprise diverse points of view on issues of contemporary and historical relevance. When we substitute "exposure" for "reasoning," our students engage in superficial cultural appreciation with, however a possibly insidious implication: they may come to see other cultures as simply aberrations of themselves, exotic people, and uncivilized, evolving cultures. For this reason, the tourist approach can cultivate the kind of sociocentricity I call "fair-minded Eurocentricity." These tourist activities can actually invite stereotyping since they are often presented as existing in an era of nostalgia and anecdotal romanticism; witness the current studies of the American Indian or the people of the rainforest. We see Native Americans in deerskins, never in business suits, and forest people as playful pygmies, never intelligent and resourceful humans at home in a different environment. We are never invited into the viewpoints of the rainforest inhabitants or the Amerindian culture. Students rarely examine the logic that inspires these diverse frames of reference. The assumptions that drive them, or cultural influences on their social and personal conclusions. Students seen them instead as "museum pieces," anthropologically atavistic and to be studied outside contemporary cultural assumptions about life, outside our own historical struggles, and outside our own thoughtful experiences.

Centering a philosophy of education on holidays, historical dates, and quaint excursions into nostalgic and exotic episodes of the lives of others both patronizes the peoples and cultures under study, and disconnects the reality of diversity from the students' concrete existence. In other words, an otherwise well-meaning approach manages to present the reality of culture and diversity as a quaint historical deviation from normal Eurocentricism.

Because the tourist approach to multicultural issues can unwittingly promote sociocentricity and present "the other" as a curiosity examined and analyzed like an interesting museum piece, its claims as a corrective to irrational thinking is itself irrational. People speaking some 146 languages live side by side in Los Angeles yet who would argue that Los Angeles has reached the pinnacle of well-reasoned and harmonious social relations? Exposure simply has not been enough. Exposure plus the opportunity to engage in dialogical and dialectical reasoning about one's own culturally informed thinking and the assumptions that guide the thinking of other diverse points of view is what we need. Well-structured opportunities to engage in reasoning about issues of social relevance within a climate of good faith and civility should characterize any approach to multicultural education.

Our students must understand prejudice as an abdication of human reasoning. Critically constructed reasoning activities rather than superficial exposure can eradicate sociocentric and racist attitudes and provide a curriculum likely to achieve social and personal empowerment through self-reflection. This goal is to provide meaningful cultural experiences for students to share and to encourage movement beyond the self-serving, dominant, condescending curriculum into the realm of critical cultural reasoning.

A critical examination and analysis of the Eurocentric, androcentric, entrepreneurial, and tourist approach to multicultural pedagogy reveals their emptiness. None promotes critical thinking about issues of race and culture. Nowhere do these approaches encourage students to confront historical or contemporary political and social problems so as to engage them in dialogical and dialectical examination, analysis, synthesis, and informed social action. If we want students to engage in metacognition (the monitoring and constant retooling of their thinking through reflection and self-criticism), we need to construct a curriculum rich in reasoning that promises relevancy, controversy, problem posing, and the exchange of cultural points of view. Without reasoning opportunities, multicultural education is relegated to memorizing cultural factoids and trivialities and results in self-delusion. On the other hand, reasoning within diverse cultural points of view on contemporary social and political concerns encourages students to detect when they reason egotistically or sociocentrically, when they construct false justifications for self-serving perceptions and beliefs, and when these beliefs and justifications are or are not supported by an historical record honestly presented.

Centrism: Afro-centrism and People of Color

Reacting to the failure of the current Eurocentric and entrepreneurial hegemony in their schools, many educators have begun to promote the idea of "centricity" or "immersion." So far the strongest voices for centricity or immersion belong to Afro-centrists. Conceding African-Americans face a serious problem in the growing inability of urban schools to educate their youth, such districts as the Milwaukee Public Schools are embarking on experimental immersion programs in middle and elementary schools. Designed exclusively for African-American children, these programs have generated controversy since their inception even though they have gained support in Washington D.C., Detroit, Minneapolis, St. Louis, Miami, New York, and Philadelphia. Immersion has been attacked as racist by the white mainstream and as separatist and sexist by some Blacks.

Meanwhile, ill-informed impressions of Afro-centricity appear in the media and within dominant educational circles, and it would be uncritical and unjust to paint the Afro-centric educational movement with the broad brush of ethnocentricity. Often described by dominant theorists as a project that attempts to raise self-esteem and self-respect among Black youths by replacing the Eurocentric curriculum with assertions of the primacy and superiority of African culture, the educational mainstream spreads stereotypic myths about the goals and claims of the centrist idea. But although proponents of Afro-centricity admit that it celebrates African Americans and the African contribution, it avoids downgrading other points of view, mainly because it does not, like Eurocentrism, parade as universal. Afro-centricity attempts to present African Americans and Africans in general as subjects of history rather than the objects of white Europeans. While this approach tends to raise Black self-esteem, this is not its primary goal. As Molefi Asante (1991) pointed out,

> I know no Afro-centric curriculum planner—Asa Hilliard, Wade Nobles, Leonard Jeffries, Don McNeely being the principle ones—who insist that the primary aim is to raise self-esteem. The argument is a false lead to nowhere because the curriculum planners I am familiar with insist that the fundamental objective is to provide accurate information (p. 270).

The Milwaukee School District directed its middle and elementary schools to follow the recommendations of Black community members, and as Murrell (1993) describes them, these "immersion schools" set out to develop a strong sense of community among staff members; to develop mentoring programs; to advance teaching practices that engender long term commitments and nurturing; to increase children's positive personal, social, and community values; to extend schooling beyond the confines of four walls; and to achieve all this by focusing on African, pan-African, and African American culture as the focus of the curriculum (p. 233).

Many rationales support Afro-centricity and immersion schools for Black children, but Peter Murrell makes the strongest point:

The models of human development many teachers apply, and to which they were exposed during teacher training, are models based upon the culture and socialization practices of white, middle-class mainstream norms. Not only are these frameworks not inclusive or representative of the experience of an increasingly diverse student population, but foundational knowledge about cognitive, moral, and psychosocial development is not integrated into an understanding of educational issues of children of color. Even though, less than a handful of teacher preparation programs (i.e. Wheelock College, Bank Street, and Pacific Oaks College) specifically work to integrate a foundational understanding of human development into the professional and clinical training of its teachers. Therefore, most teachers when accounting African American children, Hispanic children, and other children of color are only equipped to diagnose deficiencies as determined by the developmental benchmarks of white middle-class children (p. 237).

Doubtless most public schools ignore the history, aspirations, and contemporary problems of African Americans, and the proponents of Afro-centrism argue that only a program that immerses youth in the history and traditions of their cultures can address the specific needs of African American students. Moreover, as we will see shortly, our current teacher-training programs contribute to a general devaluing of children of color. Still further, statistics show that fewer and fewer people of color enter the teaching profession, thus exacerbating the problem.

Yet the failure of teachers to understand the populations they serve does not by itself justify centering a curriculum exclusively on African contributions. We know, as Black educational scholars have long argued, that current educational practices award students who "act white." Fordham and Ogbu (1986) first described the burden of thinking and acting white:

Specifically, Blacks and other minorities (e.g., American Indians) believe that in order for a minority person to succeed in school academically, he or she must learn to think and act white. Furthermore, in order to think and act white enough to be rewarded by whites or white institutions like the schools, a minority person must give up his or her minority attitudes, ways of thinking, and behaving and, of course, must give up or lose his or her minority identity. That is, striving for success is a subtractive process: the individual Black student following school standard practices that lead to academic success is perceived as adopting a white cultural frame of reference . . . as "acting white" with the inevitable outcome of losing his or her Black identity, abandoning Black people and black causes, and joining the enemy, namely white people (pp. 25–26).

I agree with Peter Murrell and many others that basing a school program on the experiences and cultures of African-American students is useful, and that current pedagogical practices rooted in the dominant culture and subtle racist ideologies fail to help teachers from the white middle-class mainstream work successfully with peoples of color. Yet I am less convinced that centering a curriculum exclusively on African culture solves this problem. Certainly African-American children remain seriously underserved in America's schools. In Milwaukee, for example, African-American males account for less than 30 percent of the students and yet they face 50 percent of the suspensions and over 90 percent of the expulsions. Only 4 percent of the 6,700 predominantly minority students who entered Chicago's poorest high schools as part of the Class of 1984 graduated with an ability to read at the national average. The pattern also holds for children of Latino descent and many newly arriving immigrants. The problem is not simply the teachers' impressions of who can and cannot learn, although impressions count. The problem is how these impressions affect the kind of learning that takes place, the character of knowledge acquisition, and the composition of the curriculum.

According to Scherer (1991–92), at Victor Berger Elementary school in Milwaukee, an African-American immersion school, first graders learn the alphabet based on African-American culture. For example they learn that A is for Armstrong, B is for Banaker, and C is for Carver. They learn to count from one to ten in Swahili as well as English. They know the colors of the African-American flag are red, black, and green as well as they know the colors of the American flag. Instead of singing "The Itsy-Bitsy Spider," these children draw Anansi the Spider from African folktales. This is a start; yet rote memorization of the alphabet and numbers, or reciting nursery rhymes is not critical learning. To clothe these activities within the rubric of African culture, or any other culture for that matter, and then to think that children are learning to think critically, is diningenuous.

In Cassandra Brown's third grade class at Victor Berger children memorize poetry. Why? What benefit comes from memorizing poetry? Would it not be preferable critically to analyze poetry, and to seek out the assumptions about life that motivated the author to write the poem? At Victor Berger, all teachers require students to do a great deal of memorizing and recitations tied to the oral tradition of griot, or African storytelling. Would it not be preferable critically to recognize the griot and then compare and contrast this historical form of storytelling with other cultural forms of storytelling? Or perhaps students could write their own stories in the griot tradition. They recite the "Pledge of Allegiance," sing "The National Black Anthem," and repeat poems they have memorized by Black poets. What benefit comes from memorizing the Pledge of Allegiance or National Black Anthem? Repeating the words of others without critically examining their claims and assumptions encourages acceptance not critical thinking.

At Victor Berger, children wear uniforms and know their class motto by heart. But democratic thinking rebels against the totalitarianism of mimicked authority, rote memorization, and mindless regurgitation of facts and details; nor is democratic thinking wedded to notions of uncritical adherence to monumentalist notions of culture. To require children of any culture to engage in a curriculum of rote memorization and regurgitation merely repeats the failures of current educational practices in most public schools. It is also crippling, for it avoids engaging reason, denies students an understanding of the nature of their assumptions and the assumptions of others, denies them the preparation for analyzing their own actions and beliefs and those of others, precludes any insight into critical discourse, and places no premium on developing values and dispositions important to life-long learning. Rather it costumes a curriculum embodying educational failure in superficial African customs, thinking, and culture. If white teachers have been unable to cultivate a sense of democratic thought in students of African descent, the question for immersion programs is whether African-American teachers and curricula can succeed by following the old theories and practices. Or can they develop a liberatory educational program that calls on students to reason? Without a commitment to fostering democratic thinking and values within the classroom it makes little difference whether the curriculum is Afro-specific or Latino-specific.

Yet Afro-centric approaches to education can reach beyond the didactic and domesticating. In a unit for teachers entitled *Africa: A Culture Kit* issued by the Oakland Unified School District, the goals are

. . . to allow students to think critically and to observe and understand the similarities and differences among different peoples of the world (p. 2).

This kit too centers on African thought and culture, but the quality of its lessons differentiates it from the Victor Berger immersion approach: It recognizes the need for reasoning and independent thinking as opposed to simply memorizing. For example, in one lesson entitled "Fact and Artifacts" the stated objective is to enhance the appreciation of cultural diversity and to sharpen geographical thinking, critical thinking, and writing skills. Teachers give their students (in groups of three or four) a different artifact. Each group discusses the artifacts and fills out a worksheet. Then they report to the full group utilizing evidence to support their conclusions. They organize their artifacts according to the areas of the world they came from, describing the characteristics of each artifact that helped them come to their conclusions. They validate conclusions and indicate through metacognition how they might have come to the wrong conclusions and why. They infer what an artifact was used for and then list their evidence. They indicate justifications for any conclusions they made. When explaining where the artifacts came from, students are asked what they were made of and the reasons the artifacts are made of the materials they are made of. They are asked to compare uses of artifacts with similar objects in their own lives and then justify their conclusions as to why they are similar or different. This approach to education embraces critical thinking and reasoned judgment.

Almost everyone agrees that the conventional approaches of contemporary urban schools fail African Americans and other people of color. Furthermore, the hopes that desegregation would close the gaps of racial inequality go unrealized despite the claims of mainstream educators. Moreover, inadequate teacher training, narrow attitudes, and the lack of diversity in teacher recruitment into the profession help assure that people of color underachieve. Meanwhile, slipcovering conventional teaching methods with a culture-specific-curriculum also fails to prepare students of color for the exigencies of critical self-inventory and historical sensibility. Cultural identification with what it means to be Black or Latino can, of course, be valuable and even essential for cognitive and affective growth. But if these cultural attachments are carried out in the interest of a curriculum centered on mindless memorization or an uncritical acceptance of any dominant ideology, they will fail to correct the problems facing people of color and could encourage uncritical nationalism and sociocentric thinking.

Only well-reasoned programs that challenge students to examine assumptions in light of evidence; to engage in critical historical discourse about issues of contemporary and historical concern; and to develop dimensions of learning that include independent thinking, empathy, civility, humility, discipline, perseverance, an insight into sociocentricity and egocentric thinking, and a commitment to dismantling systems of oppression and domination can help our children survive. We can dismiss anything less as temporary reform and misguided praxis. Learning and self-expression must rest on foundations of critique, and they must ruthlessly examine contemporary and historical claims and conclusions in light of evidence. If Afro-centric, immersion, or any other centric curriculum can build on the necessities of independent thought and action in ways that promote critical thinking, we should applaud and support them. On the other hand, if they continue to rely on and teach blind obedience to domesticating forms of didactic pedagogical practice, we should soundly critique and abolish them.

PART 2

Introduction

In his 1993 book *Beyond Eurocentrism and Multiculturalism: Prophetic Thought in Postmodern Times*, Cornel West argued that the first element of prophetic thought is discernment, or what he called an "analytical moment" in which

> [O]ne must accent a nuanced historical sense. What I mean by "nuanced historical sense" is an ability to keep track; to remain attuned to the ambiguous legacies and hybrid cultures in history (p. 4).

This awareness demands a taste for cultural criticism and an historical sensibility as we call into question romantic, simplistic appeals to pristine culture or idealistic nostalgia. It also demands that we reserve a place in the dialogue for the voices of disenfranchised narratives, thereby encouraging reasoning within the diverse cultural points of view often excluded from traditional dialogue. West is clear on this point:

> I believe, in fact, that the condition of truth is to allow the suffering to speak. It doesn't mean that those who suffer have a monopoly on truth, but it means that for the condition of truth to emerge must be in tune with those who are undergoing social misery—socially induced forms of suffering (p. 4).

In other words, we must move beyond the confines of Eurocentricity, as well as a romanticized, dogmatic representation of socio-centricity. We must resurrect the silent narratives of history and contemporary reality for reason's sake—that is, to engage students in empathetic understanding of the past and present and help them develop the ability to imagine and create a more rational and empathetic future. An appreciation for the humanity of others can be captured only by empathetic, fair-minded critical thinking. Without empathy we fall prey to our own ego or socio-centric falsehoods. Racism, sexism, homophobia, and the like result from an inability to empathize. Disunified and fractured, humans can do little to combat the oppressive structures of everyday life. Oppressive "political correctness" of any type is inimical to empathetic, fair-minded critical thinking. We should seek instead a self-critical spirit, a willingness to call into question and condemn any oppression existing throughout cultures and time. As West noted,

> There were structures of domination here before the Europeans got here. The plight of indigenous women, for example. It doesn't mean that the wiping out of indigenous peoples by disease and conquest somehow gets the Europeans off the hook. But it means that there was always, already, oppression. In new forms it was brought (p. 8).

West referred to a need to keep track of hypocrisy (p. 5), or the need to maintain moral and intellectual integrity, a willingness to discern between ideals and actual practice in reality and inner subjective life, a willingness to hold oneself up to the same epistemological and moral standards one expects of others. Moreover it is a commitment to rational self-critique in the interest of metacognition, and because of its commitment to the unknown, it demands both courage and humility.

The end of World War II heralded the start of worldwide anti-colonialist struggles: China's independence in 1949, the war in Algeria, the struggles in Guatemala, Cuba, Ghana, Guinea, and the list goes on. In this country, the civil rights and anti-war movements of the 1960s and 70s proceeded with an implicit commitment to international solidarity. Cuba sent troops to Angola and Nicaragua. National movements found identity and strength in their solidarity with international struggles. This internationalism presaged the internationalism we need today within academia. Understanding the similarities in our struggles and the forces of oppression we encounter is paramount to unification. Without unified struggle, material and psychological change will remain elusive. Nationalism, meanwhile, forces a wedge between peoples and discourages humanistic transformation. We must move beyond the parameters of dogma and design a curriculum for our students that provides meaningful opportunities for reasoning within multiple cultural points of view rooted in historical and contemporary reality. The reasoning activities should emphasize the common struggle for human dignity, biological survival, and the logic of oppression —a logic that deflects the quest for freedom, justice, and personal sovereignty.

Transcending the parameters of dogma requires us to scrutinize contemporary and historical reality. Many cultures beside European are racist, patriarchal, and homophobic; oppression is not the sole province of Europeans. We must be self-critical and sociocritical enough to recognize and critique oppression within our own cultures and heritage's. This project takes courage. Yet without the ability to excise oppressive structures from our own cultures, we commit the very oppression we attribute to Eurocentrism. Transcending the parameters of dogma means being committed to moral principles and humanity dialogue with self and society. A self-congratulatory engagement with cultures of any kind clouds the greater and wider principles we espouse. Combined courage and humility entitles us to expose the hypocrisies of our cultures and daily lives.

Finally, we must preserve a sense of history in our lives if we are to make constructive sense of our present and future. This sense of history—the ability to make sense of the living present through historical understanding—is rare in our time. From our electronic entertainments' and current popular culture, we no longer receive knowledge of the past. The market civilization places such a premium on material consumption, sexual titillation, and competitiveness that history has been relegated to the irrelevant. Yet if we are to make sense out of our political, economic, and moral existence, history remains a defining factor in our lives.

Toward this end, the balance of this book outlines three tenets that underlie a critical multicultural literacy. The first tenet is a commitment to educational equity, which entails a wider commitment to equitable social relations, which inevitably calls into question the political, moral, economic, and social reality of our current market civilization. Any defensible notion of multicultural literacy acknowledges current inequities our children face in material and psychological opportunities for learning and living. Thus a need to illuminate and change inequitable power structures.

The second tenet calls for a curriculum that encourages reasoning within diverse cultural points of view emphasizing commonalties in the struggle for human dignity. The struggle that unites us as human beings is more compelling than whatever divides us by emphasizing difference. If we are to unify in the struggle for liberation and human dignity, we must recognize our common historical and contemporary struggles.

The third tenet holds that students must come to understand the logic of oppression that has stained history and repeats itself in current reality, a logic that stands against self-actualization, freedom, democracy, and human liberty. This curriculum must arise out of reasoning activities designed to help students compare and contrast the historical record with contemporary reality and thereby use the power of historical insight to understand the present and its liberatory potentialities.

Chapter 5

Educational Equity: A Prerequisite for Higher Order Learning

Sir, he who denies to children the acquisition
of knowledge works devilish miracles.
Horace Mann "On Slavery and the
Slave Trade in the District of Columbia,"
delivered in the United States Congress,
February 23, 1849

The Scope of Educational Inequity

The argument for an effective approach to multicultural education posits the need for educational equity within schooling and society as a whole. As both Banks (1990) and the California Association of Bilingual Educators (1992) have pointed out, any critical multicultural literacy approach to education must commit itself in theory and practice to reasoning opportunities for all students regardless of race, English proficiency, class background, color, nationality, gender, age or disabilities. Any holistic understanding of the role of educational equity presupposes a general societal movement toward egalitarian economic and social democracy. By itself, education cannot cure the profound social oppression that for many defines current reality. As Horace Mann Bond (1934) observed,

Of one thing, at least, we can be sure: that is the unsoundness of relying upon the school as a cure-all for our ills (p. 12).

But he went on to expound on the social role of education as an institution:

We must think of the school, then, as a single institution which has a wide reach, and which may help transform the life of a people over a long sweep of time. To understand the place of the school and the function of the educational process, we must explore as many facets of community life that are visible. Social planning must include great improvements in educational facilities, but this improvement will fall short of its mark if each social process is not coordinated with the school in a planned order laying even emphasis upon all aspects of the forces which work upon individuals. Better schools cannot themselves save a population that is condemned by economic pressure to remain in a half-starved poverty stricken environment. No amount of health education in the classroom can overcome the effect of poor housing and the lack of space in congested cities. Character education, no matter how skillfully conducted, cannot be depended upon to reduce greatly the high rates of juvenile delinquency found in Negro communities so long as Negro children in cities suffer from the economic disabilities of their parents and are exposed to the full gamut of a variety of severe family disorganizations. Strictly speaking, the school has never built a new social order; it has been the product and interpreter of the existing system, sustaining and being sustained by the social complex. Schools for Negro children can perform the older function of the school; but even more they can adventure beyond the frontier and plan for a new order in those aspects which affect the race. To do this, however, they must function as coordinate elements of a unified system, and not in utter isolation from the world of action and social change (p. 13).

To confront the issue of educational equity directly is to confront the need for an "acute" paradigm shift toward general societal humanistic values and changes—from the classroom to the workplace, from the family to the State. It would be futile to hope that equity could exist within the institution of education, while economic and social inequities pervade the major institutions outside. Accordingly, we need to re-conceptualize the role of schooling relative to the role of community and democratic life. In *The Education of the American Negro*, Bond commented that

> The very structure of the school should be altered from its present structure. It should so adapt its physical form that its facilities might truly serve the community and the families in the community, through all of the child's waking hours. The school should conceive of itself as an agency for educating the whole child, which means the whole child's whole family; the "new school" would be supplied with facilities where entire families could come for instruction and guidance in the art and science of acculturation (p. 490).

For modern educators like Henry Giroux (1988), a holistic view of education in the service of community requires an examination and analysis of the educational workplace: the foundations, publishing companies, and wider political and economic interests and relations of production that directly or indirectly affect schooling:

Moreover, schools are understood within a framework of larger connections that allow analysis of them as historical and social constructions, embodiments of social forms that always bear a relationship to the wider society (p. 102).

The Quest for Economic Equity

A recent study by the Children's Defense Fund entitled *The State of America's Children* (1992) found that 14.3 million children—more than in any year since 1965—are poor. Furthermore, five million go hungry, eight million lack health care, and 44 percent live in families where the income falls below the poverty level. This means that many of our children come to school underfed, badly clothed, in poor health, and ill prepared for learning. The wide disparity between poor and wealthy schools and urban and suburban life has produced a dual society that remains unchallenged. In his book *Savage Inequalities,* Jonathan Kozol (1991) described the dual society he found during a recent visit to our urban schools:

> It was simply the impression that these urban schools were, by and large, extraordinarily unhappy places. With few exceptions, they reminded me of "garrisons" or "outposts" in a foreign nation. Housing projects, bleak and tall, surrounded by perimeter walls lined with barbed wire, often stood adjacent to the schools I visited. The schools were surrounded frequently by signs that indicated DRUG-FREE ZONE. Their doors were guarded. Police sometimes patrolled the halls. The windows of the schools were often covered with steel grates. Taxi drivers flatly refused to take me to some of these schools and would deposit me a dozen blocks away, in border areas beyond which they refused to go. I'd walk the last half-mile on my own. Once, in the Bronx, a woman stopped her car; told me I should not be walking there, insisted I get in and drove me to the school. I was dismayed to walk or ride for blocks and blocks through neighborhoods where *every* face was black, where there were simply *no white people anywhere* (p. 5).

Those of us who have worked within the inner city can vouch for Kozol's depressing experiences and impressions. The dual society stands out in the inadequacy of the urban schools themselves, with broken toilets, inadequate heating, antiquated texts, no running water, littered and dangerous playgrounds. Kozol quoted Bonita Brodt, a *Chicago Tribune* reporter who spent several months at Goudy Elementary School 1988:

> [T]eachers use materials in class long since thrown out in most suburban schools. Slow readers in the eighth grade history class are taught from 15-

year-old textbooks in which Richard Nixon is still president. There are no science labs, no art or music teachers. Soap, paper towels, and toilet paper are in short supply. There are two working bathrooms for some 700 children (p. 63).

When I taught in South-Central Los Angeles in 1989, my second graders received fragile wooden pencils manufactured in Chinese labor camps and a social studies text predicting that "one day man will land on the moon." In view of these growing inequities it is no wonder Kozol found that

> For children who begin their school career at Andersen Elementary School, for instance, the high school dropout rate is 76 percent. For those who begin at the McKinley school, it is 81 percent. For those who start at Woodson Elementary School, the high school dropout rate is 86 percent. These schools—which Fred Hess of the Chicago Panel on School Policy and Finance, a respected watchdog group, calls "dumping grounds" for kids with special problems—are among the city's worst; but, even for children who begin their schooling at Bethune and then go on to nearby Manley High, the dropout rate, as we have seen, is 62 percent.
>
> Reading levels are lowest in the poorest schools. In a survey of the 18 high schools with the highest rates of poverty within their student populations, Designs for Change, a research center in Chicago, notes that only 3.5 percent of students graduate and also read up to the national norm. Some 6,700 children enter ninth grade in these 18 schools each year. Only 300 of these students, says Don Moore, director of Designs for Change, "both graduate and read at or above the national average" (pp. 58–59).

Complicating urban education are the dire health problems associated with city living among the poor. Kozol noted that in East St. Louis,

> Compounding these problems is the poor nutrition of the children here—the average daily food expenditure in East St. Louis is $2.40 for one child—and the under-immunization of young children. Of every one hundred children recently surveyed in East St. Louis, fifty-five were incompletely immunized for polio, diphtheria, measles, and whooping cough (p. 21).

These statistics pointing up inequalities in urban and suburban life are shocking when juxtaposed to those indicating that one family in the U.S., the Waltons of Wal-Mart fame, has a fortune of 26 billion dollars, the annual income from which would, according to Tanzer (1992) quoting UNICEF experts, be enough to wipe out severe malnutrition for hundreds of millions of children in the Third World. Obviously the current political-economic reality and the exigencies of equity command our attention from opposite poles as we set out to provide meaningful and adequate educational opportunities for all our citizens. For radical educators like Gintis (1973) this stark social tension opens a unique opportunity for educators interested in real reform:

> The immediate strategies for a movement for educational reform, then, are political: (a) understanding the concrete contradictions in economic life and the way they are reflected in the educational system; (b) fighting to insure that consciousness of these contradictions persists by thwarting attempts of ruling elites to attenuate them by co-optation; and (c) using the persistence of contradictions in society at large to expand the political base and power of a revolutionary movement; that is, a movement for educational reform must understand the social conditions of its emergence and development in the concrete conditions of social life. Unless we achieve such an understanding and use it as the basis of political action, a functional reorientation will occur vis-à-vis the present crisis in education, as it did in earlier critical moments in the history of American education (p. 69).

Understanding the role of schooling reinforces the idea of education as a political act and calls on teachers to examine the relations of their production—the conditions of their work, class sizes, adequacy of materials, decision making in the larger context of determining social good, and their relationship to community and community struggles. Thus, according to Giroux (1988),

> Quite simply, if teachers and students are subject to conditions of overcrowding, lack of time to work collectively in a creative fashion, or rules and regulations that disempower them, the technical and social conditions of labor have to be understood and addressed as part of the discourse of reform and struggle (p. 103).

Grambs, in her early article "The Negro Self-Concept Reappraised," (1972) was remarkably prescient:

> Since the system is highly vulnerable (the American dilemma in a new dimension), the Black Power rhetoric will indeed work. For those mired in the system only the deliberate actions of alert and educated personnel can break the cycle of personal and social destruction. It will take more than an integrated *Sesame Street* or biographies of Martin Luther King Jr. to overcome the disasters, which occur daily in the average inner-city Black classroom. Here is where the central problem for the educator resides. It is the pathology of these schools, which need immediate attention. Only then will we be able to diagnose adequately, and educate adequately, *each* child (p. 207).

As a response to accelerating crisises in education, the business community makes many altruistic sounding recommendations regarding expenditures for public schools, the importance of education, and the need to shape learning and education for the twenty-first century. But the claims of business to be an ally of public schools weaken under inspection. Secretary of Labor, economist Robert Reich (1992) recently demonstrated that amid all the corporate talk about improving public schools and ensuring a trained workforce for the future, inaction is the dominant characteristic of business behavior. In fact, the rate of corporate giving to American education declined significantly in the 1980s even as the economy boomed. From the 1970s to the start of the 1980s, corporate giving to public schools jumped an average of 15 percent per year; yet in 1990, corporate giving was only 5 percent more than in 1989 and in 1989 only 3 percent more than in 1988. Moreover, of the $2.6 billion corporations contributed to education in 1989, only $156 million supported public schools. The rest went to private schools or to colleges or universities—in many instances, to the alma maters of senior executives (p. 6). In fact, corporations actually cost schools money. Forever clamoring for welfare handouts in the form of tax breaks and tax-free enterprise zones, corporations siphon off tax dollars otherwise needed for education. With the public school budget tied to regressive property taxes, corporations in many cases actually pay nothing.

The corporate prattle about needing an educated work force must also be understood within the context of an increasing corporate dependency on foreign workers to run the factories and plants of tomorrow. For example, Texas Instruments maintains a software plant in Bangalore, India, where fifty programmers are linked by satellite with the main Dallas office. Ford has situated its most modern engine facility in northern Mexico. Most of the employees of Saztec International, a $20 million a year data processing firm headquartered in Kansas, live and work in the Philippines. Compared with the average Philippine income of $1,700 per year, Saztec data entry workers welcome their princely $250 salaries.

When it comes to needing educated U.S. workers, corporations turn their backs; happy to avoid the political and economic costs of informed labor unrest. As one shocking example, when faced with a shortage of skilled workers in the 1980s, American hospitals began recruiting workers from Ireland and the Philippines, eventually granting more than ten thousand of them citizenship as a result of the grave shortage of nurses. Less an argument against immigration, this anecdote merely suggests what the corporate agenda really entails. As technology opens up the horizons of possibility, corporations will be looking for other means to trim their human capital expenditures here at home; this will mean less investment in training and education and more use of cheap mental and physical labor abroad. Furthermore, even if we believe the corporate rhetoric that trumpets the thirty billion annually spent on retraining workers here at home, we find the lion's share actually going to high-level management. Reich found only 8 percent goes into remedial reading or writing for workers (p. 6).

In view of the decreased contributions to education from a mendacious private sector and cuts in pubic funding by impoverished communities, educational institutions now face their worst crisis in years. In California, home of the second largest school district in the country, the State Board of Education voted seven to three to allow the Los Angeles Unified School District to reduce the school year by eight days during the second semester to cut costs. The California Teachers Association (1992) calculated this adjustment would mean an extension of the school day by 39 minutes, for which teachers would not get paid. These familiar bookkeeping tricks belie the public campaigns for educational reform. The implications for the communities the Los Angeles Unified School District serves are devastating: (1) Teachers have less time to teach lessons; (2) parents who can afford child care pay more; and (3) parents who cannot afford child care see their children consigned to the street. Wayne Johnson, former head of the second largest teachers' union in the country, United Teachers of Los Angeles, in a speech to striking teachers, had these remarks to say about the budget situation in Los Angeles public schools and its effect on teachers and students:

> There are more ideas for saving money. UTLA keeps on offering them, and the board keeps rejecting them. [The Board] lacks the guts to really tackle the issue of downsizing the administration. They moan, but they won't act. The Board's idea for saving the District is to shorten the school year by eight days and lengthen the remaining days. However, they will lengthen them only for teachers. No one else will be required to work a longer day for less pay. As long as at least 40 percent of the district budget is being spent on non-classroom, non-essential administration, Los Angeles students won't be able to get a quality education by raising classes, cutting textbook and supply budgets, and maintaining $80,000 to $140,000 "downtown" administrators with their cars and other perks. You won't get quality education by cutting the salaries and benefits of the people who work directly with the kids (1989).

By 1996, the Los Angeles Unified school teachers had been forced to accept a pay cut of 10 percent and the district itself faced extinction. In fact, the gap between poor schools and relatively affluent schools has widened. Meanwhile, an analysis of school funding prepared for Ohio's Equity and Adequacy Coalition found that, for school year 1980 and 1981, the fifty-state school districts with the highest per-pupil expenditures provided their classroom teachers with average annual salaries of $18,886, while the average annual salaries for teachers from those fifty districts with the lowest per-pupil expenditures was $14,650, or a difference of $4,236. According to *American Teacher* (May/June, 1993), by the 1988–89 school year, this gap in teacher's salaries had widened to $7,155. Obviously the struggle for higher teacher salaries must somehow become harnessed to the struggle for overall equitable funding.

In the California state universities, fiscal cuts now threaten the 19 colleges that comprise the system. In 1993, the California Teachers Association reported that the 19 colleges suffered $278 million in cuts in the preceding two years, imposed a 40-percent tuition hike on its students, dropped four thousand courses in 1991 alone, fired or "let go" some one thousand full-time and two thousand part-time faculty members in the last two years, combined classes to create classroom populations of 160 students or more, and shed entire academic programs.

The glaring inequalities between urban and affluent school districts coupled with the tremendous cuts in educational expenditures can be explained, to some degree, by the economics and politics that dictate how we fund public education. Tied to revenue collection based on regressive property taxes, school districts must first look to local funding as a source of sustenance. State and federal funding sources exist as well, but the local property tax remains the primary source of school funding. Because property taxes are based on the value of homes and properties, suburbs enjoy a larger and more lucrative tax base relative to the size of its student population than urban centers occupied by millions of poor people in apartments and run-down housing. When we add the fact that heavily affected cities like Chicago and New York host such tax-free institutions as colleges, hospitals, and museums, we can see the unfairness of basing a public school education on the value of the surrounding property. According to Jonathan Wilson, former chairman of the Council of Urban Boards of Education, whom Jonathan Kozol (1991) cites in *Savage Inequalities*, 30 percent or more of the potential tax base in Chicago is exempt from taxes, compared to as little as 3 percent in the neighboring suburbs.

In addition, large urban centers like New York, Los Angeles, or Chicago must spread their revenues ever thinner over schools, police forces, fire departments, and public health initiatives all significantly more expensive and deteriorating faster in crime-ridden areas than in the suburbs. As a result, the districts that face the most social, economic, and educational problems have the fewest funds to meet the challenges of providing education for their children. Although state contributions and federal funds augment to some extent insufficient revenues from local property taxes, they hardly assure equality. Statistics from the Congressional Budget Office published in the *Economic and Budget Outlook: Fiscal Years 1994–1998* indicate that federal outlays for education fall from 5.4 percent in 1980 to 3.1 percent in 1992, and are expected to comprise only 3.7 percent in 1998. Meanwhile, national defense outlays for the same years were 22.7 and 20.8 percent, respectively, and in 1998 are expected to be 14.3 percent. We are producing smart bombs and dumb kids. If, of course, you have the wealth to pay for private schooling, your child will receive an education free from many of the inequalities described here. For the rest, however, public school is compulsory, and because the choice of public school is defined by the district and financed by property taxes and state and federal funds, inequality continues for those millions of American school children whose access to quality education is limited by the value of the property in their communities.

As dedicated educators, we must act politically to replace the regressive tax system responsible for funding our nation's schools inequitably. This struggle requires a commitment to public education as a human right and the responsibility of all citizens, and thus the financial responsibility of the Federal government as opposed to local revenue schemes tied to property values or subject to the whims of corporate and political agendas. Shifting school funding from regressive property taxes to the Federal government could be accomplished in many ways: imposing a surtax on corporations, for example, or a more genuine graduated instituted income tax. Whatever system we find, it must also exhibit a deeper commitment to full employment opportunities and health care for all of our citizens. We must also seek to devise an educational policy that drastically increases the amount of educational monies available for scholarships and tuition for schools; monies that now lie beyond the cost of many students, especially students of color. And, of course, any commitment to educational equity must provide health and nutrition programs for the poor, ensure Headstart availability and access for all children, and medical care for those in need.

Confronting the Privatization of School

For nearly 150 years, public education in the United Sates has been recognized as a fundamental public good and a human right. Now, this Jeffersonian vision of democratic schooling is attacked by right-wing constituents hypocritically chanting the rubric of "choice," a new buzzword for conservative educational reformers. What they propose is the complete restructuring of our schools through the privatization of public education. The danger their arguments pose is indicated by the diverse, often well-meaning constituency they attract by their seductive analysis and opportunistic critique of public education. Capitalizing on the acknowledged inadequacies of public schooling, promoters of "vouchers" and "choice" find a receptive audience, especially among middle class whites, some of whom have fled the inner cities and now find the problems of urban schools gnawing at the fringes of suburbia.

Recently, the educational terrain has become peopled by conservative squatters braced for battles over the curriculum, "choice," text censoring, testing, back-to-basics, the teaching of tolerance, multiculturalism, and "privatization." This educationally conservative ideology that took root in the late 1970s and early 1980s was nourished in part because corporate America abroad was declining in international competition and military prowess as a result of a perceived relaxing of educational standards in public schooling. The solution, so the argument goes, was to convene a corporate partnership or "merger" between business and education in hopes of ensuring a continual supply of malleable workers poised to defend the interests of corporate America, which they interpreted as their own interests. This pipeline became more crucial as American industries developed their "service specialties." The assumption behind this "partnership" between schools and business was that schools exist for the dissemination of knowledge, skills, and entrepreneurial and moral values thought necessary for the acquisition of corporate profits and the maintenance of the capitalist life style.

The idea of the educational marketplace can be traced back to Milton Friedman, the conservative economist who in the mid-1950s proposed that every family in America receive a "voucher" of equal worth for each child attending school. The idea persists: families should be able to choose any school that meets government standards, and parents could supplement their vouchers leaving schools free to set tuition levels and admission requirements. Friedman's proposal came with the advent of the Sputnik at a time when the United States suddenly started to worry about Russia's accelerating space technology. Although coming amid a general excoriation of public schools, Friedman's proposal appeared to countermand the generally popular 1954 decision *Brown v. Board of Education* that mandated equality of educational opportunity. It surfaced again with the introduction of the Jencks proposal in the 1960s. Ivan Illich (1970) commented on what on the surface appears as a radical notion:

> There is currently a proposal on record, which seems at first to make a good deal of sense. It has been prepared by Christopher Jencks of The Center for the Study of Public Policy and sponsored by The Office of Economic Opportunity. It proposes to put educational "entitlements" or tuition grants into the hands of parents and students for expenditure in the schools of their choice. Such individual entitlements could indeed be an important step in the right direction. We need a guarantee of the right of each citizen to an equal share of tax-derived educational resources, the right to verify this share, and the right to sue for it if denied. The Jencks proposal however, begins with the ominous statement that "conservatives, liberals, and radicals have all complained at one time or another that the American educational system gives professional educators too little incentive to provide high quality education to most children." The proposal condemns itself by proposing tuition grants that would have to be spent on schooling. This is like giving a lame man a pair of crutches and stipulating that he uses them only if the ends are tied together. As the proposal for tuition grants now stands, it plays into the hands of not only professional educators but also racists, promoters of religious schools, and others whose interests are socially divisive. Above all, educational entitlements restricted to use within schools plays into the hands of all those who want to continue to live in a society in which social advancement is tied not to proven knowledge, but to the learning pedigree by which it might supposedly be acquired (pp. 23–24).

The pro-choice hucksters of today have fashioned an elaborated version of the Friedman and Jencks proposal arguing that the problems confronting public schools defy public and governmental response and require market forces for their solution. Some of these problems have been correctly identified by proposal proponents, like the inability of the principal at school sites to hire or fire teachers, the burdensome requirement of irrelevant and bureaucratic certification requirements, limited autonomy in the classroom for the teacher, inability to confer with educational colleagues in the construction of curriculum, and lack of parental influence over the schools their children attend. These valid considerations resemble concerns that students, parents, and teachers who support public schools cite themselves when discussing the failing character of American education today. The difference is in the conclusions proposal advocates reach.

Perhaps the most articulate proponents of vouchers, Terry Moe and John Chubb (1990) argue in their book, *Politics, Markets, and American Schools*, that public schools fail to offer adequate instruction because they lack the autonomy they need to create meaningful education. They lack this autonomy because they are bureaucratic and they are bureaucratic because they are tied to politics. The answer: substitute the free market for public-politics and all will prosper. Give "scholarships" to low and middle-income students to attend whatever public, private, or religious school they wish; these "scholarships" would be subsidized by tax revenues. Drawing on *A Nation at Risk* and other spurious reports of the 1980s, Moe and Chubb conclude that public financing of education simply does not work and drastic measures are required. Many educators rejected these assumptions. Lowe (1992) detailed the theoretical assumptions of the voucher movement and came to far different conclusions:

> Moe and Chubb assume that the market will create quality education for everyone through the mechanism of choice. Yet choice has certainly not accomplished this in the private sector of the economy. If the affluent can choose health spas in the Caribbean and gracious homes, the poor must choose inadequate health care and dilapidated housing. To the extent that those with limited resources have won forms of protection, it has not been guaranteed by the play of the market, but by governmental regulation. The conservative agenda of deregulation over the past decade has eroded those protections and greatly increased the disparity between the wealthy and poor in the United Sates. A market system of education is merely an extension of deregulation and promises to compound social inequities (p. 27).

Equally important and overlooked among proponents of schooling choice, private schools are not governed by federal, state, or community public policies and can, therefore, avoid many constitutional guarantees. The move toward "choice" threatens to undermine the civil rights gains this country has made in the last thirty years as private schools choose whomever they wish to attend and hire whomever they wish to teach in their institutions. In fact, "choice" permits discrimination on the basis of gender, sexual orientation, race, religion, intelligence quotient, or disability; in fact, its opponents see it as a cynical and desperate attempt to create elite schools for students and parents who do not want their children to attend racially mixed educational sites.

With increasing immigration many parents see people of color as a threat to their children's education, as anchors holding their children back. By using a voucher system to segregate students these wealthy parents believe they can achieve educational excellence for their children. At a time when we crucially need an educational commitment to all of our children and teachers, "choice" promises billions of dollars drained from public schools, the creation of privately owned elite academies subsidized by taxpayer money, and a wider chasm in social and economic benefit between the haves and have nots.

The response from the business community to school choice proposals and privatization of public schools has been, not surprisingly, cheerful and upbeat. Many companies have long been eager to tie the necessities of schooling to the rigors of production and consumption and have been discreetly involved in the education of American children. Kozol (1991) pointed out that General Motors distributes a curriculum to teach children about the environment, while Pizza Hut helps boys and girls learn to read. The Miller Brewing Company wants children to know about the contributions of African-Americans to our culture. *USA Today* will provide children with an "inside view" of the newspaper publishing business. Students can learn about good nutrition from Chef Boyardee or discover total health from sing-along handouts provided by NutriSweet. For 5,125 soup labels, the Campbell Company will provide your school with the film strip, *The Boyhood of Abraham Lincoln,* for 20,000 more labels you can get a remote projector to show it with, and for another 6,750 labels you can get a screen to show it on. Burger King operates fully accredited private high schools in 14 cities. We see the re-emergence of the modern "company store" when IBM and Apple set their sites on schools-for-profit as more and more multinational companies consider the idea (p. 17).

A new and growing group of "educational entrepreneurs" like Chris Whittle, founder and chairman of Whittle Communications and Channel One T.V., see a tremendous profit in privatized schooling. Whittle, a pioneer of television news and advertising packages for public schools, dreams of more than one thousand private profit-making schools serving two million children within the decade. As reported by the *Wall Street Journal* (May 5, 1993), his plan is to raise $750 million and he is seeking investments from such famous marketing and consumer companies as Apple Computer, Paramount Communications, Walt Disney, and PepsiCo. According to one Whittle executive, these companies, "know the real estate market, understand quality control, and run large-scale employee operations" (p. B2). Whittle's other partners include Dutch electronics giant Philips with a 25-percent share, and Associated Newspaper Holdings Ltd. Rather than build new schools as he originally envisioned, Whittle now focuses on taking over the management of existing public schools. These schools will, of course, be accessible by "vouchers" through government revenue transfers. Although Whittle is the company spokesman and namesake, Time Warner actually holds 38 percent of the stock in Whittle's "Edison Project," as the enterprise is called. While Whittle and the Edison Project currently provide more than 10,000 schools with their Channel One—now required classroom viewing for eight million students—Whittle and Time Warner gross $630,000 from four ads run each day bringing in annual revenues of over $100 million. At $157,000 for a thirty second ad—double the advertising rate of prime-time network news—Whittle and company bring commercials for Snickers, Burger King, and other products directly to the desks of our nation's schoolchildren. One can imagine why these new educational entrepreneurs find school privatization so appealing.

While studying the colonialization of education by business, Sheila Harty (1981) examined the Adopt-A-School program in several big city systems:

> Our 1977 surveys found that 64 percent of Fortune's 500 top industrial and 90 percent of the major trade associations and electric utilities provide [curriculum] materials free. Twenty-nine percent of Fortune's 500, 47 percent of trade associations, and 53 percent of utilities design these materials for classroom use in grades K-12 with teacher guides and mimeo stencils. . . . Teaching aids on the "energy crisis" distributed by local utilities, for example, become vehicles for nuclear power promotion (pp. 38–39).

Before we all acquiesce in what could easily become a ruinous agenda of privatization and neglect, we should question the supposed altruism and the specific programs the educational entrepreneurs offer. Is all this concern for our children's education simply the good faith expressions of a compassionate corporate America? Should we be grateful for the interest business shows in our teachers and children by providing curriculum, television advertisements, and hand-outs for classroom use? Are successful real estate endeavors and large-scale employee companies really knowledgeable about education? Or is this a repugnant attempt to wedge a product and brand identification into the consciousness of a captive audience of 45 million children?

All these companies concentrate first on accumulating ever greater profits. The so-called "student market" is an $80 billion segment ripe for wholesale commercial penetration. As advertisers on children's television so rightly understand, product consciousness equates to increased sales. Thus, while a concern for education enhances the public image of business, it does something more insidious: it allows business interests to monitor the ideas and content of the curriculum and to design filmstrips, simulation kits, videos, curriculum materials, and stories to influence the formation of ideas. In this way, business ensures that the reproduction and dissemination of dominant entrepreneurial and Eurocentric ideals continue to pervade educational life. In the words of John Dewey (1916), students can expect to be trained like animals instead of educated like human beings (p. 13).

Accordingly, while these companies forge a dishonest curriculum, they both carve out a market and foster the values of corporate America, the values of competitiveness and the dispositions of the capitalist mind. Furthermore, under the present tax system, these benign corporate efforts are tax deductible, which means we pay for them whether we like it or not.

Evidently the California State Senate shares the skepticism just expressed. In a 21-to-14 vote, it approved Senate Bill 1047 that prohibits California school districts from entering into contracts that would expose students to commercials by electronic media. Aimed specifically at Whittle's Channel One, the bill is now headed for the Assembly Education Committee. The Senate vote came on the heels of news that the East Side Union High School District in San Jose had canceled the controversial program after fighting Whittle in court. The support of the East Side Union High School District Teachers' Association was critical in defeating Whittle and his cohorts on the school board.

Meanwhile, within this political and social discourse on education one notices no emphasis on education for democracy; rather, as Illich (1970) has observed, the focus is on the technocratic and the need "to equip business with educated workers" or to prepare citizens for "disciplined consumption" (p. 45). Few questions surface regarding the specific kind of education and morals likeliest to foster business productivity and capital accumulation—like reverence for authority or unbridled competition. Nor do these educational discussions among corporate plutocrats verge on such issues as what it means to be an active critical thinking person in today's society. Efficiency and control, the hallmarks of efficient capital accumulation, usurp the debate over what it now means to be an educated person and no one asks how we can begin to construct a philosophy and accompanying curriculum to meet the challenges of being human. The cynical and myopic view of education—that it is the province of pedagogical pundits and business interests—mandates classroom alienation, divorcing schools from the democratization of personal and public life and substituting an education of repression, regimentation, and authoritarianism. On the business agenda for public schooling, education provides a domesticating service that legitimizes current political and economic relations in the interest of the business elite. Corporate promoters of the privatization of public schooling through market forces advocate schooling as a site for the reproduction and dissemination of cultural power. Any competing cultural power is silenced in the interest of "the transmission of knowledge."

The rhetoric of the various alarmist reports that exhort the nation to educational armament, like the National Commission of Excellence in Education (and its 1983 report, *A Nation at Risk*), have contributed to the shift from a debate over an education that helps young people develop the critical capacities for making informed choices and shaping their lives, to a debate over the manpower needs of the American industrial and military complex. The National Commission on Excellence in Education stated, in fact, that

> education is one of the chief engines of society's material well-being. . . . Citizens also know in their bones that the safety of the United States depends principally on wit, skill and the spirit of the self confident people, today and tomorrow (p. 2).

Accordingly, since industrial and military power become increasingly linked to education in a way that reduces schools to mere pawns of national power, and because these schools are in crisis, it logically follows that the nation is at risk. But according to Walter Feinberg (1989) it is a bankrupt argument:

> Yet, while students in the U.S. do not perform as well as those from France or England on a number of measured areas of achievement, there is no evi-

dence to indicate that these lower scores have resulted in a comparably weaker military. Indeed, there is sufficient evidence to indicate that during the period when test scores have declined, the military has grown stronger (p. 75).

One, of course, affirms the importance of educating students for a productive life. They definitely need the basic skills to engage in employment and to provide for their families and themselves. But learning to be productive citizens, reliable employees, and discerning consumers can easily accompany the development of the skills and knowledge to reflect critically and act on production and consumption insights. Simply stated, students must be educated for rational democratic and economic life, not irrational democratic and economic life. They must be helped to analyze those instances of economic and social oppression and domination that limit their human and economic potential. Teaching to economic and market templates reduces education to mere instrumentality and diminishes students (and their teachers) to objects in the service of the status quo rather than subjects in the service of tomorrow.

The Need to Restructure Schools

When we talk about "restructuring schools," we must also redefine what it means to be a teacher in today's society. If we accept the instrumentalist notion of the industrial vision of schools, we come to see ourselves and our role accordingly, and will restructure schools to serve those ends. If we accept the idea that schooling should be aimed at developing more critical citizens, our role as educators and our vision change correspondingly. By concentrating on the conception we have for education, we can identify and define our theory and practice.

Such major school restructuring efforts as school-based site management and shared decision making are necessary components of any meaningful school reform. But by themselves, they are not enough. Those bureaucratic regulations that impede school change must be restrained and a freedom to create alternative school models must be implemented. Experiments with different forms of school governance that could free schools and teachers from administrative micro-management removed from the teaching process should be discussed and implemented. In many countries, administrators and superintendents continue to teach in the classroom, which reduces bureaucracy and class privilege within the system. Teachers must have the time for planning, training, and growth. They must be treated as professionals and receive opportunities to improve their curricula—both the content and in the way they approach this content—and learn the principles and strategies of critical thinking, Socratic questioning, grouping techniques, and alternative classroom management ideas.

Furthermore, a curriculum with assessments and standards that reflects an understanding of critical thinking, how to teach for it, and how to test for it must be adopted. This curriculum must reflect higher-order thinking. Teachers must begin to think about the demands of creating a critical-thinking curriculum and atmosphere before we can decide what standards and assessment tools to put into place. As matters now stand, we have yielded assessment control to multinational textbook companies, more interested in profit margins than education quality. The California Teachers Association Secretary-Treasurer Lois Tinson, speaking at a members'convention in 1992 regarding the issue of national standards for teachers observed that

> Assessment, no matter how well intentioned or rigorous, must never be a substitute for significant improvements in how our schools are designed, managed and funded. There are no shortcuts to quality education. Standards certainly are central to good education. Yet standards alone, no matter how high, will not cure the ills of an education system that has been strained beyond its limits.

We must base our standards on a higher-order learning that challenges the skill-driven textbooks and tests. This project will require the adoption of institutionalized thinking opportunities and curricula that prepare both students and teachers for the demands of our rapidly growing global community. Assessments could be curriculum-based and challenging, which would allow teachers to "teach to the test" because the test itself would, in general, reflect the classroom curriculum. Furthermore, such innovative assessment techniques as portfolio testing must be explored and evaluated. Classifying students can, of course, become a form of internal tracking, and we need to move away from grouping by ability and instead examine cooperative grouping techniques that employ both heterogeneous and homogenous grouping. Group work should be collaborative and challenging, entailing more than just the answers to five or ten questions at the end of the chapter. Finally, we must accomplish all of this work with the support, advice, and understanding of the community we serve.

Ultimately, we must all recognize that a strong public school system is essential for a democracy. We need to mount a campaign that critically discusses the issue of private school education, the implications of voucher systems on the socio-economically deprived and minority groups, and the fact that so far these new private schools produce results no better than the results public schools produce. The attractiveness of private schools is attributable primarily to the promise of a learning environment free from violence, academically disciplined, and with small class sizes. We must incorporate these demands into our movement for excellence as a part of our struggle to restructure schools if we are really concerned with providing a critically rich, meaningful, and equitable learning environment for all students.

Confronting School Violence

Increased violence in our inner cities erodes the sanctity of inner city school life, contributes to a general deterioration of educational opportunities, and breeds disenchantment with public schools as sites for learning. According to a study by the Federal Center for Disease Control as quoted in *American Teacher* (May–June, 1992), one in 25 high school students carried a gun to class in just one month in 1990. An estimated 1.2 million elementary-aged latch-key children have access to guns in their homes and 41 metal detectors have been installed in high schools in New York City alone. In Los Angeles, the nation's second largest school district, students and teachers alike witness people dead in the streets. Such popular television shows as *Cops* ease the urban mind with scenes of Blacks and Latinos being herded together and forced to the ground by authorities of the state. When we confront violence "in real life," we may well be anesthetized to it.

An article in the December 1992–January 1993 issue of *American Teacher* entitled "Pulling the Pin on School Violence," Della Monica, a teacher at P.S. 214 in Brooklyn, New York, described the sample of 75 grenade alarms handed out to the colleagues. The instructions read, "Grasp firmly, pull the pin, and toss away from you." Monica remarked that the new devices made her feel safer. "Anything that helps stop a potential problem, "she said," makes us feel safer." (p. 6) The need for alarms arose after two Brooklyn teachers were mugged at knife point in an elementary school in 1991. The "grenades," which set off a piercing scream, came compliments of the United Federation of Teachers.

I used a similar "pull-pin" security alarm when I taught in a California prison for youth offenders, and I admit it is difficult to talk about critical thinking and reforming education when teachers are afraid of working with their students and the students are afraid to attend school. Yet rather than recommending that the teachers organize with the community to construct safe school environments and deal with problems of crime in the schools, United Federation of Teachers' safety director Ed Muir commented in the aforementioned *American Teacher* that

> our plan is to pressure the board of education to buy [the grenade alarms] for all elementary schools (p. 18).

The issue of teacher and student safety is, of course, of crucial concern; however, the failure of teachers and authorities to work directly with the community to reduce the violence, and instead to substitute technological protection devices analogous to car alarms is dangerously atavistic and, on behalf of the rest of society, fails to address the wider problem of community deterioration and moral and economic responsibility for that decay. How much longer can the public avoid the deeper problems of poverty, disenfranchisement, inadequate health care, urban deterioration, and loss of hope among many citizens and expect to teach? What will teachers demand next in response to a deteriorating moral and material educational climate, full body armor or bulletproof vests? What kind of atmosphere of critical inquiry can exist in a school where students know the teachers come "armed" with security devices, where teachers know students could be armed with guns or knives, and where schools come to resemble prisons? What does this miniature arms race tell a youngster about school life, society, and the value of education? Teachers and their unions must abandon symptomatic treatments and begin to confront the overall economic and social reality that creates these problems in the first place, or there will be little progress. Nat Hentoff (1966), interviewed a former principal of an inner city New York school, who commented on the role of teacher unions:

> You see with this kind of protection from their union, teachers could be so important in advising, participating in, and stirring up community action. Not only about education, but also about neighborhood rehabilitation and other problems that directly concern the children as well as their parents. Think of masses of teachers marching with parents and with other people in the community! That's an important new role for teachers to play—instead of being dropouts as teachers, and human beings (p. 117).

Addressing Teacher Attitudes and Morale

Any discussion of educational equity should confront the issue of teacher training and teachers' attitudes. Lack of teacher recruitment among minorities and effective teacher training with diverse populations remain serious problems and obstacles in assuring students educational equity and reasoning opportunities. Another serious problem is the current state of teacher attitudes toward those they instruct. Teachers often bring their own sociocentric and egocentric predispositions to the classroom, and wittingly or unwittingly allow these attitudes to influence their conclusions about who can and cannot learn. Many teachers feel unprepared for, alienated by, and even unaware of the cultural and historical backgrounds of the students they serve. All too many classrooms fail to accommodate the cultural and historical voices represented by diverse populations. Furthermore, with growing language disparities between teachers and students, many educators find communication difficult with many of their students and leave the teaching of these limited-English students to classroom aides who, though they may show sincere compassion and commitment, generally have little experience with critical pedagogy.

Teachers themselves must develop a critical attitude, an inward questioning through which they come to see the reasons they teach what they teach, what they do in the classroom, and why they believe and decide as they do. Teachers must develop the critical faculties and see the need to unmask the dominant curriculum. This dominant curriculum—in the form of prepackaged materials, texts, audio-visual material, and so forth—subtly encourages uncritical thinking among teachers as they try to separate execution from conception. Teachers often become pawns in the dissemination of "knowledge" or "purported facts" without having analyzed these curriculum materials critically. In fact, presented with prepackaged materials like character programs, teachers are actually encouraged to avoid asking questions about and seeking answers to problematic situations; they are invited to rely instead on the corporate materials whose authors have already asked the questions and formulated the answers. As Giroux (1988) stated,

> Needless to say, teachers may ignore such packages, or may fight their use in the schools. But the real issue is understanding the interests embedded in such curriculum packages and how such interests structure classroom experiences (p. 4).

For example, a young boy I was teaching wanted to know why we never answered the questions at the end of each chapter in the social studies book. This boy had been conditioned by his teachers and curricula to expect that doing well in school meant answering the questions at the end of the chapter. When I surprised him by telling him that we would not answer them but he could if he wanted, he seemed bewildered and then looked at me with suspicion, so thoroughly had the conditioning taken hold of his mind. Bruce Romanish (1992) noticed the same tendency in students:

> If school experiences are not devoted to a democratic ethic, students become socialized to accept power differentials between groups. They become willing to consent to their own sense of powerlessness and alienation. They become accustomed to inaction in the face of unfairness and inequity. In anti-democratic settings their critical skills cannot develop and their education soon becomes one better suited for citizenship in places where words such as "freedom" and "democracy" are empty (p. 27).

Once we come to see that ideology, or the way in which meaning embodied in schooling practices, plays a significant role in formulating the underlying assumptions that inform our curriculum, we can begin to look critically at our own experiences and ask ourselves about our own assumptions regarding human nature, social class, culture, and how these assumptions originate, are rewarded, and influence school life for both ourselves and our students. In this way we can realize that education is a process that includes us, and we can begin to question the assumptions that underlie our ideas of student achievement, tracking, learning capabilities, and the relationship between teaching and learning.

Rather than serving as passive agents of political power and cultural elitism, teachers should constantly strive to become more socially and culturally literate. They must understand that they too have biases to be critically examined. They must question their own often associational assumptions concerning diversity, the influence these assumptions have on their curriculum, who they decide can and cannot learn, and how they distribute learning opportunities to their students. It would be intellectually dishonest and harmful to students to ask teachers who avoid the critical quest for social and cultural literacy to teach students from varied social and cultural backgrounds. In her studies of urban adolescents in public schools, Michele Fine (1989) found that

Conservative administrators and teachers viewed most of their students as unteachable. It was believed, following the logic of social studies teacher Mr. Rosaldo, that "If we save 20 percent, that's a miracle. Most of these kids don't have a chance" (p. 158).

Teaching in a Los Angeles inner-city elementary school, I often observed this attitude, especially in response to newly arriving Latino or Asian students without the English language skills the monolingual curriculum demands. The teachers saw these students as inhibitors of educational growth for the rest of the English-speaking community simply because they lacked English proficiency and required "special programs" like bilingual education. With a 50 percent dropout rate in Los Angeles schools, the ideology of "dropout" came significantly to effect negative conservative teacher attitudes toward the students they taught. When I began teaching migrant children in central California, I found the attitude prevalent there as well. Many teachers thought of their students as migrants, "here today and gone tomorrow." These children, they reasoned, would never be in one place long enough to gain the skills the dominant curriculum expected and could, therefore, be "written off." I often heard such instructions as, "His family is leaving for Washington to pick fruit in a month, so just make sure he doesn't misbehave during the time he has left here."

We can trace some of these negative attitudes to the theoretical and moral decay that infect the training programs that produce most of our teachers. These programs emphasize task-oriented behavioristic activities and courses far removed from the realities of classroom life. Giroux (1988) aptly remarked that these programs are more concerned with "simply turning out technicians, students who function less as scholars and more as clerks" (p. 9). These programs are responsible for distributing a managerial "code of ethics" or qualities supposed to guide functioning educators. These codes address both the affective and cognitive domains, as teachers learn "how to behave" in the classroom, not simply what to present their students. As currently constituted, these programs are really nothing more than ideological gatekeepers to an irrational educational system. Until we teachers begin to see the logic of social relationships that define our work, and the logic of literacy and the underlying epistemological notions of knowledge acquisition, we can do little more than perpetuate an unjust system. In another December, 1992–January, 1993 article in *American Teacher* entitled, "Learning to Teach in the Inner City,"

Cheryl Anderson contributed some salient observations about how we prepare teachers for dealing with the diversity of inner city life

> Very little of the training I received in college or as an intern teacher prepared me to teach in the inner city (p. 14).

She commented that for some teachers straight out of teacher training programs, the experience could be "a culture shock." She went on to say that

> It's important that the [teaching] interns get to know the children, their cultural background, and the area they live in (p. 14).

In *Foxfire*, Elliot Wigginton (1985) described his interaction with a young high school student who decided to quit school for a week to hunt for "sang." This young boy had been a "discipline problem" throughout the class refusing to work, engage in activities, or comport himself properly. When Wigginton displayed an interest in the boy's hunt for sang, their relationship assumed a new empathic dimension. Not only did "sang" involve a traditional craft long ago abandoned by most, but this boy also knew everything there was to know about the root—from its location to the way one removed it from the ground. Wigginton accompanied the lad:

> I've thought about that day many times since. Its most immediate effect, besides from the ache in my legs, was that I never again had a disciplinary problem with that boy (or his friends whom he apparently talked to behind the scenes). The change was instantaneous. Whereas before our friendly encounters—our arm wrestling matches and such—had tended to make things worse, this event had the opposite effect. Instead of being a "pal," someone with whom it was safe to clown around with, I had stumbled into a different kind of relationship of a much deeper quality. For one thing, our roles had been reversed and suddenly I was the pupil, he the teacher. I was amazed at the depth and quality of his knowledge about the woods. He knew far more on that score than I, and I could not help but respect him. He had his areas of knowledge and ignorance, and I had mine, and in that respect we were equal, each potentially able to share something with the other, to the enrichment of both (p. 72).

Sound teacher-training programs should afford teachers the opportunities to gain an insight into their own unexamined attitudes as well as societal attitudes toward cultural reality and the students they teach. For Paulo Freire (1985) these opportunities carry the responsibility of ongoing evaluation:

All of this requires not only rigorous conviction from base educators but also ongoing evaluation of their work. Evaluation, that is, and not inspection. Through inspection educators just become objects of vigilance by a central organization. Through evaluation, everyone is a subject along with the central organization in the act of criticism and establishing distance from the work. In understanding the process in this way, evaluation is not an act by which educator A evaluates educator B. It's an act by which educators A and B together evaluate an experience, its development, and the obstacles that one confronts along with any mistakes or errors. Thus evaluation has a dialectical nature (p. 23)

We must have genuine opportunities for critical cross-cultural training to serve all our students, regardless of gender, sexual orientation, race, or culture. Teachers need continual reactions and advice from communities and peers to help them see how they distribute educational opportunities to their students. A recent Public Broadcasting television program focused on sex bias in the classroom, and one fifth grade teacher was shocked when she watched a video of herself in the classroom and noticed how more often she questioned the boys than the girls. According to the American Association of University Women (1992),

(1) Girls receive significantly less attention from classroom teachers than do boys.
(2) African-American girls have fewer interactions with teachers than do white girls, despite evidence that they attempt to initiate interactions more frequently.
(3) Sexual harassment of girls and boys—from innuendo to actual assault—in our nation's schools is increasing (p. 2).

The AAUW Report goes on to recommend that state certification standards for teachers require course work on gender issues, including new research on women, bias in the classroom, interaction patterns, and the ways in which schools can develop and implement a gender-fair multicultural curriculum.

Unfortunately, many teachers consider their students "marginal" or outside the "middle class" mainstream. Unconsciously perhaps, they treat these students as inferior, subordinate, devoid of reason, incapable, and inherently valueless or intrinsically dysfunctional. Alexander Moore in his essay "The Inner City High School, Instructional and Community Roles," (1970) declared himself

. . . convinced that the great problem [of teaching disadvantaged students] is not the low aspirations of parents and students, but rather those of their teachers (p. 225).

Moore found the race of the teachers less significant in designing learning than their social class outlook. Many of the teachers he surveyed
were middle class, upwardly mobile, and, no matter what their color,
tended to imbue lower-class children with fewer educationally powerful attributes. Many similar studies reveal the same pattern. Long before Moore, Leacock studied the differential perceptions of learners.
Moore reported that Leacock too had found differences in expectation levels produced as much by social class as by race. In the lowest
socio-economic Black school, teachers clearly conveyed their low expectations of their students. In the Leacock study, said Moore (1970)
one researcher observed that

> The teacher working with white middle-income fifth grade children took re-
> sponsibility for her own limitations and spoke of reacting to lack of attention
> as a cue to her, indicating the need for her to arouse their interest. On the
> other hand, the limitations of the teacher working with low-income Negro
> children were ascribed to the children, and boredom on their part was attrib-
> uted to their presumably limited attention span (p. 203).

I found these same perceptions in my teaching career both in the
way teachers behaved with their students and how they talked about
them. Leacock and Moore's studies, although launched in the late
1960s and early 1970s, represent the current reality in many schools.
The ideology of lower-class stupidity, or race stupidity, or gender inadequacy runs rampant through our schools today. Teachers burdened
with such an ideology must begin the cultural dialogue with their students and their communities. Through critical reflection and experience with other cultural points of view, they may come to find that
alcoholism, crime, slums, sickness, drug addiction, and dysfunctional
families are not the sole province of "a wicked or insignificant popu-
lace," but are pervasive evils in all our social structures; structures
now deeply needful of social and political transformation. Furthermore, as we have seen, teachers often become unconscious agents of
a political agenda inherent in classroom texts and life. To engage in
critical reflection, they must unceasingly evaluate their own work and
seek to understand how the world of culture and history becomes a
created product capable of conditioning men and women to unexamined
falsehoods and social justifications for continued dominant practices.
Hentoff (1966) described a teacher at P.S. 119 in Harlem, New York,
discussing teacher attitudes with another instructor

"It would also be valuable for some of the teachers in other schools to get to know our kids. Those stereotypes about children of the poor are still so pervasive. 'They can't learn. They won't learn.' It's surprising how much they do learn with all the obstacles against them. Last year I had thirty-three in my class." "Oh they have strengths," Mrs. Boone said mordantly. "The ability to survive for one. And look at the amount of responsibility these children have to take. Little children picking up littler children and bringing them home. They can't enjoy growing up because they can't be children" (pp. 13–14).

In an *Educational Leadership* (December 1992–January 1993) article, Barbara Ries Wager shared her experience as a principal at James P.B. Duffy School No. 12 in Rochester, New York. She spoke of the deplorable conditions at the school, including violence directed both at teachers and students, and she described the teachers' attitudes when faced with this classroom madness:

In the face of these outbreaks teachers reacted in different ways. Some, who had frozen into passivity, did nothing to control problems and neglected any available preventative measures. Others became petty tyrants, harassing children with abusive lectures or insisting on formal public apologies following misdemeanors. Some teachers expressed their anger in physical forms: one teacher tipped over desks of second graders if their content was not organized in a prescribed way; another assigned, as punishment for misconduct, the performance of 100 push-ups. Some fought violence with violence: one teacher threw a pail of water over squabbling nine-year olds as if they were fighting dogs. While there were no instances of outright battery by teachers, neglect and retaliatory actions were sufficient to keep the faculty in a state of chronic agitation and to breed angry gossip about peers (p. 35).

One can easily imagine what these teachers thought about their students, what assumptions they had made about their abilities to become fully human, what their actual connectedness to the community and culture of these students was, and what their ideas of education were.

Theodore W. Parsons (1972) discussed teachers' attitudes and the assumptions they bring to the classroom when he quoted a teacher in a Mexican-American community who explained why she put an Anglo boy in charge of a group of Mexican-American students:

I think Johnny needs to learn how to set a good example and how to lead others. His father owns one of the big farms in the area and Johnny has to learn how to lead the Mexicans. One day he will be helping his father and he will have to know how to handle Mexicans. I try to help whenever I can (p. 32).

Here is a teacher who internalized the culture of power and rotely disseminated "learning opportunities" that ultimately perpetuate the inequities in social life. Unaware of her own assumptions, this teacher not only discriminates in learning opportunities, but more insidiously will also fosters cultural and socio-political inequities.

In his essay "The Black Revolution and Education," Donald Smith (1972) concluded that

> What Black pupils want and need are teachers who believe they can learn, who expect them to learn, and who teach them. Not teachers whose naiveté or cultural biases have conditioned them to believe that Blacks, Indians, poor whites, or Spanish-speaking children are inferior and they can never teach them. It is extremely difficult for most teachers to understand how their own perceptions of the worth and ability of their students actually affect the emotional development and achievement of the children (p. 46).

It is also difficult for them to understand how these perceptions influence the opportunities for learning provided for some students as opposed to others.

Winnie Porter, a kindergarten teacher in San Francisco, described in *California Tomorrow* (1992) how her assumptions and conclusions about her students changed as a result of experiencing and then coming to understand the realities of her students' lives:

> When I came back from the first time I visited the projects, the kids' behavior didn't bother me that much anymore. When you realize what home lives some kids come from and what they have to deal with, you realize they're not naughty kids but just expressing their frustration and anger. . . . One of my little girls comes in without socks in the morning. If I'd never been at her home and seen that mom has eight kids, one year apart, and she's on welfare and on crutches, I'd probably get angry with the mother and ask why the hell she can't get socks on her child in the morning. But after the visit, I realize that this six-year-old not only has to dress herself, but her three brothers and sisters in the morning and help her mom! It gives me such a sense of respect and pride in that little girl (pp. 1–13).

Winnie Porter became more culturally and socially literate after taking the point of view of the community and her students. Similar opportunities to participate in and analyze these types of experiences elude most teacher training programs and are uncommon in school-site life. Teachers rarely receive encouragement to reason within the cultural and economic points of view of the students and parents they serve. Thus, they are less inclined to think critically or analyze their own assumptions about their students, decide who is potentially gifted, or critically examine the implications of this lack of cultural awareness on the design of their curricula. This insularity limits the thinking opportunities they provide for their students, the issues they choose as vehicles for transforming reality, the questions they ask their students, any reluctance to track students of color and newly arriving immigrants, and the overall implementation of a rich critical-thinking environment that benefits all students.

We educators must see ourselves as more than just vendors of pre-ordained truth but as dignified public servants devoted to a transformative education. We must demand the dignity that accompanies the teaching mission and develop an appreciation for theory, practice, and the development of praxis both inside and outside the classroom. This new stridency requires reflection and a willingness to share ideas, problems, and solutions. It also calls us to re-map the political agenda of teacher unions, and force the fight for restructuring in education with such changes as more preparation time in the elementary schools, collaborative teaching, more classroom resources, more money for authentic in-services a redistribution of power between administrators and teachers, authentic assessment, and a commitment to involving community in the struggle for educational equity.

But our new stridency also means confronting our own classroom authoritarianism. Too often teachers refuse to tolerate student challenges only because they "undermine my authority." Fine (1989) cited an example of this reaction in her story of a high school teacher who structured an in-class debate on Bernard Goetz, New York City's vigilante. This teacher asked her class to divide into two groups: one that supported Goetz and one that condemned his use of a revolver on the subway. As the students divided up in groups several of them stayed in the middle of the room. The teacher admonished them, "Don't be lazy! You have to make a decision. You can't be passive!" Six of the students remained in the middle, refusing to join either side. One of the students, Deirdre, an outspoken Black senior, remarked,

> "It's not that I have no opinions. I don't like Goetz shootin' up people who look like my brother. But I don't like feeling unsafe in the projects or in my neighborhood either. I got lots of opinions. I ain't bein' quiet because I can't decide if he's right or wrong. I'm talkin'" (p. 164).

For Deirdre, the issue was far more complex than the black-and-white dichotomy the teacher tried to establish. Yet the teacher resented her decision not to take one side or the other as an attack upon authority and on what the teacher considered to be an exercise in reasoned judgment. For Deirdre and other low-income minority youths, schooling in this sense represents an orientation to the corporate workplace polarities where they are expected to obey authority and refrain from complexity or contradiction. In this way, they learn subordination early, and the function of schooling is fulfilled.

Finally, we educators need to embody and exemplify the politics of hope and optimism as we go about our daily activities. In light of drastic pay cuts, intolerable working conditions, excessive bureaucracy, over-populated schools, influential technocrats removed from the classroom, increased violence in the schools, parent alienation, racism, sexism, and the rest of the problems facing our society and public schools, it can be difficult to maintain and resonate hope about the future of our students and the democracy we are attempting to build. It can be difficult to transcend the politics of despair, and there is no question that we confront real despair that limits our hopes for freedom each and every day. As an educator, I must continually confront misery while I try to imagine a better world and a pedagogy that exemplifies and conveys critical-thinking opportunities for my students. I want to avoid the politics and polemics of nihilism, and I resist preoccupation with the negative side of the dialectic. I want to hold the hope that we can make relevant and liberatory "educational theater" for the masses of people in this country, that we can make metacognition an actual part of their personal reflection and daily activities. For Sharon Welch (1985), the pedagogical notion of hope is embodied in a theology that combines a vision of liberation with an understanding of past and present oppression:

> This theology emerges from the struggle to create, not merely to proclaim, a human community that embodies freedom. The verification of this struggle is not conceptual, but practical: the successful process of enlightenment and emancipation, a process that is open and self-critical. This theology emerges from an effort to live on the edge, accepting both the power and peril of discourse, engaging in a battle for truth with a conscious preference for the oppressed. . . . It is a discourse embued with a particular tragedy of human existence—the dangerous memory of despair, barrenness, suffering—and with the particular moments of liberation—the equally dangerous memory of historical actualization's of freedom and community. . . . [This] type of theology. . . affirms with Bloch "that learned hope is the signpost for this age—not just hope, but hope and the knowledge to take the way to it" (p. 214).

As Henry Giroux (1988) observed, by embracing pedagogical hope, teachers can begin to view themselves as more than simply school teachers—but as intellectuals:

> Viewing teachers as intellectuals also provides a strong theoretical critique of technocratic and instrumental ideologies underlying an educational theory that separates the conceptualization, planning and design of curricula from the process of implementation and execution. It is important to stress that teachers must take active responsibility for raising serious questions about what they teach, how they are to teach, and what the larger goals are for which they are striving. This means that they must take a responsible role in shaping the purposes and conditions of schooling. . . . If we believe that the role of teaching cannot be reduced to merely training in the practical skills, but involves, instead, the education of a class of intellectuals vital to the development of a free society, then the category of intellectual becomes a way of linking the purpose of teacher education, public schooling and in-service training to the very principles necessary for developing a democratic order and society (p. 126).

This conceptualization affords teachers a new respect and a sense of integrity both for themselves as agents of social change and for the profession of pedagogy in general. Redefining ourselves as intellectuals restores the dignity and esteem so viciously expropriated by the recent and current power relationships within the educational system.

Recruiting and Training Teachers Comfortable with Diversity

Teacher recruitment to meet the needs of our diverse student population remains an issue of central concern to anyone propounding a critical multicultural pedagogy. Innovations like providing bilingual classroom aides with opportunities for teacher training and education can help meet this challenge. The task of recruiting minorities and people of color to serve the demographic and language needs of our students is a goal multicultural education must confront and meet. In their 1980 report entitled *Minority Teacher Recruitment Initiatives*, the National Education Association noted that 12.5 percent of all public school teachers in the United States were minorities. Yet by the year 2000, the NEA expected less than 5 percent of the teaching force to be minorities. Compare these figures with the fact that 45 percent of the student population nationwide is made up of minority students, and one can appreciate the alarming nature of the trend.

Promoting Educational Relevance
and Personalized Learning

Educational relevance and personalized learning are also essential to any meaningful multicultural curriculum concerned with equity. In the words of Paulo Freire (1985),

> [An educator's] objective shouldn't be to describe something that should be memorized. Quite the contrary, he or she should problematize situations [and] present the challenge of reality that learners confront each day (p. 22).

Freire recommended an active curriculum that involves students in thinking about reality with the purpose of acting upon those thoughts. This project, of course, requires critical writing about reality, critical speaking about reality, Socratic questioning of reality, critical reading about reality, and critical listening to diverse narratives of reality. Horace Mann Bond (1934) advocated the active curriculum and recognized a need for authentic assessment:

> One of the best examples of the "activity curriculum" ever known was inaugurated at Tuskegee Institute by Booker T. Washington several decades before the name became current in educational literature. At rhetorical exercises, students at Tuskegee did not give the expected orations about efficiency, or cleanliness; Washington aimed at these ideals but his students spoke about the efficient way of milking a cow, or the clean way to make butter. Under Washington's tutelage, they went much further. A cow was introduced upon the platform, and the student went through the activity of milking while delivering his "oration." A girl giving an essay on butter-making had on a platform beside her a churn, milk, and molds. It is hardly necessary to remember that there is no "Negro way" of milking a cow: there is a right way and a wrong way (p. 12).

Educators should take advantage of all opportunities to stimulate their students, even by sharing their own doubts, viewpoints, and criticisms. They should encourage active student involvement as opposed to sedentary passivity. According to Boyer (1983),

> Students suffer from information overload—not to mention boredom. Some pass notes to each other; others doze in the heat of the afternoon, heads down on the desk. Nevertheless, the teacher feels it has been a successful class. He has "covered" the material and there have been no serious interruptions (p. 147).

Unfortunately, what typically passes for multicultural education does little to encourage critical thinking and exploration into self through reality, or reality through self. Nor do these exercises provide engaging opportunities for informed social inquiry and transformation. As currently constructed, multicultural education tends to be non-transformative, intellectually domesticating, and unable to offer active voices to the students it purports to serve. Relegating students to mere educational spectators, current multicultural educational programs both fail to invite critical multicultural discourse through dialogical and dialectical thinking, and reinforce schooling as a trivial pursuit removed from the living realities of everyday life. Dewey (1916) commented on this externality of school:

> Another influential but defective theory is that which conceives that the mind has, at birth, certain mental faculties or powers, such as perceiving, remembering, willing, judging, generalizing, attending, etc., and that education is the training of these faculties through repeated exercise. This theory treats subject matter as comparatively external and indifferent, its value residing simply in the fact that it may occasion the exercise of general powers. The outcome of the theory in practice was shown to be an undue emphasis upon the training of narrow specialized modes of skill at the expense of initiative, inventiveness, and re-adaptability, qualities which depend upon the broad and consecutive interaction of specific activities with one another (p. 80).

Many students today live nightmarish lives, especially in our inner cities. They face drug addiction, unemployment, inadequate educational opportunities, racism, sexism, dysfunctional families, teenage pregnancies, and even the status, for some, of being "illegal." These conditions redefine what it means to be an educator and a student, and a citizen in today's society. Students bring legacies of oppression and resistance to our classrooms and they seek and expect critical exploration, critical listening, and critical evaluation through radical discourse and rigorous analysis. In his book *Sometimes a Shining Moment*, Elliot Wigginton (1985) described student attitudes toward teachers. He asked his students to comment on teachers they had known and to offer any opinions about the experience, positive or negative. The following comments remain salient a decade later:

> Most of you are alike. A teacher doesn't need to put on an iron mask each morning before coming to school. I know your job is to teach us, and I also know a lot of kids are almost impossible to get through to. It does take a strict and powerful approach—but pounding our heads is not how to get through.

> To me a teacher who is understanding and can see my problems and wants to help is the kind of person who does help. The other kind of teacher—the one who will teach by not getting involved but by standing in front of the room (apart from students and students' problems) repeating over and over again his facts is nothing. In too many classrooms the world is only what's there in the classroom. There is no such thing as war, love, religion, or individualism. The teacher is master. The students do what the teacher says (p. 35).

For many newly arriving immigrant students and students of color or from the lower socioeconomic classes, schooling divorced from reality becomes an exercise in alienation as they develop two worlds and two identities. One world and one identity is the notion of one's self outside of school, the "real self"; the other is the notion of the academic self, the "good student." The academic self or good student learns the logic of teacher expectations: to speak standard English even if one is of Creole or Latino descent; to give the teachers back what they want at test-taking time. Donning this academic self is a way to survive in school for a great many students, and many teachers encourage it. Many teachers expect students to leave their "cultural baggage" outside the classroom, adopt this conformist schizophrenia, and live bifurcated lives: self-actualization and identity versus prescription and regimented passivity. Michelle Fine (1989) interviewed a young black, female, urban high school dropout who observed that

> In school we learned Columbus Avenue stuff and I had to translate it into Harlem. They think livin' up here is unsafe and our lives are so bad. That we should want to move out and get away. That's what you're supposed to learn (p. 163).

Tony, another high school dropout Fine interviewed, reported that

> I never got math when I was in school. Then I started sellin' dope and runnin' numbers and I picked it up right away. They should teach the way it matters (p. 163)

Yet far too often the curriculum silences dialogue about our students' lived lives, imaginations, dreams, and social realities. What constitutes the lives of newly arriving immigrants and people of color is often deemed irrelevant to academic life. This separation between the lives of students and the curriculum's ideology of silence promises to turn schooling into a compulsory obligation and against a life-long commitment to education and enlightenment. As early as 1933, W. W. Charters recognized the need to link critical thinking in the curriculum to reasoning about material necessity and human experience:

The impossibility of deriving subject matter from the aims of Plato and Comenius is due to the fact that their aims are statements of ideals isolated from activities. For the curriculum is properly concerned not only with the ideals which govern life, but also with the things which a person does and thinks about. . . . Some ideals, such as virtue, or swift-footedness, piety, or social efficiency, must be set up in the system of education; but in order to determine the curriculum, it is absolutely essential for the teacher to know the activities, problems, thoughts, or needs which those ideals are to influence and control (p. 9).

Building on the lived experiences of our students can make a lively subject for public and private debate, legitimizing these experiences and affirming those who live them. It means offering critical educational opportunities for students to articulate their language, dreams, hopes, values, and encounters with others. It welcomes reflection, metacognition, and insight into these experiences on the part of both students and teachers, while offering opportunities for critical thinking about social and personal issues. Students need to see that the purposes and implications of education go beyond the classroom. As currently structured, education remains so disconnected from the struggles in the community, neighborhood, churches, and workplace that students come to assume that being educated has nothing to do with the social institutions or their daily lives. In their June 1992 report entitled *Creating a Gender Fair Multicultural Curriculum*, the American Association of University Women concluded that

It is therefore imperative that the formal curriculum which conveys the central messages of education, provides students with "mirrors" reflecting their experience as well as "windows" revealing those of others. But for most students, particularly girls and minorities, the present curriculum provides many windows and few mirrors (p. 1).

Banks (1990) went further, pointing out that teaching about the contradictions of American history and reality is essential for accommodating humanity in the future:

When the schools fail to recognize, validate, and testify to racism, poverty, and inequality that students experience in their daily lives, the students are likely to view the school and the curriculum as a contrived and sugarcoated place that is out of touch with the real world and the struggles of students' daily lives (p. 213).

As we have seen, the classroom rarely addresses the needs, goals, and lives suggested by our changing student demographics. Texts compound this failure by offering the dominant narrative of reality on issues of contemporary and historical concern, thereby providing few opportunities to see the world from alternative cultural points of view. Texts and lesson plans require less independent thinking in favor of rote dissemination and memorization alienated from the discourse of everyday life. Freire (1985) asked, "What meaning is there to a text that asks absurd questions and gives equally absurd answers?" (p. 9). Freire meant that this type of divorced instruction—the instruction of accommodation and trivialization, of decontextualization and alienation, of subjugation and domination—can have no appreciable effect on human growth and potential, and can provide no catalyst for transforming the human mind or the world. This anesthetized approach to learning hides behind its claim to social and political neutrality. Education, we are told, is not a form of political expression, but rather generic or value free. The generic curriculum pretends to wide appeal among students while shunning controversy, depersonalizing learning, and trivializing reality. Giroux (1989) suggested some valuable questions we teachers should ask:

> What relationship do my students see between the work we do in class and the lives they live outside of class? Is it possible to incorporate aspects of students' lived culture into the work of schooling without simply confirming what they already know? Can this be done without trivializing the objects and relationships important to students? And can it be done without singling out particular groups of students as marginal, exotic, and "other" within a hegemonic culture? (p. 243).

Social, economic, and cultural conflict beg for acknowledgment and recognition as current realities. They provide relevant, real-life subjects for independent thinking, democratic decision making, and intellectual character building. With all its complexities and contradictions, current reality is hardly too controversial or intimidating for classroom discourse and should be embraced. In one school, Fine (1989) found a biology teacher, one of the few Black teachers in his high school, using creative writing assignments. He infused such assignments as "My Life as an Alcoholic" and "My Life as a Child of an Alcoholic" quite appropriately into the biology class curriculum. But when this innovation came to the attention of the principal, the teacher was severely reprimanded for introducing extraneous materials (p. 165). My own primary school experience in South Central Los Angeles confirms this silencing of teachers by administrators. I had enlisted the help of an independent filmmaker and wanted to work with a group of children on antigang messages. The principal told me this was not the role of a teacher and my students could not participate in this activity.

A curriculum devoid of conflict reduces the need to reason about issues of social and personal relevance. It reduces the role of education to that of disempowerment—a pedagogy separate from the real world. The implications for the teacher laboring under this restraint is that he or she works on students, never with them. Students so treated become mere receptacles to be filled with predigested truths. On the other hand, teachers who critically understand the role of education and society tend to work with students—helping them explore the complexities of their personal and social existence relative to the social structures around them. These educators can provide profound opportunities for students to develop the values and dispositions of learning, encouraging them to see the relevance of learning and to be ready to apply educational insights in other domains. In speaking about the male students attending his inner city school, Hentoff's (1966) principal Shapiro stated that

> I don't believe they're beyond help. Look at those boys. I know them. They can hardly read but they certainly do have hostility; and if they could become involved, let us say, in action against slum landlords and in similar projects to change the community, they'd be motivated to learn to read in order to be more effective in what they are trying to do (p. 132).

In her essay "Enhancing the Black Concept Through Literature," Arnez (1972) encouraged the use of popular culture as relevant educational material. Although more than twenty years old, her example of Aretha Franklin's song "Think" for classroom use applies today, if one substitutes (for example) rap. She also advocated the use of poetry, dance, visual arts, and contemporary new literature by young Black authors to help students understand the relevance of education. Popular culture used as classroom text can empower students, can profoundly affect students' lives, and can help students read culture critically as they begin to see how their own self-interests are manipulated or reproduced by cultural forms.

Teachers concerned with relevance see education and learning as a political act that requires reasoning within diverse and often opposing points of view; reflective thought, theory, practice, and transformation; interdisciplinary learning transfers; and personal and social commitment. For these educators, student and teacher are not objects but living subjects in the process of critically learning and knowing. This idea of critical learning and pedagogy rejects authoritarian impositions dictated from above and alienating obligatory relationships that end when youngsters reach 18. Rather, the idea promises an empowering journey into humanity. Understanding that human beings are inherently creative, thoughtful, and capable of knowing is paramount to offering them honest and empowering educational opportunities. Teachers should seek to develop high expectations for all of their students, to listen to their personal narratives, to enter into their subjective lives, and to express confidence in their abilities to develop fair-minded reasoning while simultaneously maintaining a vision that they are also potentially gifted.

The Need to Strengthen Bilingual Education for Newly Arriving Immigrants

For many newly arriving immigrants, a low English proficiency level limits their ability to enter into reasoning activities. The race is on between language acquisition and alienation from the educational discourse in the monolingual classroom. Any comprehensive and theoretically sound critical multicultural pedagogy must be committed to providing effective bilingual education to students limited in English. This task extends beyond simply the transition to English and should also respect the student's cultural and linguistic heritage. As Gabelke (1988) noted, without the ability to discuss issues of relevance, newly arrived immigrants are far too often relegated to remedial activities and viewed as deficient in both ability and character. Krashen's (1988) research revealed that developing literacy in the ("native") primary language both speeds the acquisition of English reading, writing, and speaking skills overall and contributes to superior levels of cognitive development. Constructing effective bilingual programs that lead to the acquisition of the English language, without the abandonment of the primary language, is essential if we are to construct an equitable curriculum. Furthermore, the absence of such programs practically ensures the abandonment of the cultural and linguistic identity of the student, creating problems with self-esteem and reducing appreciation among all students for bilingualism or multi-linguistic diversity.

Enlisting Parents and the Community in the Struggle for Social Equity

Because schools belong in the social structures that dictate everyday life, parent involvement is imperative in the struggle for educational equity. Parents and teachers must work together to mobilize all adults in the community to encourage critical academic and social development skills for all students. Parents should have the chance to participate in a rich and relevant curriculum. Parents need to be recruited as more than just den mothers in the classroom or servers for student birthday parties, but recruited as decision makers in the construction of an equitable educational practice designed to accommodate their children democratically. Parents must feel a sense of participation in their children's education. Already familiar with alienated decision making and administrative disregard, parents need to be encouraged to help build an educational life for their children, themselves, and others. In this way, the Jeffersonian vision of the "common school" extends to parents as well as students. Parents and students begin to see education as a life-long commitment to social responsibility, structural transformation, and social action. Long ago, Hentoff (1966) reported the remarks of a principal in Harlem about the parents' hesitancy to involve themselves with schooling:

> Well, for a long time it was difficult here too. The parents didn't trust us and they had good reason not to. One of the problems of parents in this kind of neighborhood is supposed to be that they're non-verbal. But they often have very good reasons for not saying much to school administrators. They're thinking, "Why don't the children have readers to take home and why don't they have more of other things to do?" But often parents don't ask because they suspect that principal is loyal to the system and not to the children and they figure, "What's the use? He's not going to do anything to change the system." So it's an act of intelligence on their part to refuse to enter into what would be phony dialogue (p. 30).

He went on describing how he attempted to develop a relationship between educational and community struggle:

> As for housing, our middle income housing is the low income St. Nicholas housing project. Across the street a house built for eight families has forty-five. Next door there are two houses with serious heating problems. Two winters ago, I spent hours trying to track down the owner, and finally I told the man who said he was only the agent, that if the heat wasn't provided there'd be a picket line of teachers and me. There was heat for the rest of the winter (p. 30).

When this principal experienced a response from the community, he welcomed it:

> Our school has to have an organic relationship with the community. If the staff tries to take action, that indicates to the community that there is hope.

Then the parents come alive; and in any case, what happens in the street affects our children. Education that stops at three in the afternoon is mis-education (p. 30).

Nancy Arnez (1972) described the plight of Chicago Black youths who, disillusioned with the educational system, left high school before graduating to establish an alternative school system for the people in their community. Arnez discussed their negotiations with priests to occupy an empty convent on a one-acre lot. The men and women cleaned the area and began to arrange the school when the priests reneged and called the police to evict them. A fight ensued and many young people were injured. Following the incident Arnez, described how an Open House Affair was designed to combat the racist atti-tudes, including those of notable Black politicians and leaders in the community. Again the priests sent in the police, again a fight ensued, and again youths were injured. The students were advised to move to a structure offered by another religious group. This they did, and they drew up a charter for their school setting forth its purpose:

To provide educational facilities for all age groups in the community with specific emphasis on health, recreation, and training programs. These pro-grams will be designed by the youth with full participation of the community (pp. 102–103).

Here we have an example of educational equity in the real sense of the term. Here students fought for and achieved an educational institution with the support of the community for the community. We need to revive this form of community involvement to encourage education as something desirable and accessible for all.

Commenting on the importance of community involvement in schooling, Grambs (1972) noted that

The achievement of the educationally crippled can be drastically improved by establishing the legitimacy of teacher accountability, bringing in many more adults in every educational level, many of whom may well be from the school community, utilizing cross-age tutoring, grouping, gaming, and playing. Older children are superb teachers; no one learns more than a teacher about what he is teaching. Understand that no child should learn to read a textbook: he should learn to read books, faces, music, moods, pictures. Commercial televi-sion can be as useful in any classroom as in any home, though the lessons may be different—but this is the real world. Use the new technology such as video-taped lessons, to help every teacher see his own teaching, and every child to see his own learning—every year, or every month, or oftener. Open

up the school day, lengthen it, lengthen the school year also so that ample
time is available for the leisure to learn (p. 207).

Relevancy and community involvement became political for Hentoff's
principal, Shapiro:

> Take this neighborhood. It's poor, stores go out of business leaving many
> vacant storefronts—some with backyards—that could be used as classrooms.
> From 110th to 145th St. and between Seventh and Eight Avenues, there are
> the equivalent of forty to fifty potential classrooms. Why not use them prima-
> rily for young children—with backyards as school yards, and with libraries
> interspersed here and there? The libraries could be for parents as well as
> children and could be open until eight or nine in the evening. We would be
> coming right into the heart of the community, creating the kind of reciprocal
> relationship between the community and the schools that you don't find any-
> where in this city—or in this country. We'd be on constant display, and people
> would be welcome to come in and see what we are doing. And if they wanted
> to, they could help as parent aides. The plan would take care of classroom
> shortages and would represent real decentralization. It could be the stimulus
> for the creation of a new society. But we couldn't have an adult-to-pupil ratio
> of one to twenty-eight in those storefront schools. The classes would have to
> be quite small.
>
> Some of these basic improvements can be put in motion by teachers spurring
> the parents. In our neighborhoods, action for beacon schools, smaller classes,
> educational parks can start that way. You know, it's very often said that the
> schools reflect the social order. Actually that often means that schools are
> institutions of apology for the social order. But it doesn't have to be that way.
> The schools could be an instrument for changing the social order into a more
> truly democratic society. But for that to happen we have to break the circle in
> which professional personnel tend to remain loyal to institutions rather than
> to the human beings that should be served by those institutions (pp. 46–50).

Helping parents help their children should a principal goal of a
critical multicultural literacy. Parents should come to understand the
underlying goals of a critical pedagogy. Too often I hear parents la-
ment that their children cannot read, write, regroup numerals in mathematics, and accomplish other "skills." While these skills are of course
important, parents still labor under the impression that schooling is
reading, writing, and arithmetic and expect little more. Parents need
to enter the restructuring dialogue, weigh the principles and strategies
of critical thinking, discuss assessments of higher-order learning, and
respond to the challenges of becoming educated in a critical sense in
today's world. Unless parents become involved in the struggle to achieve

a new critical pedagogy, the coalition of educators and administrators interested in restructuring education will remain feeble.

In its 1991 publication *Teaching Young Children to Resist Bias: What Parents Can Do,* the National Association for the Education of Young Children (NAEYC) makes the point that parents can help their children combat prejudice and develop critical-thinking skills by first recognizing the need for anti-bias development and creating an environment of critical inquiry and dialogue about cultural heritages, self-identities, and diversity. The NAEYC emphasizes that meaningful empathetic opportunities with different people, materials, experiences, and activities reinforced by critical dialogue and reflection can help young children develop minds that resist associational thinking and stereotypes. The NAEYC is committed to helping parents help their children develop into critical thinkers, and it publishes materials for parents to use at home. For example, advising parents how to deal with bias and prejudice, one NAEYC pamphlet proposes the following hypothetical situation: Lisa, Peter, and Elana are playing hospital when Lisa's dad hears an argument break out over who will be the doctor and who will be the patient. Dad hears Lisa declare, "I don't want to be your friend anymore you stupid Mexican!" The NAEYC suggests that the father intervene by comforting Elana and saying, "I am sorry Lisa said that to you." Then the pamphlet portrays him asking all three children what the problem was. Here is his conclusion:

> Sounds like the real problem is that you both want to be doctor. That has nothing to do with Elana being Mexican. Elana, who you are is just fine, just like you Lisa, and you, Peter are also just fine. But you all have a problem with taking turns. How can you work that out? (p. 1)

Although I would prefer to ask the children what the problem was instead of telling them what the problem was, the message is that by intervening critically at home in everyday problems that arise between young children, parents can, like teachers, shape the characters of their children.

In another scenario, Elana and her family have just moved into the neighborhood and Lisa's parents invite them over for a visit. When they arrive, Lisa refuses to play with Elana in her room. After the family leaves, Lisa says, "I don't like them. Mexicans are stupid!" Mom is encouraged to ask Lisa why she thinks that way and learns that Cindy, Lisa's friend, told her so. Mom responds:

> Lisa, Cindy is wrong! To say that Mexicans are stupid is unfair and hurtful! Mexican people are just as smart as everyone else. Tomorrow let's go to the library and get some books on Mexican-Americans so that we can learn more about them. We want you to get to know Elana and her family because they are our neighbors (p. 4).

Lisa's mother wisely ascertains the origin of her thinking about Mexicans, but I would encourage her to ask Lisa why she believes what Cindy says. Does Cindy have any evidence for her thinking? Does Lisa? Can Lisa think of any reason why Mexicans would be stupid? Rather than telling Lisa it is wrong to suggest that Mexicans are stupid, I would help Lisa arrive at this understanding herself. I would want her to see the implications of her thinking by (perhaps) asking her, "How do you think Elana felt when you wouldn't play with her?" "What do you think she was thinking?" I would then do exactly what the pamphlet suggests and invite Lisa to study Mexican people ourselves and arrive at our own conclusions. By suggesting these activities, parents model critical thinking and the values and dispositions of a reasoning mind for their children. In both scenarios, the parents model intellectual empathy, humility, courage, fair-mindedness, civility, and curiosity, as well as such cognitive dimensions of thinking as the elements of thought.

Another important point the NAEYC brochure makes is the importance of showing children that injustice can be corrected and changed. To make this point, the pamphlet suggests that parents

> (1) Talk to a store manager or owner about stocking more toys, dolls, books and puzzles that reflect diversity;
> (2) Ask the local stationary store to sell greeting cards that show children of color, and
> (3) Take a child to a rally about getting more funding for child care centers.
> (p. 1)

Engaging in emancipatory movements that challenge inequality and injustice helps prepare children for engaging in critical activities outside of their schooling.

In a section of its publication headed "Common Questions Children Ask and Ways to Respond," the National Association for the Education of Young Children suggests inappropriate and appropriate responses to children's comments. The following paragraphs offers some useful examples along with my own suggested responses:

"Why is that girl in a wheelchair?"

Inappropriate
"Shh, it's not nice to ask." (admonishing)
"I'll tell you another time." (sidestepping)
Act as if you didn't hear the question. (avoiding)

Appropriate
"She is using a wheelchair because her legs are not strong enough to walk. The wheelchair helps her move around."

Suggested
"Why do you think people use wheelchairs?" (This response encourages independent thinking and challenges the child's assumptions.)
"If your legs were not strong enough to move you around real well, do you think a wheelchair might be a good way to get around? Why?" (These questions encourage thinking independently about assessing solutions to problems and exploring the purposes of wheelchairs, thus connecting the question at issue with the function of the chair.)

"Why is Jamal's skin so dark?"
Inappropriate
"His skin color doesn't matter. We are all the same underneath." (This response denies the child's question, changing the subject to similarity when the child is asking about difference.)

Appropriate
"Jamal's skin is dark brown because his mom and dad have dark brown skin."
(This is enough for two or three year olds. As children get older you can add the next explanation of melanin.)
"Everyone has a special chemical in our skin called melanin. If you have a lot of melanin, your skin is dark. If you only have a little, your skin is light. How much melanin you have in your skin depends how much your parents have in theirs."

Suggested
"Lots of people have different colored skin. What color is your skin? Why do you think you have white skin? What color is my skin? Do you think the color of your skin has something to do with the color of my skin? How about your dad (or mom)? Why? Do you think the color of your skin has something to do with the color of my skin? How about your dad (or mom)? Why? Do you think the color of Jamal's skin might have something to do with the color of his mom?

How about his dad? Why?" (Questions like these ask children from four or five years old on, to think independently about the color of skin and discover for themselves through Socratic questioning the genetic connection. Furthermore they are encouraged to see similarities and differences as they compare and contrast the color of their skin. Finally, they are asked for reasons for what they might be thinking, which provides more information for parents to use to question their children further.

"Why am I called Black? I'm brown!"
Inappropriate
"You are too, black!"
(This response fails to reduce the child's confusion between actual skin color and the name of a racial or ethnic group.)

Appropriate
"You're right; your skin color is brown. We use the name 'Black' to mean the group of people our family belongs to. Black people can have different skin colors. We are all one people because our great-great-grandparents once came from a place called Africa. That's why many people call themselves 'Afro-American's.'"

Suggested
"You're right; your skin color is brown isn't it? We use the name 'Black' to mean the group of people our family belongs to. Do you think that Black people can have different skin colors? Why? How about other Black people you know? Do they all have the same skin color?" (This response asks the child to think independently about evidence in reality about the skin color of people who are from the African-American race.
"We say that 'Black' people are all one people because our great-great grandparents came from the same place. Do you know where that might be? Have you ever heard of Africa?" (This questions and responses respect the child's prior knowledge and assumptions.)

"Why does Miyoko speak funny?"
Inappropriate
"Miyoko can't help how she speaks. Let's not say anything about it." (This response agrees with the child's observation that Miyoko's speech is "funny"—that is, unacceptable—while also instructing the child "not to notice" and be polite.)

Appropriate

"Miyoko doesn't speak funny, she speaks differently than you do. She speaks Japanese because that's what her mom and dad speak. You speak English like your mom and dad. It is okay to ask questions about what Miyoko is saying, but it is not okay to say that her speech sounds funny because that can hurt her feelings."

Suggested

"Do you think Miyoko speaks funny because she speaks differently than you do? How do you think Miyoko thinks that you speak? Have you ever thought about that?" (Though this type of questioning should proceed gently with younger children, it encourages them to gain an insight into reciprocity and intellectual empathy while questioning their assumptions about the criteria for "speaking funny.") "Miyoko just speaks a different language than you do. What language do you speak? What language do I speak? Do you know what language Miyoko speaks? Miyoko speaks a language called Japanese. What language do you think her mom speaks? How about her dad? Do you think they might speak English too? Why? Do we speak Japanese? Why?" (Questions like these help children appreciate differences in language and at the same time challenge assumptions about bilingualism.)

"If you don't understand what Miyoko is saying, what do you think you should do? Why? What should Miyoko do if she can't understand what you are saying? Why? What should I do if I don't understand Miyoko or her mom or dad? If you didn't understand each other could you play and have a good time? Why or why not?" (This line of questioning emphasizes the need to encourage and value questioning in children.) It also provides an opportunity for parents to model fair-mindedness, empathy, and humility.

A Postscript

If we are serious about the development of schooling as a community resource, we must realize that quality schooling is impossible without adequate funding. The current regressive property tax funding system must be replaced with an alternative that funds schooling equally for everyone. We might achieve this equality if the Federal government fairly taxed large corporations, most of which avoid paying their share but loudly whine about the quality of schools and complain about programs that would mandate an equitable distribution of educational opportunities. College loans, scholarships, grants, health and nutrition programs, Head Start, and universal medical care must remain part of the equation and be strengthened. The lack of financial resources threatens the very infrastructure of schools and must be quickly addressed. The struggle must be two-pronged: (1) a battle for policies with parents and the community participating that increase funding and relevant educational opportunities for schools; and (2) a battle for financial support for communities with increasing poverty and sheltering populations heavily at risk.

Chapter 6

Reasoning Within Different Points of View: The Common Struggle for Human Dignity and the Logic of Oppression

"Suggestions for Further Study"

If one is talking about critiques of racism, critiques of patriarchy, critiques of homophobia, then simply call it that. Eurocentrism is not identical with racism. So, you deny the John Browns of the world. You deny the anti-racist movement in the heart of Europe. Eurocentrism is not the same as male supremacists. Why? Because every culture we know has been patriarchal in such an ugly way that you deny the anti-patriarchal movements within the heart of Europe. And the same is so with homophobia. Demystify the categories in order to stay tuned to the complexity of the realities. That is what I am calling for. That is the role of prophetic thinkers and prophetic activists who are willing to build on discernment, human connection. Who are willing to hold up human hypocrisy, including their own, and are also willing to hold up the possibility of human hope.

—Cornel West
Beyond Eurocentrism and Multiculturalism (1993)

Because valuing diversity entails learning to reason within and about different cultural, social, historical, and economic points of view, a critical multicultural literacy that promotes and accelerates diversity appreciation through reasoning must also value what unites us all in the quest for our humanity. But when our various historical struggles for humanity go unnoticed, it can be difficult to imagine a unified future among diverse lifestyles, points of view, and frames of reference. Helping students analyze differences and similarities in the historical and contemporary struggles for self-determination, personal freedom, and social justice should be a fundamental component of a critical multicultural literacy. Catherine Christie, a kindergarten-second grade combination teacher in Los Angeles, described this necessity for *California Tomorrow* (1992):

> Essentially all our students are immigrants, so you'd think that there would be a common thread. But sometimes it is not so easy for them to see it. Our students who come from Armenia are considered to be fleeing a repressive Communist regime. They're given resettlement allowances, money by our government. Sitting next to them is somebody from El Salvador or Guatemala who left because their uncle was shot while standing with them on a street corner. They've walked across countries and across borders to get here. They come here and their mothers work as cleaning ladies for minimal pay and they're living next door or sitting next to someone who's being given a resettlement allowance and housing help. One of my biggest challenges is getting these two groups to see themselves as more similar than different. (pp. 1–13).

Questioning these students Socratically about similarities and differences in their social and personal lives would require long term reasoning activities designed to confront the contradictions in their social realities. The students would then have to critically analyze, evaluate, and synthesize these social realities uncovering the logic of commonalties and disparities.

This reasoning within disparate cultural points of view serves in the interests of human unity, and both students and teachers should both strive to unmask the common human struggle for authenticity and validity, and engage in the critical analysis of exploitation, oppression, authority, power, homophobia, sexism, racism, social class, and domination so evident throughout history. Acknowledging that students need abundant examples for reasoning within different cultural points of view is not to diminish the need for students to study their own cultures—a study often foreign to classroom life. While knowledge of one's own cultural group does not convey an understanding of the enormous diversity of American social life, knowledge of one's own culture helps one acquire an understanding of other cultures since no culture exists in a vacuum. To comprehend the American experience fully, one must reason within multiple perspectives informed by culture, gender, race, and socioeconomic class.

All students profit from a rich, multicultural curriculum when they are encouraged to see the world, its history, and contemporary reality from diverse cultural perspectives. They learn to develop a critical social discourse that includes self-inventories and historical sensibilities. This frame of mind increases opportunities for students to examine their sociocentric thinking and engage in transformative metacognition—the ability to reappraise their thinking. Furthermore, it allows them to recognize the commonalties and differences in the forces of oppression that shape historical and contemporary reality, giving them the ability to engage in a praxis that challenges this oppression. Understanding multiple perspectives informed by differing cultures helps students understand the totality of human experience. Therefore, a multicultural literacy avoids teaching an *us* about a *them* or teaching others to be like us. Individual and social freedom can be realized only in a common unified struggle for liberty and justice coupled with a recognition of the logic of oppression and domination that orchestrates much of our social structures and our lives.

Students and teachers can both become so immersed in everyday concerns that they fail to reflect on the logic that serves the interests of the dominant order—a logic whose image and thoughts they far too often internalize. Hearing the muted voices of struggle and oppression that comprise the political, social, and economic realities of our human history adds meaning and critical consciousness to those in the process of learning and transformation. On the other hand, robbed of our heritage by inadequate teaching and faulty renderings of history, we can treat our struggles as isolated episodes in a linear human evolutionary process, as opposed to seeing them as constants in the dialectical process of *becoming* on behalf of the whole human species. In cultivating an awareness and appreciation for and of others and their gender, economic, ethnic, or cultural differences, educators then strive to create meaningful opportunities for students to understand both the differences among people that lead to distancing and the historical and global nature of human relations and the interrelatedness of us all. Although this interrelatedness hardly cancels our diversity, it does provide opportunities for developing relationships that confront racial intolerance and thus serves to unite us in the common struggle for human dignity, justice, critical self-evaluation, and freedom. What unites us as human beings, after all, is just as important as our various distinctions.

Providing opportunities for students to reason within different cultural points of view encourages them to reason their way to their humanity and overcome egocentric and sociocentric attitudes and prejudices. As students begin to reason about this historical cultural point of view or that contemporary socio-cultural issue, they begin to see the parallels in history with other economic and cultural struggles. For example, a student who reasons about the plight of the United Farm Workers in this country begins to take the farm workers point of view. But more, given the reasoning opportunities, this student can begin to see the commonality between this struggle and the struggle for civil rights as enunciated by Malcolm X or Martin Luther King, or the struggles of the labor movement throughout this century and the last. This student is better able to transfer intercultural insights into everyday life and to understand that a common humanity transcends cultural or race barriers. In her award-winning essay, Elizabeth C. Kim (1993) asked, then answered a particularly significant question:

> What can be done to form a progressive movement in light of such seeming hopelessness? The answer to this vital question can be found in history. During the Second World War, when every Japanese American on the West Coast of the United States, regardless of citizenship or generational status, was interned in concentration camps, a substantial movement of African Americans formed who stood up and denounced President Roosevelt's Executive Order 9066. They saw the obvious racism of this order, and, although its enactment had no direct effect on their own lives (and in fact, their opposition to it incited the FBI to create files on their "subversive" activities), spoke as a voice when the voices of their Japanese American sisters and brothers were silenced. Similarly, during the Gulf War, the Japanese America Citizen's League (JACL) issued statements warning of the possibility that Arab Americans could face internment motivated by the same racism. Just as African Americans were not the only ones to "March on Washington" during the civil rights movement to demand racial equality, migrant farmworkers of many races, Japanese and Mexican Americans, and Filipino and Mexican Americans, built coalition movements for improved pay and working conditions. They were able to join together for a common cause against a common oppressor, so that all of them could reap the benefits together. In the process they learned the truth of the fable of the bundle of sticks. One stick can easily be broken, even by the weakest people, but a bundle of sticks tied together by the cord of solidarity stands up to the most stringent tests of strength (p. 54).

In his article, "Citizenship Education for a Pluralistic Democratic Society," James Banks (1991) discussed the idea of teachers incorporating a unit on "The New World and the European Discovery of America":

> The students can then study about the Aztecs and other highly developed civilizations that were established in the Americas prior to the arrival of the Europeans in the fifteenth century. After the study of the Native American cultures and civilizations, the teacher can provide the student with brief ac-

counts of some of the earliest Europeans, such as Columbus and Cortes, who came to America. The teacher can then ask the students what they think the term the New World means, whose point of view it reflects, and what other and more neutral words describe the Americans. The students could then describe the European discovery of America from two different perspectives: the point of view of an Arawak Indian, the tribe that was living in the Caribbean when Columbus arrived in 1492, and the point of view of an objective, or neutral, historian who has no particular attachment to either American Indian or European society (p. 212).

The object of Banks's lesson is to illustrate for students how knowledge is socially constructed and can serve the interests of dominant powers. I would also want to give students brief accounts from the Taino Indians of Puerto Rico, now an extinct people, thus introducing an additional perspective. Such concepts as the New World and European Discovery are Eurocentric and ethnocentric terms that serve a purpose, rest on a specific set of assumptions, and have a logic that shores up dominant social forces. By reasoning critically within different points of view on history or contemporary issues, students come to see how knowledge becomes constructed and how history can revised and institutionalized so as to justify exploitation and subjugation. They can gain insights into how we human beings can uncritically come to accept history exclusively from the point of view of the conqueror to the exclusion of the conquered.

Reasoning from within culturally diverse points of view also gives students a chance to feel empathy, which they may later transfer into other personal and social domains in their lives. When conflict prescribes the curriculum, when varying juxtaposed perspectives invite critical exploration, analysis and evaluation, students must engage in activities that exercise their reasoning skills. Moreover, they begin to pay particular attention to the elements of their thinking and the thinking of others. As they engage in such fair-minded reasoning activities as those Banks and I describe, they become better able to develop the affective domain of critical thinking—the values, attitudes, and dispositions of life-long learning with others that translate into a productive life and the personal relationships we acquire.

Reasoning from a multicultural perspective broadens an understanding of diversity. Furthermore, when students ponder the common struggle for human dignity and the logic of oppression they consider their own behavior—the decisions they make and the actions they engage in. The connection between history and contemporary reality—between the choices the actors of history made and those we make today, between the assumptions that guided past choices and claims and those that guide them today—places students in a better position to see how inhumanity affects their lives and how they can avoid acting inhumanely toward others. These crucial insights allow for transformative metacognition in the interest of an individuality defined not outside of humanity, but by humanity.

Reasoning toward humanity by reasoning multiculturally presents students with the opportunity to capture the logic of oppression, "oppression" meaning any situation whereby one person or group exploits another or interrupts that person in pursuit of self-actualization. Having recognized another as a human being, one finds it difficult to objectify that person to gain ego-driven interests. But one can understand and reveal the purposes and inner workings of oppression as motivated by the individualistic quest for power and material possessions. For an oppressor, the only human beings are the other oppressors; the rest of humanity, the oppressed, are "others" or "things." Underlying oppressive thought and behavior is the assumption that humanity can be possessed and used as an exclusive right. For the oppressor, the earth, property, production, sexuality, and human creations can all be possessed as the objects of self-interests. To be is to have. Eric Fromm (1966) discussed the necrophilious characteristics of oppressive thinking:

> While life is characterized by growth in a structured, functional manner, the necrophilious person loves all that does not grow, all that is mechanical. The necrophilious person is driven by the desire to transform the organic into the inorganic, to approach life mechanically, as if all living persons were things. . . . Memory, rather than experience; having, rather than being, is what counts. The necrophilious person can relate to an object—a flower or a person—only if he possesses it; hence a threat to his possession is a threat to himself; if he loses possession he loses contact with the world. . . . He loves control, and in the act of controlling he kills life (p. 41).

Perhaps one reason for the persistence of oppression is the presentation of history as the devaluation of insignificant others—an historicity wedded to sociocentricity, or a sense of cultural superiority that invites one to devalue others in accordance with insidious dominant attitudes and acquisitive desires. Bigelow (1992) applied this point in his treatment of the Amerindian Holocaust and especially regarding Columbus's "discovery" (p. 28). Moreover, issues of authority and the way human beings actualize their lives and orientate themselves in face of authoritarian institutions and situations can subtly encourage the continuation of oppression. Here the work of the Frankfurt School—especially Horkheimer, Marcuse, and Adorno as well as many of the little-known writings of Wilhelm Reich—is revealing.

One of the important consequences of oppression is that the struggle of the oppressed for liberation is viewed as radical subversion in the minds of both the oppressor and the oppressed. Accordingly, the oppressor must control and the oppressed expects to be controlled. The maintenance of this oppressive order historically proceeds through active repression and subtle manipulation, both ideologically and materially. Oppression seeks to silence and domesticate the population. Specifically how the maintenance of oppression has historically evolved and developed, what forms it takes during specific historical junctures, and the particular interests it serves at any one moment should all be the subject of critical historical inquiry. Furthermore, the manifestation of oppressive forms of life in contemporary reality can be elucidated only by a commitment to critical analysis of and social discourse about both historical and contemporary reality.

An apt example of how oppression can pass as sincere scientific research for purposes of ideological control appeared in a popular book published in 1932 and used for many years in several universities and secondary schools. The book is *The Races of Man* by Robert Benneth Bean, who was a professor of anatomy at the University of Virginia. In his last chapter, Bean wrote that

> In general, the brain of the white race is large, the convolutions are rich with deep fissures. The mental characteristics are activity, nervousness and physical vivacity, strong ambitions and passions and highly developed idealism. . . . The brain of the Yellow-Brown race is about medium human size, with medium to good convolutions, which are sometimes varied and deep. The mental characteristics of the Yellow-Browns need further study, but they seem to be less vivacious, with emotions and passions less evident than in the other two races. They possess moderate idealism and some love of sport, but have less spirit for exploration and adventure than the White Race. The size of the brain in the Black Race is below the medium both of the whites and the Yellow-Browns, frequently with relatively more simple convolutions. . . . The psychic activities of the Black Race are a careless, jolly vivacity, emotions and passions of short duration, and a strong and somewhat irrational egoism. Idealism, ambition, and the co-operative faculties are weak. They love amusement and sport, but have little initiative and adventurous spirit. . . . They have poetry of a lower order, are rather free from lasting worries, are cursed with superstitious fears, and have much emotionalism in religion (pp. 94–95).

Imagine yourself a student exposed in class to an ideological philosophy of oppression like this accompanied, no doubt, with demonstrative evidence in the form of charts, skeletal demonstrations, and other images of propaganda and hate. Exposing students to this type of philosophy of hatred and oppression and then asking them to look for similar contemporary philosophies for purposes of comparing and contrasting nourishes an understanding of oppression. Thinking critically, students would want to ponder such questions as these six:

(1)   What are the common cultural assumptions that are inherent in Bean's theory that we can find in racist ideologies apparent today?

(2)   How are they alike and different?

(3)   Where do they originate?

(4)   What are their implications?

(5)   How do we critically examine and analyze the cultural assumptions of intolerance and oppression?

(6)   Whose interests do these assumptions serve?

The common struggle for human dignity and freedom diametrically opposes the logic of oppression. To achieve personal and social justice, freedom, and liberation one must struggle for the complete elimination of oppression. As Freire (1990) noted,

Concern for humanization leads at once to the recognition of dehumanization, not only as an ontological possibility but as an historical reality (p. 27).

Helping students study contemporary and historical examples of oppression places them in a better position to avoid reproducing the logic of oppression both externally in the world of men and women and internally in the life of the self. This contribution is extremely important for without an historical understanding of oppression, men and women can become its embodiment. Again, Freire is instructive:

To surmount the situation of oppression, people must first critically recognize its causes, so that through transforming action they can create a new situation, one which makes possible the pursuit of fuller humanity (p. 32).

For Freire and other liberatory pedagogues, dehumanization is the distortion of the true calling of human beings—humanity. For this reason, oppression and its causes should consistently be the objects of critical scrutiny, reflection, and social action. When studying the Emancipation Proclamation, for example, students should be encouraged to discern the purpose of the document. To begin with, the Proclamation applied only to the states of the Confederacy. Given this, we might ask students

> What was the purpose of the Emancipation Proclamation? Was the Emancipation Proclamation cosmetic or real? In what ways? What assumptions underlie the document? What point of view did those African Americans who were not freed have? Did the fact they did not fight the Union have anything to do with the slaves' continuation in bondage? Why did the Act not free them?

Regarding the rise of white supremacy after the Civil War, students could be asked

> What exactly was "white supremacy" after the Civil War and how did it affect freed Blacks? What underlying assumptions guided the white supremacists? What underlying assumptions guided the resistance to white supremacy? What conclusions did both the resistance and the white supremacists reach during this time in history and what reasons did they give for what they decided to do or believe?

Students could research the different viewpoints on the issue and discuss them in groups, role playing the interests served by the white supremacy movement and those served by resisting it. This issue could be related to current developments in white supremacy, including skinheads, American Nazis, the Aryan Brotherhood, and other such white supremacist organizations. Linking past and present realities gives students the opportunity to reason historically and the intellectual and moral ability to act humanely. Yet we find little in our schools on white supremacy and the resistance to it, especially in the upper primary grades where the Civil War is often a mandated subject. We also find little on the Reconstruction and the roles African Americans played for the first time in government and civil life. By failing to provide students with the raw data of human history, we ensure that they learn to reason Eurocentrically and sociocentrically from one point of view unprepared for any comprehensive understanding of the past, present, or future.

Linda Christenson (1991), author of *Rethinking Schools*, wrote of constructing units on cartoons and fairy tales with her students to expose the underlying myths concerning race, class, and treatment of women (p. 15). She brings critical discourse to the dominant depictions of men and women, and she encourages her students to use their writing to keep journals about cartoons they see or fairy tales they read. Then they organize these articles in a publication for parents and teachers. They kept track of how these stories depicted people of color, gender, and the poor. They then related these depictions to their own lives. How these stories treated different colors, sexes, and races became the object of cultural study. All the students could see how various stories treated African Americans, Native Americans, people of color, women, race, and social class. Students began to comprehend how points of view informed by culture are mediated by the dominant culture. They began to recognize how issues of race, class, and gender affect us all. These students could see where their own culture fit into the dominant myths. In this way, they could begin to find their own voices and develop their own perspectives. In short, promoting a critique of dominant ideology through popular culture is an excellent way to stimulate student thinking on issues of contemporary concern.

James Loewen (1992) made a similar point in his critique of renditions of Thanksgiving reenacted each fall in elementary schools as our national origin myth. Complete with paper Pilgrim hats and Indian feathers fashioned from multicolored construction paper, children throughout the United States learn that the Indians and Pilgrims feasted together on Thanksgiving dinner. But the textbooks leave out the embarrassing facts. To begin with, the pilgrims did not introduce Thanksgiving to the American Indians. Eastern Indians had celebrated the autumn harvest for centuries. Furthermore, our modern Thanksgiving celebrations date back only to 1863 and not until the 1890s were the Pilgrims included in the tradition or were even called "Pilgrims." Add to this deception the other false, feel-good historical accounts: "The Pilgrims served the Indians pumpkin and turkeys and corn and squash. The Indians had never seen such a feast!" The fact is the Pilgrims had never seen such a feast; all these foods were indigenous to the Americas. Nor do students receive historical information about the Black Plague and other diseases that beset the fleeing "Pilgrims" and which they brought to the American continent as their gifts to the American Natives. Instead the whole Thanksgiving scenario becomes a rustic party complete with the *Mayflower*, Squanto, a fish in each cornhill, and a bountiful harvest.

No one suggests that students engage in "Pilgrim bashing," for indisputably the Pilgrims displayed courage during their difficult voyage and settlement; yet the glorification of the American myth of Thanksgiving does marginalize the Native Americans at the expense of European culture, and it need not be the case. As Loewen pointed out, committed educators can use this Anglo and Native cultural holiday as an opportunity to promote tolerance and understanding. They can concentrate on the commonality between Native peoples and the escaping European settlers, debunking the Eurocentric myths while celebrating both the culinary diversity of the Americas and the diversity of both the newcomers and the Native Americans.

One of the central questions that confronts a multicultural philosophy of education is precisely how the study of human oppression can direct students to question contemporary examples of victimization critically and then translate this understanding into concrete action that simultaneously elevates the struggle for human dignity and combats oppression. Consider the now-famous 1991 case of the Korean-American grocer in Los Angeles, Soon Ja Du, and the shooting death of Latasha Harlins ignited by a dispute over a $1.79 bottle of orange juice. The conflict is often framed as a simple cultural crisis between a Black and Korean arising out of their differences as people. But now consider what Itabari Njeri (1991) wrote in the *Los Angeles Times*:

> An honest description would say [of the so-called Black-Korean conflict]: How capitalism and white tribalism fueled Black-Korean tensions (p. B5).

This remark highlights the role of economics in defining cultural conflict. Economic and political points of view must be addressed if we are to understand thoroughly the sources of what we routinely refer to as "cultural differences" between (say) Koreans and Blacks. This might inspire interesting and useful points for dealing with reasoning if this conflict were to become the subject of a high school debate. On a recent public television show, I watched Asians in front of guarded, grate-fenced businesses pleading those in the L.A. rebellion not to steal. One of the Asians asked,

> Why is the Asian merchant conceived as the enemy? I put all my money in my business.

Yet from the point of view of many in the African-American community, bitter questions are more appropriate:

> But what part of yourself did you put in the community? What endeavors towards humanity have you made? Are you happy exploiting an economically

disadvantaged community? You want to sell liquor but you fail to dispense hope. Is your dream to be a businessman, a merchant, or a human being?

University of California sociologist Edna Bonacich (1991), also writing in the *Los Angeles Times*, suggested that we cannot study this conflict fruitfully if we take only the point of view of culture or race; instead

> To put it bluntly, the larger problem is the way capitalism works. Koreans to a certain extent, are fronting for the larger white power structure. They are both beneficiaries of the arrangement and victims of it (p. B5).

The point Bonacich made, one with which reasonable minds might argue, is that this conflict must be understood from an economic point of view exacerbated by culture. Critically understanding the role of Korean merchants and the complex community in which they find themselves is an essential step toward understanding the wider parameters of the conflict. Proceeding Socraticly I would ask my students a vast array of questions like these:

> What role does the Korean merchant play in the ghetto where he has his shop? Can he be called a middleman for larger economic powers? What about the Korean merchant's sale of liquor to a Black community ravaged by substance abuse? Are the multinational liquor corporations using the Korean merchant? How? Who profits? Why? What about the point of view that argues that the Korean merchant is exploiting Black people by selling not simply articles of poison like liquor, but selling them at inflated prices in light of the fact that most large supermarkets have chosen to leave South-Central Los Angeles? What about the point of view of the Korean merchant who argues that if he doesn't sell the commodities of the multinational liquor companies someone else will, be they Latino or Anglo, and that he or she has to make a living, and if he or she is not the foot soldier for internal colonialism someone else will be? What should the Korean merchants do, sell their businesses and go to work for one of the liquor stores owned by Latinos that sell these commodities in the community? What is the question at issue? Is it culture or economics or both? How does culture play a part in this argument if we agree that the problem is structural? How does economic injustice lead people to target specific cultures for abuse and blame and how does this lead to prejudice or racism? How does ethnic stereotyping impede or help generate and assess solutions to problems like the so-called Korean-Black conflict? Why has it been referred to as the "so-called" Korean-Black conflict? Do you agree? Why? Are there such things as intra-minority group tensions? Why do they exist? Who profits from them? What assumptions are they based on? What are the origins of those assumptions? Evidence? Implications? What is it, if anything, that the Asian-Americans and the Black Americans have in common? (The Koreans carry with them the subjugation under the Japanese not

to mention the daily abuse of anti-Asian prejudice in Los Angeles.) How have the Asian Americans been treated historically? How have the Black Americans been treated historically? What economic interests were served by this treatment? Why is it difficult for many ethnic groups to see the similarities in what they have all endured throughout history? What would be the implications if we saw that we had much in common as human beings both in our struggle for determination, and as objects of the forces that oppress us and block our path to humanity? What happens if we take only one cultural point of view on a problem as immense as the Korean-Black shooting? How does this discussion affect your life? Is there anything in your own life that raises similar questions? How do the structural necessities of the political, social, and economic system define the roles of both Blacks and Koreans in South-Central Los Angeles? Are there structural inequalities in the production, distribution, and consumption of goods and services? What role does the Anglo population play in this scenario?

A similar, perhaps more general inquiry could use case studies of the Jewish Holocaust, the Amerindian Holocaust, the Armenian Holocaust, or the African slave trade. These episodes invite students critically to analyze oppression and injustice to learn how conformity, uncritical acceptance, and misdirected thinking can foster and perpetuate inhumanity. Students might confront the power inherent in the "concepts" or labels we use to describe ourselves and others. Critically analyzing the lessons Nazi schools used, the lessons used in Eurocentric curricula, and lessons oppressive societies use might challenge ideological obedience and transform uncritical student thinking into critical student action.

Lessons from the Holocaust

Stoskopf (1991) reported on *Facing History and Ourselves*, an innovative curriculum for Junior and High School students, in which Michael Berenbaum, Director of the U.S. Holocaust Memorial Museum, argues that a thorough investigation of the Jewish Holocaust can serve as a paradigm for studying modern instances of genocide and the assumptions that fuel them. Berenbaum recommends that to keep the Holocaust from being considered an aberration, students should study and make critical connections between the Holocaust, the Armenian genocide, the Amerindian Holocaust, the Killing Fields of Cambodia and the atrocities in Bosnia and Herzegovina. Gathering the narratives of victims and oppressors from various genocides and holocausts, which regrettably comprise quite a wide range of human experience, allows students to see the logic of oppression that fuels this incredible inhumanity. Included in these studies should be narratives of *resistance*—for example, the Christians and others who often took enormous risks helping Jews escape the Holocaust. Analyzing narratives of altruism, students meet the possibility and the language of hope and can see that human beings not only create oppression but also have the capability of defeating it.

Using the history of the Holocaust, *Facing History and Ourselves* helps students gain insights into issues of morality and specifically the implications of moral deterioration or breakdown. The program includes such social problems as abuse of power, unquestioning obedience to authority, and how abuse and obedience can be resisted. Students attempt to understand the logic of oppression: why neighbor turned against neighbor; and how indifference, denial, and opportunism, along with a lack of critical thinking allowed a government to implement genocide. Through the example of the Jewish Holocaust, students can examine contemporary reality more critically, observing how racism, anti-Semitism, homophobia, anti-feminism, and violence can affect the decisions they make, the actions they choose, and the lives they live. Students also become aware of the collaborative power of resistance as they become aware of the common struggle for human dignity and humanity during this period and associate this struggle with contemporary examples of resistance and unified campaigns for freedom and dignity. This exercise helps students raise oppression and the common struggle for human dignity beyond the realm of abstraction into the realm of the actual where active participation can make a genuine difference. *Facing History and Ourselves* would have us ask the following six questions:

(1)   How does an environment of mass conformity and racism come about?

(2)   How does a nation move from protecting its minorities to defining them as the enemy?

(3)   Why did doctors, nurses, and teachers, all trained to care for human life, participate in the systematic dehumanization and murder of so many millions?

(4)   Why did lawyers trained to pursue justice participate in the systematic denial of the most basic human rights?

(5)   Why and how did some individuals defy the power of the state despite the dangers they incurred?

(6)   What are the consequences of avoidance, denial, and distortion of history?

The text in Facing History and Ourselves states the following awareness and goal:

> The curriculum must help students whose newly discovered notions of subjec-
> tivity raise the problem of differing perspectives, competing truths, the need
> to understand motives and to consider the intentions and abilities of them-
> selves and others. . . . Methodology has been developed to encourage stu-
> dents to understand more than one perspective in a dilemma, to place them-
> selves in a position of another person, and to be willing to express ideas in
> class without fear of ridicule (p. 14).

When studying genocide, for example, it would be important to ask
questions like these eight:

(1)   What were the perpetrators' motives or goals?
(2)   What questions at issue or problems did these perpetrators
       see and react to?
(3)   What information or empirical dimension did they rely on for
       their conclusions and assumptions and how did they create
       information and disinformation?
(4)   What concepts and labels did they use to dehumanize one
       race at the expense of another? What concepts and labels did
       they use to appeal to sociocentric behavior and thought pat-
       terns? What language of oppression did they rely on?
(5)   What conclusions did the perpetrators come to regarding other
       members of humanity and what reasons did they offer for these
       conclusions?
(6)   What assumptions guided the thinking of those engaged in
       genocide? What did they believe about themselves and
       others?
(7)   What were the implications of their thinking for other mem-
       bers of the human race?
(8)   What point of view or frame of reference did they demon-
       strate and why?

Furthermore, I would want to ask the same sorts of questions of the
so-called bystanders who, by their compliance and fear, condoned the
genocide in question.

Using personal testimony and historical literature in their studies of
these issues, students naturally start to analyze the logic of oppression
both within external reality and within their own internal reality. For
example, does a popular television show like *Cops* glorify oppression

of one group? If so, how? Do the mass media and mass culture glorify the concept of dehumanization, and if they do, whose interests do they serve? What, if anything, is similar in the depiction of Jews, gays, or Gypsies in the middle 1900s in Germany and that of the depiction of African-Americans in television shows like *Cops* today?

In their review of *Facing History and Ourselves,* Martin Sleeper, Margot Stern Strom, and Henry Zablerek (1990) noted that

> *Facing History and Ourselves* approaches citizenship education through a case study of the rise of totalitarianism that led to the Holocaust. We selected the history of Nazi Germany and the Holocaust as the primary case study for the curriculum because it is a watershed historical event—one that is exceptionally well documented, that encompasses the full range of ethical choices and perspectives on human behavior, and that engaged every political, social, economic, intellectual component, and institution in society. Its issues defy simple answers and superficial treatment. By examining the circumstances of this piece of history, classes explore the fundamental issues of citizenship, responsibility, and decision making in a democracy (p. 2).

Some consequent questions for critical classroom inquiry in junior and senior high school might be

> What parallels if any are there between the "ethnic cleansing" of Bosnia or Nazi Germany and treatment of the homeless on our urban city streets? How do these concepts relate to and epitomize the logic of oppression? What other comparative situations in contemporary reality resonate the ideology of inhumanity? Who would you try for crimes against humanity at this moment in history, and why?

This Socratic approach links educational relevance to the topic under discussion. Additional questions might include

> What is there, if anything, in your life that parallels the atrocities of yesterday? What are you doing, if anything, to disseminate and reproduce atrocity in your own life? What are you doing to assure that you don't repeat the atrocities of the past?

Students might also ponder the following five questions as they gain exposure to the material of historical reality:

(1)   What assumptions create an ideology of racism and from where do they come from? How are associational assumptions distinguished from reasoned judgment?

(2) How does sociocentricity operate to create assumptions of superiority that redefine minorities as victims to minorities as enemies? What is the purpose of sociocentricity and how does it hinder or help human behavior?

(3) Why were so-called educated people—nurses, doctors, lawyers, social workers, and teachers—propelled by assumptions of racism and sociocentricity that allowed them to become complicit in the dehumanization of Nazi Germany? Are these assumptions present today in the educated community? How do these assumptions parade as scientific truth? What is self-delusion? What role does the affective and cognitive elements of thought play in the realization of hope and despair?

(4) What cognitive and affective dimensions of thought allow one to resist oppression at any cost? What implications do the lack of these dimensions of thought have on avoidance of the issues, denial of oppressive ideology, and individuality?

(5) What are the implications of dependent thinking on self, society, and history?

In exposing students to the logic of human oppression, curricula like *Facing History and Ourselves* relate history to the present in ways that call for critical reasoning. In one of their videos, for example, Frank, a German Jew in his fifties, recalls an experience he had in elementary school. He recounts having been forced to stand in front of his classmates while his teacher, a member of the Nazi party, pointed out his Semitic features. Forty-seven students are then asked why German-Jewish students were picked on this way. Describing the reactions of her students, Melinda Fine (1989) provided this narrative:

> Bobby yells out, "Because they were Jews and Hitler taught the Germans to hate Jews." Several students nod; a few others raise their hands. Bobby continues, "But you know, everybody picks on some people. It's not a nationality thing." Katie [the teacher] asks the class to consider why this is so. "They feel like they get power to do it," Maria replies. "Were the German people bad?" Katie asks. "Not the German people," explains David, the one Jewish student in the class. "That's the way they had to act. If you don't, you'll get picked on." "It's not that they're bad; it's that they were brought up that way. It's society training them," confirms Bobby (p. 47).

This discussion reveals young students' remarkable abilities to evaluate intellectual cowardice, question over-generalizations, confront the issue of intellectual integrity, compare similarities and differences in dehumanization, and understand and articulate power and domination.

By asking students to relate history to their daily lives, *Facing History and Ourselves* encourages historical analysis toward the goal of critical thinking and critical action. Questions like Fine's—"Do people besides the Germans do this too? What about in our community? Have you seen behavior like this?" (p. 47)—encourage students to examine the social and political tapestry of their lives and notice how dehumanization, or the logic of oppression, can produce analogous situations in contemporary society. In Fine's discussions such issues as whites versus Blacks, skinhead supremacy, misogynism, homophobia, and sexist behavior all surfaced as her students attempted to translate historical insights into an understanding of contemporary reality. Fine encouraged her students to look for evidence of oppression at their school and in their communities. In an exercise at Harriet Tubman Junior High School, a public school serving many Haitian students in Boston, Fine asked the students to write about an instance they had seen at the school where students were discriminated against. The following comments emerged:

> I see people making fun of the bilingual students because they're different and often because they will say something to you or laugh and point at people, and people don't know what they're saying. Also because they dress different. People make fun of their clothes and hair.

> I saw two people chasing a Haitian boy down the hall and into the boys' bathroom. I went in, and I knew the two boys that were bothering the Haitian. I laughed and said leave the poor boy alone.

> In school I see Haitians being picked on for no reason. Is it because they are stupid, or Haitian, or what? (p. 47).

These young minds already know the horrors of cruelty and oppression. By asking them to make the link between oppression within their present reality and the oppression of the past, they can readily develop moral attitudes and critical reasoning faculties to combat antisocial behavior.

Encouraging students to role play incidents of oppression as they occur in their lives invites them to enter into different points of view and reason empathetically and critically about human behavior. For example, Fine noted that in the social studies class where she observed the *Facing History and Ourselves* curriculum, students were encouraged to devise skits that dealt with some of the behavior they had mentioned in their writing. Divided into groups, they chose skit-conflicts that involved discrimination or dehumanization. One skit depicted conflict between an American and a Haitian player on a basketball court. The Haitian dropped the ball and racial slurs issued from the American player. A fight began and the principal arrived but because of a lack of bilingual skills, neither student could communicate. Another skit also addressed Haitian-American relations. Two students were cast as white students, two as Haitians, and one (whose nationality and race went unspecified) as the mediator. The Americans whispered to each other and pointed to the Haitians. Overheard were phrases like "smell bad," "nappy hair," and "dumb Haitians." The Haitians also pointed and whispered but their words were unintelligible. The mediator encouraged each group to talk to each other.

With innovative curricula like *Facing History and Ourselves*, teachers have an unusual opportunity to address issues of multiculturalism through the strategy of reasoning within points of view informed by different cultures. Furthermore, they can do so understanding that there is a logic to the common struggle for human dignity and oppression. Helping students understand the material and psychological conditions of oppression that inform and often define their reality can equip them with the abilities to transform this reality as well as their thinking. Fine (1989) described Jacques, a young Haitian student, explaining the program's value this way:

> A kid might come from another country to this country. The kids in this country don't respect them because they're different from them. The course shows the kids movies of Jewish people in concentration camps. The kids learn that they did that to the Jews because they were different. The kids learn that they shouldn't make fun of other different kids because they're different; if they do they'll think that they're as cruel and mean as the Nazis were to the Jews. Because they've learned that it is cruel to bother someone because they are different (p. 48).

For students like Jacques the lessons in this curriculum are particularly important and resonate loudly. Many immigrants students—particularly those victims of exploitation or war with no real desire to be here beyond the need for safety—find in a curriculum like *Facing History and Ourselves* a relevance and a determination to struggle against discrimination and oppression.

The horror of Nazism reminded Jacques of his experience as a political refugee:

People really joined together to get rid of Duvalier. . . . Even though they were different from each other, they helped each other when there's danger. I thought that was right. And my people did it, and I felt proud. Well, that didn't happen in Nazi Germany (p. 46).

Students who bring legacies of oppression, victimization, and resistance to the classroom find themselves in an excellent position to capture the logic of dehumanization and can readily identify with and understand the commonalties in the struggle for human dignity and freedom. What Jacques conveys is his ability to meld historical understandings with contemporary reality. His ability to empathize, identify, and even consciously question personal and social responsibility arises out of the impoverishment of his own daily life and the constant struggles he and his people face. It is comparatively easy for a student who knows social injustice, inequality and cruelty, to gain an insight into the logic of oppression, probably because these students have an empirical dimension to their reality that cries out for critical understanding and analysis. It is as if to say that those who have met oppression face to face have a better ability to identify it when it operates in other dimensions.

Furthermore, I contend that those who have known resistance to oppression either personally or through loved ones are apt to appreciate another group's struggle against dominant forces. This seemed, in any event, to be the case with Jacques. Oppression was familiar to him so he could identify its operations at school, in history, and in community life. The resistance—at school, in the community, or in Haiti—had become a permanent force in Jacques' life which is why he could identify with it and question those who would not resist. This "at risk" child brings a brilliance to the classroom that many so-called gifted children do not. Jacques brings both concrete and psychological material to the classroom applicable to the issue of dehumanization and resistance. The so-called "gifted" are often sheltered from the realities of inequity and critical inquiry and, therefore, bring no historical or autobiographical material that can help them personalize and make relevant the echoes of resistance and oppression. Their ability to empathize and analyze is notably dulled by this sheltering. Their giftedness often lies more in their abilities to pass standardized tests than in their abilities to analyze, synthesize, empathize, and evaluate the logic of everyday life.

Commenting on the efficacy of the program for all students, the principal at Tubman, David Vellucci, remarked,

> Unlike the kids from Haiti, the American kids haven't had this sort of larger
> political context that takes them out of themselves, to another level. We should
> be able to somehow incorporate that raised consciousness on the part of our
> bilingual kids to help the monolingual kids understand their moral responsibil-
> ity (p. 46).

But it is more than just a raised consciousness among bilingual children; it is a raised consciousness among all those who have struggled
to resist inequality, oppression, and injustice. Those with a history
of struggle can use their knowledge to discover similarities and differences in the struggle for humanity. Recognizing that so-called "at risk
students" are often those with the greatest ability to empathize,
reciprocate, and think fair-mindedly is paramount to providing meaningful opportunities for these children to sort out their lives and
responsibilities.

Lessons from American History

Facing History and Ourselves affirms what Art Costa (1993) noted—
by helping our students think critically

> Our view of instruction will shift from learning of the content to learning from
> the content (p. 50).

Similar critical pedagogical analysis can, of course, apply to the
subject of American history. In studying slavery in the South, students
rarely discover that of the nine million Southerners in 1860 half were
Black and nearly all of them were slaves. Yet only a quarter of the
white families owned slaves. The "poor whites" or what were considered at this time to be, "white trash," were pushed out of the fertile
valleys into the hills of the back country where many of them barely
eked out a living. In fact, back in 1905 Philip Bruce wrote that these
families lived much like the Black slaves themselves:

> The narrowness of their fortunes was disclosed in many ways—in the sallow-
> ness of their complexions, resulting chiefly from insufficient and unwhole-
> some food—in the raggedness of their clothing, in the barrenness and dis-
> comfort of their cabins, which were mere hovels in the most slovenly
> surroundings, and in the thinness and weakness of the few cattle they pos-
> sessed. Nowhere could there be found a population more wretched in some
> respects than this section of southern whites, the inhabitants of the ridge and
> pine barren, men and women who had no interest in the slave system whatso-
> ever (p. 427).

It would probably be safe to say that these poor whites not only had little interest in the slave system, but the slave system also represented for them a familiar oppressive situation. Wasserman (1972) estimated that only ten thousand families owned slaves in 1860, each family averaging about fifty slaves each. What these slaves had in common with the poor whites of the pine barrens and ridges were the fundamental inhuman conditions of life, the loss of lived reality, and the smothering of hopes. Yet this commonality, this shared oppression, does not appear in the history texts. Our students grow up believing gross generalities about slavery and white complicity, never understanding that the economic conditions that faced the poor whites and slaves were similar in many ways—rendering the struggle that much more common, even if it never got played out in reality.

Discussing Reconstruction after slavery, Bennet (1967) pointed out that

> In some cases Reconstruction brought to power blacks and poor whites who had been completely colonized by the slave owners. At the same time, Northern radicals fought to break up the old plantations and redistribute them to the blacks. Thaddeus Stevens, leader of the radical Republican Congress, fought hard on the principle that "forty acres of land and a hut" would be more valuable than the immediate right to vote. "With their own land," he argued, "real freedom would come to the ex-slaves naturally" (p. 40).

Thus different points of view existed among the African-American community as to the importance of planning and power after Reconstruction. And it is important to note that many whites and Blacks fought side by side against the exploitative colonial system that defined social reality in the South before the Civil War. Students should have the chance to understand the logic that informed these points of view, perhaps engaging in role playing and other classroom activities that require empathetic critical reasoning.

Reconstruction met fierce resistance from many whites determined to kill all Blacks. They burned schools, churches, homes, and beat, raped, hanged and shot Blacks. In 1868, some Arkansas whites assassinated Black government officials. A U.S. attorney estimated that a thousand Blacks a year were killed in Texas from 1868 to 1870. General Philip Sheridan estimated that 3,500 people, mostly Black, were killed or wounded in Louisiana in the ten years after the war (all these estimates come from Wasserman, 1972.) Black militias organized resistance to this intimidation, violence and continuing white terrorism during Reconstruction. Students could usefully study Reconstruction from the point of view of these militias. In New Orleans, the resistance was particularly dramatic. After the election of 1872, armed bands of Blacks and whites filled the streets of the city supporting rival candidates for legislature.

In the late 1870s the Ku Klux Klan, Knights of the White Camelia, Red Shirts, and White League, all racist supremacist organizations, roamed the Southern countryside terrorizing both Blacks and whites who would not support the Democratic Party. That the issue was as economic as it was racial somehow eludes the texts. Students should study the logic of oppression by focusing on the aims of these groups and their respective incentive. They should be examined with an eye toward unmasking the similar kinds of oppression that persists in our country. For example, the Democratic Party represented not simply white supremacy after the Civil War, but also the interests of the rich land barons, bankers, and speculators. The Republican Party earned the label "the party of War and the Negro." Students should be encouraged to examine, analyze, and synthesize critically this surprising record and produce critical writing, engage in role playing, or stage debates that explore the historical questions at issue. It might be useful to know, for example, political parties supported by corporate power used penitentiaries to punish the masses who revolted, white or Black. In Arkansas alone in one year the death rate for prisoners was 25 percent (Wasserman, 85).

Similarly, students could critically examine American cities in the early twentieth century to compare and contrast their situations with cities today. As we read Jacob Riis's descriptions of the urban tenements that awaited most European immigrants to America at the turn of the century, we can easily see the waves of Latino immigrants crowded into garages in Los Angeles at this moment—sometimes five families to a building, working and sharing what little clothing, food and hope they have. Here is Riis (1957) in *How the Other Half Lives:*

[A] man, his wife, and three small children shiver in one room through the roofs of which the pitiless winds of winter whistled. The room was almost barren of furniture; the parents slept on the floor, the older children in boxes, and the baby was swung in an old shawl attached to the rafters by chords by way of hammock. . . . Perhaps this may be put down as an exceptional case, but one that came to my notice some months ago in a seventh ward tenement was typical enough to escape that reproach. There were nine in the family; husband, wife, and an aged grandmother, and six children, honest, hard-working Germans, scrupulously neat but poor. All nine lived in two rooms, one about ten feet square that served as parlor, bedroom, and eating room, the other a small hall-room made into a kitchen. The rent was seven dollars and a half a month, more than a week's wages for the husband and father (p. 35).

Cities teeming with immigrant workers looking for a better life after their hardships in Europe became hell-holes of despair. Industry's need for cheap labor produced in America in the 1890s some of the worst cities in the world, a situation analogous to the realities of urban life today. In 1894, for example, New York's Sanitation District A included 32 acres on which more than 31,000 people lived, a density of 986 people an acre. The density in Bombay at the time was 759 people an acre. Prague, well-known for the worst ghettos in Europe, reported only 485 people an acre. New York was four times larger in 1900 than it had been in 1860. Chicago grew by 35 percent in the same period.

Students need to explore, analyze, and evaluate the conditions of life and the struggle of the immigrant masses in our largest cities this century. In this way they can come to appreciate the enormous crises of contemporary urban life. Currently, cities today face health problems worsening at alarming rates. Diseases like tuberculosis have returned to our cities. Other diseases like AIDS; new strains of syphilis, gonorrhea and hepatitis; and other developing health problems affect the poor in our inner cities just as the poor of our cities were plagued by disease in the early part of this century. Students need to see the commonalties and differences in the city life of yesterday and today. They could actively involve themselves in researching urban problems, gathering statistical information about cities, analyzing that information, and proposing solutions to current urban problems. Students could, for example, examine the health care system and its effectiveness in the early part of this century. They could examine our current health care system and formulate public health policies in cooperative groups, drawing on their own experiences and resources or lack of them thereby adding the dimension of relevance to their study. Similarly, they could work cooperatively to advance urban policies for various cities in the United States and critically debate and analyze these policies in light of the evidence that supports them and the existing rationales found to be irrelevant.

We should certainly study immigration historically. Students need insights into how the American cities formed. The new city dwellers in the 1800s were largely the displaced peasantry of Europe. Between 1840 and 1890, four million Germans and three million Irish made their way to the U.S. In a country of thirty million, this group comprised almost 25 percent. From 1880 to 1920, four million Italians, four million Austro-Hungarians, and three million Russians came to the U.S. Between the Civil War and the start of World War I, thirty million immigrants entered this country. Taking the viewpoints of these immigrants, students might come to see their differences and commonalties and the logic that compelled them to leave home. Students might draw upon immigrant narratives from yesterday and today, noting what these immigrants faced as a group and the parallels with what immigrants face today. What hopes and aspirations did the Italian immigrant and the Hungarian immigrant share? What assumptions drove them both?

Similarly, children in the early primary grades can develop the critical sensibility and passion for critical discourse that is essential if we expect them to address both historical and contemporary issues as they grow older. The whole-language approach helps young children both develop the skills they need to understand the so-called three R's, and gain insights into the elements of their own thinking and the thinking of others. Furthermore, if students are to develop a sense of critical inventory, see the value of independent thinking, engage in civil discussions about issues of controversy, and acquire the values and dispositions essential to fair-minded critical thinking, then we educators must begin early. Administrators and teachers too often assume that primary school children are too immature for critical thinking and that they should concentrate first on teaching skills divorced from critical discourse: the skill of reading, the skill of writing, the skill of mathematical computation, and the skill of decoding. Students, they say, will have time enough to engage in reasoning activities as they grow older; kindergarten and early primary school should be places where children learn to play—and learn the skills of cut-and-paste, reverence for authority, and responsibility.

But this obsession with teaching skills detached from thinking signals the neglect of reasoning about conflicts and problems in favor of trivial pursuits, the hallmark of most skill-intensive curricula. Basic instruction is, of course, crucial to successful learning, and in shaping critical thinking activities for children in the early grades we take their developmental readiness into account. Yet as Jerome Bruner has argued, if you appraise the nature of a child's thought by reasoning within the child's experience, "any subject can be taught to any child in some honest form." What one does is to gear the instruction to the student's dominant mode of representation and development. Beginning with the child's experience and spiraling out, one can make remarkably weighty conceptualizations accessible to young children. Critical thinking about issues of personal and social justice in the early primary grades is more than developmentally appropriate, it is a developmental necessity. Helping children in early grades learn to enter into diverse points of view can be accelerated by role playing and critical evaluation of problem-based classroom rules, conflicts, literature and stories, as well as visual and audio presentations that confront issues of commonality, difference, and oppression.

Visual presentations generate strong emotional responses among young children and can help them reflect critically on their daily experiences. One excellent curriculum, Moment's (1992) "Reframing Resistance" published by the Jesuit Center for Social Faith and Justice in Ontario, Canada, helps children speak to their own experience of resistance and hope. The educational kit consists of a selection of photographs designed for students to decode. In one photo a poor young boy peeks through a fence. He is framed by the wooden planks and his hands extend through the holes. Students in a group are asked to decode the image, then connect their thoughts to their personal experiences. Some questions the teacher might ask follow:

> What do you see in the photo? Why is the fence old and broken? What might
> have caused the fence to get that way? Why is the boy peeking through? Why
> are his hands sticking out through the holes in the fence? Why do you think
> he is poor? Are there broken fences or structures in your neighborhood?
> Why? How could we fix them?

A teacher can integrate activities like these into language experience approaches to reading, thus helping students develop both critical insight while enhancing their written and oral language skills.

Another useful series prepared by Law and a Free Society (1986) encourages grade students to think critically about issues attending responsibility and authority. One of the first lessons on authority asks children to identify situations where persons act on their own initiative, distinguish situations in which persons' actions are controlled by others, and develop an understanding of power relationships. Using film strips and videos, the lessons introduce children to conflicts that involve the use of power. For example, in one scenario Laura and her friends explain that they go to the park each day and play kickball, or softball, or hide-and-seek. One day, a group of older, bigger children stopped their kickball game and threatened to take their ball unless they moved off the grass onto the dirt field. Laura and her friends were angry but too afraid to argue. Students can be encouraged to describe power relationships like these and discuss issues of social justice while attempting to generate solutions. With Socratic questions teachers can ask students what they think authority is, whether it is always right, and in what ways they can resist oppressive authoritarian situations like the one Laura faced in the park. Helping young students develop critical sensibilities to issues of authority can equip them for the task of resisting unjust authoritarian situations as they mature.

Lessons in Literature

One of the most useful vehicles for increasing young children's ability to critically analyze and reflect on the common struggle for human dignity and the logic of oppression is a literature-based curriculum. It can both expose young children to issues of racism, domination, oppression, authority, and resistance, and help them learn to write, speak, and reflect critically on their own experiences. Using conflict-based literature as opposed to trivial stories is the key here. Children's Book Press publishes beautifully illustrated, bilingual legends, stories, and fables that concentrate on issues of compassion, power, authority, and oppression and reflect a diversity of cultures and viewpoints. In one story, Garcia's (1987) "The Adventures of Connie and Diego," students read about how twins born with rainbow faces are laughed out of their town for being different. The twins try to live with animals but eventually discover the beauty of their humanity and return to the village. By addressing physical differences and race in the early grades, students can begin to develop an insight into racism and oppression while connecting their own experiences to stories like these. Another story, "The Little Weaver of Thai-Yen Village" by Tran-Khanh-Tuyet (1987), describes a young Vietnamese girl, Hien, who loses her family to war and comes to the United States for medical treatment. Like most refugee children, Hien faces a new language, a new culture, and perhaps a permanent relocation in the United States. The story shows how Hien maintains her pride, her language, and cultural beliefs as she struggles to adjust to the American way of life. Literature that addresses the problems and conflicts newly arrived immigrants face is meaningful for all children, not simply immigrants, for they can see the commonality and differences between people and the oppression and fear that immigrants often face.

But as useful as it is for early primary school students, powerful literature is not by itself enough. Teachers must know how to ask Socratic questions and probe for the elements of their thinking while guiding them toward insights into the elements of thought the storybook characters express. For example, in *Crow Boy*, a Caldecott honor book by Taro Yashima (1955), children learn about a strange, shy, small boy isolated by his differences from the other schoolchildren. The setting is a Japanese village school, but the situation arises in schools everywhere. How Chibi, as he is called, comes to find his own dignity is a poignant story that resonates in children's experiences. Yet teachers must be able to recognize and question critically the assumptions that other students and teachers make of Chibi, what they infer about him in light of those assumptions, the implications of their thinking about Chibi and how these implications translate into their oppressive treatment of him. Furthermore, they must understand the assumptions that Chibi makes, the evidence that guides his thinking, the conclusions he draws about how to learn and act in school, and the implications of his thinking and actions for his quest for dignity.

Moreover, teachers must look for opportunities to capitalize on student experiences with similar themes. Without an understanding of Socratic questioning and the purposes behind literary accounts like *Crow Boy*, teachers can fall back on asking students merely to sequence the story, respond to recall questions, engage in didactic episodes of rote memorization, or express their own subjective responses with little or no critical reflection and thinking. Applying children's literature to promote critical reflection while helping children see its relevance for their own lives requires an understanding of the principles and strategies of critical thinking as well as the subjective lives of students themselves.

In his book *Teaching Strategies for Ethnic Studies*, James A. Banks (1990) provided an excellent resource for teachers interested in pursuing reasoning from within diverse cultural points of view. The beauty of Banks's book goes beyond his clear approach; he recommends both teacher-education books focused on contemporary and historical experiences of the childrens'cultures and children's books for use in the classroom. His own book includes an extensive annotated bibliography of the books he recommends. In addition, he advocates student role playing combined with critical writing, debate, and discussion. This regimen encourages fair-minded critical thinking while helping students grasp the logic of various points of view. His questions need to be more Socratic with an eye on unity and diversity and on to the elements of thinking. But, by offering classroom lesson plans a teacher can use to encourage critical thinking, Banks has provided a valuable resource for promoting critical multicultural literacy. Furthermore, Banks's central point is well taken: if we are to teach history we must do more than rely on the points of view in simulation games or textbooks; we must begin to educate ourselves about the history of this country.

In encouraging the study of culture and ethnicity, Banks emphasizes that values play an integral part of what should be studied, "not chow mein, basket weaving, sombreros, or soul food" (p. 87). Instruction of this type reinforces stereotypes in the name of fighting prejudice. While I agree with Banks, I find his contention that values are pertinent to the study of cultural points of view problematic. Banks himself acknowledges that "it is important to realize, however, that the values of all of America's ethnic groups are changing, especially in urban areas" (p. 87).

This is an important insight, for what we often think of as culture is rarely characteristic of all those we think of as constituting that culture. Furthermore, by embracing an essentialist or universalist approach to values, Banks overlooked the fact that morality can be understood only relative to history. What requires examination are the elements of thought that guide the assumptions people from all cultures make when deciding how to behave or what to believe within a specific period. People use assumptions to form their values and these assumptions arise from specific historical realities. Therefore, those assumptions and the realities that produce them must be analyzed critically lest the values remain ambiguous. Because these assumptions relate to the social structure of society, that society itself must be questioned. We often think of values as somehow separate from cognition and thus separate from social structures. Multiculturalism recognizes the influence of history and the unity of values and attitudes necessary for affective and cognitive critical thinking about self and society.

In one of the units he developed for teachers on Native Americans, Banks paraphrases an old Wintu holy woman who describes her viewpoint on the relationship between Anglo culture and the Earth:

> The white people never cared for Land or Deer or Bear. When we Indians kill meat we eat it all up. When we dig roots we make little holes. When we build

houses we make little holes. When we burn grass for grasshoppers, we don't ruin things. We shake down acorns and pine nuts. We don't chop down trees. We only use dead wood. But the white people plow up the ground, pull down the trees, kill everything. The tree says, "Don't, I am sore. Don't hurt me." But they chop it down and cut it up. The spirit of the land hates them. They blast out trees and stir it up to its depths. They saw up the trees. That hurts them. The Indians never hurt anything, but the white people destroy all. They blast rocks and scatter them on the ground. The rock says, "Don't, you are hurting me." But the white people pay no attention. When the Indians use rocks they take little round ones for their cooking. . . . How can the spirit of the earth like the white man? Everywhere the white man has touched it, it is sore (p. 86).

Students given passages like this can critically analyze the frame of reference and the assumptions that guide it. Students can be encouraged to look for the elements of thought in the holy woman's argument, the purpose of her thinking, the information she relies on, the concepts she uses, the assumptions that underlie her inferences, the reason and evidence upon which she bases her conclusions, the history that informs her thinking, and the implications of her description. They can also see if her criteria for ascertaining environmental damage remain operative today, and if so, how and where. They can be encouraged to see comparisons between this cultural point of view and other similar environmental viewpoints outside the Native American community. They can be encouraged to analyze those points of view that conflict with the logic of the Wintu woman.

Banks's thoughtful chapter on Native Americans discusses culturally appropriate instruction, or "teaching strategies." For the primary grades, he proposes the subject of family relationships and suggests that teachers ask children such questions as these:

Has one of your parents ever gone away for a long or short trip? Did you miss your parents? How do we feel when someone we like very much goes away? Why do we feel that way? (p. 160).

Banks goes on to advance the idea of exploring with children the concept of the family itself—that is to say, specific types of families and how one would feel if an important family member went away. He recommends that

Through further questioning and discussion, [teachers] help students to understand how emotionally difficult it might be if they no longer had one of their family members (p. 160).

Banks also recommends the famous children's book *Annie and the Old One* by Miska Miles. The story describes how Annie's grandmother attempts to teach her about life and death. Although written by a Native American, it hardly takes an exclusively Native American point of view. African legends and folktales often describe the relationships between elders and the young, as do the stories in many other cultures. What Banks finds particularly constructive are the questions we choose to ask children, and not simply whether they have grandmothers. For example,

> Why does Annie have this relationship with her grandmother? What is grandmother thinking? Why? What is Annie thinking? Why? Because this is a story about Native Americans, do you think this might have something to do with the point of view of Annie and her grandmother? Why? Have you read any other books from any other cultures that have the same point of view about family? What did Annie believe about death? Why? What did grandma believe about death? Why?

While continuing this line of questioning with an eye toward helping students develop an understanding of our common struggle for human dignity, I would ask them if any experiences in their lives were similar to Annie's experience. If so, I would want to see if they thought Indians have specific family needs. Are they different from our family needs? Why or why not? In this way students understand that, yes, some cultures have specific family relationships, and their practices show these relationships. But this view of family is informed by culture and is not necessarily cultural itself. Thus, reasoning from the point of view of Annie and her grandmother is not reasoning within the point of view of a particular culture per se, for a particular culture is never stagnant or "handed down" to all its members.

Culture does, however, inform points of view about family, and we can find through critical reasoning and discourse that many kinds and types of cultures share similar ideas about family. I would want my students to understand that there are diverse families so as to help them understand our common need for family. To complement this unit, I would introduce literature that exemplifies the diversity of families, including single fathers, single mothers, extended families, lesbian and gay families, and traditional nuclear families. I would also engage students in upper primary grades in a discussion of patriarchal and matriarchal families, perhaps suggesting research on these family structures for comparison and contrast purposes.

For teachers of upper primary, intermediate, and upper grades, Banks introduces the concept of cultural diversity and similarity. In presenting this concept, Banks makes the general point that "Native American cultures used both different and similar means to satisfy common human needs and wants" (p. 161).

The first question is specifically what are Native cultures? Every Native tribe or only some? Native Americans definitely appear to evince a different point of view attributable, no doubt, to their cultural relationship with the earth and people, than (say) European Americans evince. Yet theirs is a point of view about needs and wants informed by culture. Of course, many other cultures viewed needs and wants similarly, and when reasoning about the Native American point of view on needs and wants, we should call attention both to differences and to similarities. Banks points out that the unit should ideally include four (at a minimum two) Native American cultures to avoid stereotyping *all* Native Americans.

Yet Banks's approach is still to study Native Americans as an early people. Though an important period for critical inquiry, this conception of Native American needs and wants as rooted in time deceives. They have changed as Native culture has modified in response to displacement, genocide, and economic and political neglect. Banks can be criticized for presenting an image of Native Americans different from the reality of Native American life today. What retains interest on the more mature grade levels are the assumptions that guided the historical points of view of various Native American Indian tribes. Students might also study contemporary tribes to see which values and assumptions that inform them have remained consistent or have changed and why. To restrict student activities to gathering information about how American Indian tribes a hundred years ago ranked their needs and wants is to invite them to ignore contemporary conditions and to preclude contemporary linkage to a common ongoing human struggle.

Furthermore, some of Banks's questions—

What kinds of food did the people eat? How was the food usually prepared? By whom? What goods and services were produced? How were they produced? Was some form of money used?—

mask more fundamental questions about what specific historical assumptions account for the points of view toward these questions, about the origins of these assumptions, about their implications and how they might conflict with other assumptions. The lesson also uncritically advocates focus on getting students simply to produce information, not to advance it to reason about the contemporary assumptions that drive their own realities. Finally, Banks's lessons fail to encourage dialogue about the oppression Native American peoples faced and face. Revealing this oppression is essential if students are to grasp the logic of Native American subjugation.

In her book *The Seminole Wars,* Henrietta Buckmaster (1966) described the relationship between the Seminole Indians and Black slaves who joined forces against this oppression during the Seminole Wars. Buckmaster made an important contribution for her book points out current pedagogical practice ignores many disenfranchised American Indian narratives. Rarely do we encourage students to see relationships between the common struggle for human dignity among Native Americans and Black slaves. Unearthing important historical examples of unified struggle against and resistance to a common oppressor provides students with authentic multicultural reasoning opportunities that foster a sense of shared humanity. Teachers could have students research (say) the Seminole Wars paying particular attention to the common struggle, the historical identities, and the questions at issue that faced both cultures. They could work cooperatively researching and analyzing the historical period, eventually role-playing historical voices and even scripting dramatic narratives.

In his Native Americans unit meant for the high school grades, Banks advocates discussions of the concept of "Federal Policy," and he posits this generalization:

> Most Federal Policy on Indian Affairs was made without Indian input and usually sought Indian assimilation and termination of federal-tribal relationships (p. 167).

First, this generalization could and should be presented at every grade level, not just high school. The youngest students are ready to understand the logic of oppression. Second, students should have the chance to develop insights into how matters of American society are decided without the advice and cooperation of the groups involved. Banks wisely suggests that students critically examine treaties between the U.S. government and Indian tribes and then divide into groups, representing an Indian tribe and government agents and argue for or against terminating or maintaining their ties (p. 167). Critical collaborative opportunities for dialogical and dialectical thinking like these are es-

sential for multicultural reasoning and promote the affective and cognitive dimensions of critical thinking. Students should be encouraged
to use the elements of thought in their preparations and also to examine the logic of the position against which they debate. They should
be encouraged to reason civilly and independently and to exercise intellectual humility by forming discussion groups that further a critical
social discourse.

Although this lesson focuses on important historical comprehension, especially since it includes disenfranchised narratives, we must
encourage students to see the present as it affects possibilities in the
future. Students in both primary and secondary grades must see Native people as they exist today; understand their struggles, thinking,
and the oppression they face now; then link this understanding with
the Native historical experience. They must see the Native American
in today's garb, not just the deerskin jerkins and moccasins of yesterday. Children's books for primary grades like *Kevin Cloud: Chippewa
in the City* depict contemporary urban Indian life and shows how a
young boy bridges the gap between his culture and the Anglo culture.
Another excellent book, *Eskimo Boy Today* by Byron Fish (1971),
takes a contemporary look at an Eskimo boy who bridges the two
cultures. Opportunities exist here for recently arrived immigrants to
integrate the understanding inherent in these books into their own
lives. Students could critically examine and analyze similarities and
differences between these narratives and their own experiences while
identifying obstacles that faced both the Indian cultures and their own.

In a unit for primary grades on African Americans, Banks proposes
that the focus fall on

> Afro-American and African folktales [which], like all ethnic folktales, reflect
> the cultural traditions of the people and explain how things in the world be-
> gan (p. 258).

Although I would question whether folktales "explain how things in
the world began" (for some cultures yes, for others no), Banks has
found an excellent way to address the issue of the common human
struggle while honoring the cultural differences in early renditions of
human development. As Banks correctly assumes, many folktales have
a great deal in common; all cultures have their folktales; and many
human values emerge from those legends and folktales that are cross-
cultural. Also, folktales can give students insights into the logic of

oppression, especially when tricky animals deceive, connive, lie, and cheat to get their way. By finding similarities and differences between folktale characters across cultures, students can see that those differences and similarities are important aspects of being human.

Banks proposes that intermediate and advanced students studying African Americans focus on slave rebellions and role play the stories they read. This approach invites students into those elements of thought that propelled the notion of slavery and the logic of oppression that inspired slave rebellions. By Socraticly questioning students about this period, teachers can help them gain insights into the ideology of racism. Connecting these rebellions with the African-American urban rebellions of these past three decades, students can see a sense of how history helps one understand the present and infer the future. They would also come to recognize those elements of thought that explain the racist mind—the assumptions behind racism and the interests it serves. Banks also suggests units on the idea of racial separatism for high school grades. Students and teachers addressing this issue would need a familiarity with African-American protective organizations that appeared in the 1800s, Black-led colonization attempts, the NAACP, and the National Urban League. He suggests that students compare and contrast the views of these eleven men:

(1)   David Walker,
(2)   Martin R. Delaney,
(3)   Richard Allen,
(4)   Prentice Hall,
(5)   Paul Cuffey,
(6)   Marcus Garvey,
(7)   W.E.B. Du Bois,
(8)   Stokely Carmichael,
(9)   Malcolm X,
(10) Adam Clayton Powell, and
(11) Jesse Jackson.

Teachers could add many more names to this list, but Banks intends here to make three basic points:

(1)   It is imperative that teachers become acquainted with the historical record if they expect to teach for historical thinking;

(2)   The resources we use are of paramount importance so as to avoid conveying a trivialized revisionistic history; and

(3)   When we study historical figures we study their thinking, and we concentrate on the elements of thought that presented themselves in specific historical conditions.

Students also need to see how historical figures changed their thinking as a result of metacognition—that is, their ability to critique their reasoning—and how these transformations affected the organizations they were involved in, the goals of those organizations, the questions they confronted, and the underlying assumptions and inferences that guided them. Malcolm X provides an excellent example of someone able to view his own thinking and then act to change his assumptions in light of new evidence. Students should be clear about the assumptions that guided the thinking of the historical figures or organizations under critical examination. A critical analysis of the elements of their thought would provide students with opportunities to represent the viewpoints of others clearly, precisely, fairly, and consistently, even if these points of view vary from their own. Students should be encouraged to work collaboratively researching, critically writing, and orally presenting the ideas and claims of these figures.

Lessons from the Recent American Past

Finally, students should find examples of similar struggles involving racism in contemporary reality and should engage in panel discussions or political debates formulating policy to address the problems of the African-American community or for that matter, the problems of or with racist America. Teachers can encourage students to see the similarities and differences in the way Mexican Americans or Filipinos, for example, formed organizations of resistance and their struggles early in this century. Reasoning multiculturally, students will recognize both the differences and similarities in how we adjust to oppression or perpetuate struggle. Encouraging students to take points of view they might not necessarily agree with gives them opportunities to engage in reciprocity, metacognition, and empathy. Assuring that they do so with standards shows them the importance of representing the thinking of others fairly, clearly, and accurately. These activities naturally involve critical writing, cooperative group work, critical reading, critical speaking, and critical listening. Most important, teachers should be educated about the viewpoints being represented so they know how to question their students and help them assess their thinking and the thinking of others. Having linked this historical inquiry to contemporary reality, students can connect the lived reality of the past with the present while developing their own critical perspectives.

Those teachers broaching the Mexican-American experience in the United States will want to acquaint their upper primary, middle school, and high school students with the Bracero program and then ask them to assess its purpose, the questions that inspired it, and its consequences for Mexican Americans and other Americans. Violence and race riots greeted many Mexicans who immigrated to the U.S. in the early part of this century, and students should study these episodes and assess the thinking behind them. They could create historical accounts in the form of scripted narratives or dramatic presentations. The Sleepy Lagoon case, the Zoot Suit Riots, film colony stereotypes, and other racial antagonisms affected many Mexicans in the 1940s. Students would want to assess critically the role of the Anglo press and dominant culture in fueling this racial hatred. Students could be encouraged to investigate such historical data as the Hearst newspapers in California that inflamed anti-Mexican sentiment with their racial propaganda. They could identify concepts and labels used to depict Mexican Americans and the assumptions that accounted for them. By critically examining these issues students could come to see that many of the problems facing Mexican Americans are the same problems facing the Asian Americans, African Americans, Puerto Rican Americans, and European Americans who immigrated to this country. Students should be urged to explore the similarities and differences in the oppression that Mexican Americans and other immigrants faced. How did they respond culturally to that which they found similar and different? Who represented the forces of oppression and what logic explains their points of view?

In studying the whole Chicano movement, students in intermediate and upper grades can learn about figures who have struggled since 1848 throughout the Southwest to establish humane conditions for Mexicans. The supportive organizations that arose in the late 19th century paralleled the African-American organizations, Chinese organizations, and Filipino organizations. Why did they exist and what were the similarities and differences? How did these organizations develop? What problems confronted them and how did they solve them? Since some of the early Chicanos' resistance took the form of union organization and strikes, how do these activities resemble and differ from other concerted action on behalf of human rights among other cultural groups? (This raises the issue of commonality.) How does the Chicano movement resemble and differ from other resistance movements among Latinos in the United States? What assumptions guide it? On what conclusions is it based? Do the same assumptions and conclusions attend strikes in, say, the garment industry in the early part of this century? What was the same about the strike in California's Imperial Valley in 1928 and various other strikes? By understanding the history of Mexican Americans and then linking this understanding with the broader issues of humanity, students come to see historical commonalties and the logic of oppression. What elements of thought gave rise to unions and civil rights organizations and in what ways did they resemble and differ from civil rights organizations formed by African Americans, Jews, or Italians?

Students should have the chance to discover how Mexican-American struggles today relate to history. What problems that existed in the Imperial Valley in 1928 have been resolved and remain unresolved? Why? In this way students see history as made minute-by-minute by human beings and essential for understanding the present and inferring the future.

When studying leaders like Cesar Chavez, students should read critically with an eye for Chavez's elements of thought. Why did he do what he did? What historical forces did he and his labor union face? What assumptions did he make? In this way students come to understand the humanity and the thinking of Chavez, not just didactic facts like when he was born and when he died.

Again, the teacher requires a thorough understanding of Mexican history and appropriate resources and materials for students to examine and analyze. Unfortunately, since most texts present a revisionist position on history or simply exclude struggles, early movements, and lives of the Mexican immigrants in this country, many teachers find it difficult to teach these histories. Furthermore, few teacher preparation courses address such issues adequately.

For yet another intermediate and upper grade lesson, Banks suggests a unit on European Americans. He advises that students base their study upon specific multicultural books that share information and diverse viewpoints about the experiences and realities of the immigration of English, Germans, French, Norwegians, Swedes, Jews, and other groups represented in the early colonies. He suggests group discussions with students to adduce from their reading why they think these groups came to the United States. He recommends that teachers list the student-generated reasons on the board and help them group these reasons into categories like "economic," "political," or "social." Banks then suggests that teachers assign readings on immigration in the late 1800s and early 1900s and ask students to compare and contrast the reasons why these groups of immigrants left their homelands.

Emphasizing the importance of role playing for developing intellectual empathy and humility, Banks recommends in one example that students take the parts of a poor Italian farmer and an agent of a steamship company who tries to persuade the farmer to immigrate to the U.S. The more men Mr. Rossi, the steamship company agent, can recruit, the more money he makes. Drawing upon accounts of the diverse viewpoints of immigrants like the poor Italian farmer, students can come to understand the exploitation and oppression that faced many immigrants before they left and after they arrived. In the role play, Mr. Rossi approaches Mr. Pareto, the poor farmer with eight children who lives with both his parents. Mr. Pareto cannot feed his family because of crop failures. He has heard of the American wealth and has often thought of immigrating. But he realizes that if he goes to America he must leave his family behind. Approaching him at village market, Rossi tells Pareto he can get a great job in America and that America is a magical place of instant success. Pareto will become wealthy after two or three months and can then call for his whole family.

Banks's exercise can intrigue students for at least three reasons. First, it invites them to reason empathetically within diverse points of view and see their logic. They should be questioned in ways that lead them to see the assumptions that drive the logic of each point of view, given the experiences the individuals faced. Based on these assumptions, both men decided what they chose to believe and how they would act. Their thinking was influenced by the socio-economic realities of the times and had profound implications on their lives and on their families.

Second, by exposing the logic of Rossi's point of view, students gain insights into egocentrism, social class, greed, socio-centrism, fair-minded critical thinking, integrity, honesty, and moral and ethical dimensions. Reasoning within the point of view of exploitation, students can come to see how individuals can become victimized by manipulation and propagandistic appeals. They can learn how people use sociocentricity and nationalism to obfuscate the truth. They can gain an understanding of egocentrism posing as individualism and of how greed and exploitation accompany sophistic thinking as opposed to fair-minded critical thinking.

Third, seeing the world from the point of view of Pareto, students gain a better understanding of what it was like to be poor and desperate in Italy during the late 1800s. They can come to know the goals, problems, and questions that Pareto and his family faced and compare and contrast them with the goals, problems, and questions Rossi faced in his search for profits.

Students should examine contemporary reality for any material or psychological examples of this same phenomenon either among immigrants today or in other spheres of daily life. They could be encouraged to draw analogies by focusing for example, on the coyotes, current traffickers in human beings, at work along the American-Mexican border. Writing scripts, plays, and stories, they could critically construct dialogue to match contemporary realities. In Silicon Valley, for example, a small stretch of so-called clean industry that serves the largest communication and electronic conglomerates, newly arrived immigrants currently face the conditions their European predecessors faced. Here, as Kadetsky (1993) reported, 172,400 electronic production workers—60 percent of whom are female and 70 percent of whom are Latino or Asian—work tediously to produce printed circuit boards for such giants as I.B.M., Anthem, Digital Microwave Corporation, Telebit, and Apple computers (p. 517).

Production does not, however, take place at these companies; instead, they farm it out to assembly companies that often simply rent garages and hire people off the streets. Many of these newly arrived immigrants work with toxic substances on assembly lines resembling the assembly lines in Thailand, Malaysia, Tijuana, and the New York garment district in the early 20th century. They receive six dollars an hour with no health benefits or none of the occupational safety protections afforded other workers. Kadetsky described Chong Kun Yi, a Korean pharmacologist who immigrated to the Silicon Valley in 1986 with hopes of studying medicine, became an assembly worker instead, attaching bits of coil and solder slabs of circuit board at a small electronic assembly house (p. 517). Working up to twelve hours a day for his six dollars an hour, Yi worked with toxins and solvents without gloves, eye-safety equipment, masks, or safety sheets—all in violation of health and safety laws. Unlike many work places in America, these fly-by-night companies sponsor no beer busts, volleyball tournaments, employee health clubs, childcare, paternal leave, company baseball games, or profit-sharing for their immigrant workers. In fact, Yi's company, U.S.M. Technology, slipped into bankruptcy owing Yi $3,000 in back wages and owing another 150 workers more than two months pay totaling $300,000 (p. 518). This scenario continually repeats itself as Chinese immigrants and others are lured to the land of golden opportunity only to find unbearable working conditions and false promises.

Students in middle school and high school could be encouraged to examine the working conditions of these immigrants in the multi-million dollar Silicon Valley electronic industry, researching and then comparing and contrasting contemporary reality with the conditions immigrants faced in the sweatshops in earlier periods of our industrial development. They could compare and contrast the needs of the industry, the needs of the immigrants, the working and safety conditions, and the nature and amount of worker resistance to exploitation. They could work collaboratively to suggest solutions to the problems these newly arrived workers face. With the benefit of critical historical analysis, students can reason abstractly but constructively about poor working conditions, inadequate health protection and safety equipment, exploitation, and sixty-hour work weeks.

Having concretized these historical understandings within everyday contemporary realities, students can look for parallels and connections between immigration, discrimination, exploitation, and oppression historically and today. Equipped with multicultural literature, students can critically explore what happened and what continues to happen to those immigrants who, like Mr. Pareto, accepted the promises of the Mr. Rossis and arrived and continue to arrive in America with more or less unattainable dreams and aspirations. With videos, movies, filmstrips, and literature, students can come to appreciate the struggles of these newly arrived immigrants who once helped and still help build our country.

It would be important to study how the national media contributed to the anti-immigrant mentality during the early part of the century and how the media continue to fuel anti-immigrant sentiments today. Those who stood up to the bosses and industrialists during the early part of this century were labeled, as Wasserman (1972) pointed out,

long-haired, wild-eyed, bad-smelling, atheistic, reckless foreign wretches, and they should have to pay (p. 484).

This type of demagoguery inspired pogroms against the immigrants in our cities and increased cultural hate and sociocentricity among the masses, dividing them further from themselves and from the struggle for justice and self-determination they all had in common. Similar demagogism currently rings out against immigration. In 1997, some 21 bills restricting immigrant rights and services faced the California State Legislature. Having students critically examine the role of the dominant media in the early part of this century regarding immigration policy along with the character of the media today guides them toward insights into the struggle among all immigrants for human dignity and the obstacles and issues that once confronted and still confront them.

Yet, one should note that several groups favored immigration during the early part of this century. For example, the International Workers of the World tolerated no racial disharmony designed to disrupt the natural alliance between human beings trying to better their lives. Among the Eastern immigrants and across the Mississippi among the workers of the West, the IWW spread like wildfire during the early part of this century. The dues were low and membership was open to all-Blacks, women, and immigrants of all varieties. IWW ("Wobbly") newspapers appeared in ten languages, unifying ideas that had been fragmented by racism and xenophobic hysteria. Although inner city immigrants displayed diverse cultures, they had much in common. For one thing, in the early 1900s they shared an admiration for Eugene V. Debs, who spoke on behalf of the working people. Coleman (1930) described the love the immigrants had for Debs and the ideas he stood for

> The picture of Gene was on their walls alongside those of Sir Moses Montefiore, the Rabbi of Libawich, "Goan of Vilna" and other heroes of these immigrants. For them Debs was the liberator, the first who had come to them from the ranks of American workers, holding out his hands and saying, "I am your brother." They had respect and admiration for radicals of their own race. But they worshipped Debs (p. 249).

They knew that Debs had much in common with them. Their struggle for humanity far outweighed any differences that marked these disparate cultures united in squalor in our cities and plagued by ceaseless exploitation. The call to the poor for freedom crossed all color and cultural boundaries among the early Wobblies, and they described their oppression and the common struggle for human dignity in the songs, stories, and cartoons in the Wobbly literature. A culture of commonality and mutual respect presented a clear-cut diagnosis of who the oppressive enemy was. This IWW culture pictured in the great labor songs of the early century advertised the struggle and bonded cultural identities to the cultural craving for freedom and dignity. Private life became public life, as workers of all cultures and ethnicities "traveled the rails," or occupied the hobo camps where the campfires lit meetings and strategy sessions. Amid this reality there was no place for false ideas of national superiority or racial inferiority. The goal was clear, and a unified struggle was the ticket. Students should learn about this thinking and point of view. Having tracked down the remaining oral histories or narratives, students could critically examine the early American resistance movements, analyze and produce journals and stories, and role play historical scenarios.

Women's voices also filled the halls of early and fairly recent American history, even though contemporary texts rarely suggest it. As C.V. Woodward (1951) reported, Mary Lease of Kansas, an important figure in the late 1800s, said of the farmers that they were going to "raise less corn and more hell." She went on to observe

> Wall Street owns the country. It is no longer a government of the people, by the people, and for the people, but a government of Wall Street, by Wall Street, and for Wall Street. The great common people of this country are slaves, and monopoly is the master. The West and South are bound and prostrate before the manufacturing East. Money rules, and our vice president is a London banker. Our laws are the output of a system which clothes rascals in robes and honesty in rags. The parties lie to us and the political speakers mislead us. . . . There are thirty men in the United States whose aggregate wealth is over one and a half billion dollars. There are a half million looking for work. . . . We want money, land, and transportation. . . . We will stand by our homes and stay by our firesides by force if necessary, and we will not pay our debts to the loan shark companies until the government pays its debt to us. The people are at bay, let the blood-hounds of money who have dogged us thus far beware (p. 270).

Contributions like these are silenced in education today. Few adults would recognize the movement she represented, much less her name. Yet during the 1890s voices of women like Mary Lease filled the air.

By the early 1890s farmers everywhere were losing their farms to corporate business and land speculators. Twenty-five percent of the farms in Kansas, Nebraska, Iowa, Missouri, Illinois, Indiana, Ohio, and Pennsylvania lay in the hands of Wall Street investors and their cronies. The figure was more than 50 percent in the South. The farmer revolt numbered in the millions of Americans and the membership included women, and Blacks, and immigrant farmers. Mary Lease's viewpoint was less *feminist* than populist. Yet the contributions of women in the struggle for farm rights and freedom have been relegated to the out lands of history. Students can learn the logic of the farm movements in the late 1800s by taking the farmers' points of view—critically identifying and examining their assumptions and reasons they believed and behaved as they did. Students can also size up the situation from the viewpoint of landsharks, bankers, and railroaders. They can then translate these insights into an understanding of the plight of contemporary farmers who continue to face some of the same forces, with bank foreclosures and the need to accept charity from country musicians just to survive. These men and women have legacies from early United States history, and one can understand the role and plight of the contemporary American farmer only by entering critically into the points of view of the men and women who made up the huge populist movements. Unfortunately, we rarely see their position in texts and classroom materials. We see only the side of capital. Students need to examine critically the underlying assumptions that guide both perspectives. It would be dishonest to pretend that capital and labor operate from the same points of view with the same purposes, arriving at the same conclusions, based on similar or the same assumptions. It would also be dishonest to pretend they operate independently of one another. In fact, the lack of the labor point of view on historical and contemporary reality leaves students and future workers without the critical faculties to distinguish between ideals and actual practice or arrive at reasoned judgment on issues involving labor and capital as they arise.

In an article entitled "On Being Busted: The Death of a Union," reporters at the *Santa-Barbara News Press,* a California newspaper now owned by *The New York Times,* made a salient point:

> We've seen a lot of turnover since the Times took over. The new hires have been young people with no union experience. They entered the work force during the Reagan era. They did not understand why they were earning so much more money at the News-Press than at the sweatshops they came from. Most of them voted against the union (p. 16).

These worker-reporters noted that the new hires seemed unlikely to reach a reasoned judgment on whether to keep or disband the union. They had matured in an era of union busting in the 1980s with no access to or understanding of the historical struggles working men and women had waged in this country. Therefore, they could hardly reason critically about their reality at the newspaper—about, that is, the relationship between their current wages and benefits and past struggles with management. They had only one point of view, one set of assumptions, and little historical understanding of the role of labor in the human struggle for self-betterment, fair income distribution, and work-site control. As a result, they made decisions they might not have made had they known the hidden history of this country—had they the benefit of an education that advanced reasoning from the point of view of labor as well as capital.

Students in the upper primary grades who study American history in the late 1900s should know that as third party movements gained power in the late 1870s, especially among the Farmers Alliance, whites and Blacks formed many cordial and productive alliances. This unified notion of struggle disappears from most history texts, perhaps because these Black-white alliances posed (might still pose) a formidable threat to the banking interests that had replaced the old plantation-slavery systems. This unity, this common struggle for human dignity, threatened monopolists and bankers. A united humanity overcoming the petty distractions of racism could actually force change. Racism muddies the water of human similarities and aspirations, inviting disruptive in-fighting among the oppressed.

Wasserman (1972) quoted Tom Watson another American hero conspicuously absent from the history books, on the coalition between Blacks and whites:

> The Negro Question in the South has been for nearly thirty years a source of danger, discord, and bloodshed. It is an ever-present irritant and menace. . . . Never before did two distinct races dwell together under such conditions. The problem is, can these two races, distinct in color, distinct in social life, and distinct as political powers, dwell together in peace and prosperity?. . . The white tenant lives adjoining the colored tenant. Their houses are almost equally destitute of comforts. Their living is confined to bare necessities. They are equally burdened with heavy taxes. They pay the same high rent for gullied and impoverished land. They pay the same enormous prices for farm supplies. Christmas finds them both without any satisfactory return for a year's toll. Dull and heavy and unhappy, they both start the plows again when "New Year's" passes. Now the Peoples Party says to these two men, "You are kept apart that you may be separately fleeced by your earnings. You are made to hate each other because upon that hatred is rested the keystone of the arch of financial despotism that enslaves you both. You are deceived and blinded that you may not see how this race antagonism perpetuates a monetary system which beggars both" (p. 89).

We see these same problems today. By understanding the populist movements and alliances of Blacks and whites during the late 1800s in the strong Farm Alliances throughout this country, students can gain insights into contemporary problems of race and class and see how the former is used to distract and weaken potential resistance.

Along with the immense Farmers Alliance that spread through Texas and over the Southwest, by 1890 the Northern Alliance (of farmers) in the West had over a million members, while the Southern Alliance had as many as three million, and the Colored Farmers Alliance also centered in the South had another million and a half members. These groups all worked together against the railroads, cattle barons, and land sharks. Students could critically explore these alliances, paying particular attention to the issues they confronted, the claims they made, the decisions they reached, the assumptions that guided their thinking, and the implications of their thought and actions. Students could cooperatively engage in critical research, writing, and reading activities specifically about these alliances, using role playing as a vehicle for critical social discourse.

Similarly, few students know that populist white farmers spent the days before the 1892 Georgia election armed and on horseback trying to protect Black allies from white lynch mobs. In 1896 the chief victory for the populist movement came in North Carolina where a coalition of Blacks and whites gained control of the state government. The Democratic Party, fearing damage to their industrial empire, proclaimed the election the "return of nigger domination" and vowed to take back the South for the white race. White "jubilees" celebrated spontaneously and gangs of white supremacists roamed small towns and the countryside beating and killing Blacks—all in the interest of the capitalist who controlled the party; for as Tom Watson observed, as long as one half the population fights the other the ones above the fray win. Finally with the imposition of poll taxes, literacy tests, and property qualifications, Blacks lost the ballot. In Mississippi, the Mississippi Plan also disenfranchised poor whites in the 1890s. Yet even though the Mississippi Plan disenfranchised whites in much the same way that poll taxes had disenfranchised Blacks, many poor whites supported the plan. The issue as they saw it was racial supremacy. Wasserman (1972) described an Alabama politician justifying the new voting laws designed to place power firmly in the Democratic Party:

[A]ll those who are unfit and unqualified [do not vote], and if the rule strikes a white man as well as a Negro, let him go. There are some white men who have no more right and no more business to vote than a Negro and not as much as some of them (p. 107).

As this racism took hold, the Black-white alliance in the South found itself in a cul-de-sac. The Jim Crow laws of the day established the ideology of racism in the minds of many southern whites by segregating trains; separating residential areas, parks, restaurants, and hospitals; and making sure that even in courtrooms and schools Bibles and texts were stored separately on the basis of race. In some states it became illegal for whites and Blacks to play, fish or boat together. Where there had once been two classes in the South—slave owners and slaves—there were now three owners over poor whites over "freed slaves."

The logic of oppression operated in the cynical use of Black militias from Brownsville, Texas, to quell the 1899 populist strike in the copper mines at Coeur d'Alene, Idaho. Although a regiment of white soldiers was stationed nearby, President McKinley ordered the Blacks to put down the strike, thereby fomenting racism among the workers and Black militiamen, racism being the actual policy of the federal government. Adamic (1958) quoted Big Bill Haywood of the Western Federation of Miners on the situation:

We always believed that the government officials thought it would further incite the miners if Black soldiers were placed as guards over white prisoners (p. 126).

In his book *Dynamite*, Adamic described this racial divide-and-conquer strategy. Black, Asian, white, Native American, and immigrant were all played off against one another by the wage system. The mine owners routinely used Blacks as strikebreakers. When the Blacks left the South for the northern cities in the early part of the century, labor problems intensified as many whites saw Blacks as driving down wages and worsening working conditions. Samuel Gompers, the head of the American Federation of Labor, quoted by Nash and Weiss (1970), played the racial card himself:

The Caucasians are not going to let their standard of living be destroyed by Negroes, Chinese, Japs, or any others (p. 115).

Students need to experience this history so as to explore and analyze how the forces of oppression use race to promote their interests. Students must understand race socio-economically and politically, not just viscerally. Students must have opportunities to assume the points of view of both racist whites and pro-alliance forces. They should be encouraged to examine critically the assumptions that motivated both the efforts to unify and efforts to divide by race. They should be encouraged to compare and contrast the interests and forces facing poor whites and non-whites during this period. They could examine speeches from members of the Democratic Party and compare and contrast these with the Republican and third party positions. They might consider questions like these:

> What problems faced the country and farming regions at this juncture in history? What competing claims and points of view were put forth by the various historical forces? On what assumptions were they based? Where did these assumptions come from? On what reasons and evidence did these competing claims and assumptions rest? What were the implications for deciding one way or the other on problems facing the farmers at this time? Why did some whites and not others come to the aid of Blacks? Why did the farmers form alliances and a third party? What were the underlying assumptions that fueled these third party movements?

They might want to question the divide-and-conquer tactics of the mine owners and the federal government:

> What was the purpose of using strike breakers? Why did McKinley not use white workers even though they were closer? What was McKinley assuming about race relations? Why did the federal government adopt this policy? What were the mine workers striking for? Why did the AF of L leader Gompers make the statement he did? What assumptions fueled his thinking? Did all AF of L members agree with Gompers? How might we find out?

In considering the common struggle for human dignity we might usefully ask ourselves these questions:

> What kinds of people refuse to engage in or comply with policies of racism, homophobia, sexism, anti-Semitism, and hatred? What kinds of people comply? Why do some people choose this manner of actualization rather than coming to the aid of victims in times of trouble? What is it about the dominant attitudes of discrimination and equality that members of the population internalize? How might critical thinking influence these decisions?

Similar opportunities for cultural learning wait in a host of contemporary controversies surrounding the drug problem, sexually and racially offensive speech prohibitions, feminism, gay rights, and homophobic attitudes. Teachers might ask their students to examine Los Angeles life in the 1940s from the point of view of the pachucos. They might interview parents and community members as a way to elicit culturally informed points of view from the community. Another teacher could make the contributions of various cultural groups to the labor movement between 1900 and 1950 a subject of inquiry. Differences in viewpoints on the labor movement between whites, Blacks, and Asians in the early part of the century could be analyzed. For example, Chinese coolies were paid slave wages to build the railroads of the West in the late 1900s, driving down the pay of native whites and creating anti-Oriental riots all over the West. Meanwhile, Blacks distrusted organized labor, especially in light of the Eurocentricity and sociocentricity of Samuel Gompers who founded the AF of L. Students might identify and analyze critically the different points of view from Blacks, women, and immigrants, all of whom were barred from the AF of L in the early 1900s.

The great literature that flowed from the struggles of the masses in the early part of this century are, themselves, sources for and subjects of critical analysis. Workers' viewpoints that appear in Upton Sinclair's *The Jungle*, (1906). Frank Norris's *The Octopus* (1901) and *The Pit* (1903), illustrate the point of view of the farm culture, following the flow of wheat from California to the Chicago markets. The great muckraking periodical journalism around the time of the publication of *The Jungle* presents points of view rarely mentioned in history texts. In 1912, James Weldon Johnson published *The Autobiography of an Ex-Colored Man*. The principal figure, a mulatto, hides his Black identity to become successful in the business world. Johnson presaged sentiments in the Black community today about race and "passing" and business. More historical attention could usefully focus on such figures as Timothy Drew who in 1913 founded the Moorish Science Temple in Newark, New Jersey, or Marcus Garvey who in 1916 landed in New York to promote the Black Nationalist United Negro Improvement Association. We rarely find Garvey mentioned nowadays outside of ethnic studies courses. Great American thinkers like E. Franklin Frazier rarely appear in texts. Explaining why he writes about a great African American like Frazier, Tony Platt (1990) commented that

Writing about Frazier, [I] recognize his contributions and put him back into our collective memory. Frazier's work—and the work of countless Afro-American artists, writers, and intellectuals—has not been taken seriously. This is another form of racist exclusion that is very much a fact of academia today. Let me give you a typical example. For five years from 1922 to 1927, Frazier built and directed the Atlanta School of Social Work, the first of its kind in the South. In these five years, he administered the program, taught classes, did fundraising, wrote and published some 33 articles, wrote short stories and a play, started a French club on campus, painted water color portraits, and had his photographs published in several journals. The unique social-work program that he developed does not appear in any history of social work. His contribution, as Sheila Rowbotham has said of women, was "hidden from history" (p. 45).

Students might analyze the cultural point of view of the Black Muslims historically and currently on issues of race and urban economic development. They might also discuss the point of view leaders like Booker T. Washington, who considered Black participation in white politics a mistake. The African American League he began in 1890 to promote Black banking and cooperative industry has many current parallels in the realms of economic self-help and inner city banking in the Black community. But those leaders like W.E.B. Du Bois had a wholly different opinion on what role African-Americans should play in political life. Students could be asked to discuss the differences between Washington and Du Bois by examining the statement by Du Bois (1924) that he and other Blacks

. . . feel in conscience bound to ask of this nation three things: The right to vote, civic equality, the education of youth according to ability. [s]o far as Mr. Washington apologizes for injustice, North or South, does not rightly value the privilege and duty of voting, belittles the emasculating effects of caste distinctions, and opposes the higher training and ambitions of our brighter minds—so far as he, the South, or the Nation does this—we must unceasingly and firmly oppose them (pp. 50–54).

These remarks raise important contemporary issues, particularly since Du Bois helped found the National Association for the Advancement of Colored People in 1910 and a year later Washington founded the National Urban League. Both organizations remain powerful forces within the Black community and the country and a similar debate is still present in the African-American community.

We should wonder, furthermore, why students rarely encounter the personalities and thinking of such contemporary African Americans as Ron Dellums, who has served in Congress for more than twenty years and now heads of the House Armed Services Committee. What assumptions inform his thinking on issues of defense and base closures? How have they changed, if at all? At what conclusions has he arrived? On what evidence has he based his assumptions?

For students in upper grades, critical discussions and debates could usefully focus on current affairs of interest to students. Consider the controversy over whether Heavyweight Boxing Champion Mike Tyson raped the young beauty queen Desiree Washington. Some women in the Black community consider Tyson a hero and contend that Desiree Washington chose to be raped. Why would some women in the Black community think this is so? Could the answer lie in how Black women are socialized to treat the crime of rape? What about the idea of the image, a Black athlete or Black celebrity must project? What about the argument heard in the Black community that hegemonic racism requires celebrity Black men to comport themselves with decorum, and that this burden would be lighter in other racial communities? Questions like these call for critical thinking, metacognition, and reflection, and they could easily be subjects of inquiry among students of all races. Students should be encouraged critically to explore the similarities and differences in how different ethnic communities view the crime of rape.

At Sarah J. Hale High School in Brooklyn, New York, students critically examine issues like these. In 1988, the students of this inner-city high school founded The Society for Social Analysis, and its journal *Crossing Swords* determined

> to construct the foundation of a splendid journal covering the whole field of civic affairs, drawing on free, responsible and committed students in charge of their destinies, in touch with their cultures and moved to spread the message of their love and their aspirations by the device of literary articulation. [This journal promotes critical dialogue and discovery by] encouraging critical analysis of political, social, and cultural issues (p. 1).

The Hale students use their journal to engage in critical writing about such issues such as multicultural education, all-male Black schools, socialization practices, abortion, teenage pregnancies, drugs, international affairs, power, authority, neighborhood, child abuse, parenting, school life, popular culture, art, music, freedom, history, and street life. Mauricia O'Kieffe (1990), a Sarah J. Hale High School graduate, commented this way on her experience with The Society for Social Analysis:

As I look back at my high school career, I see many things. Some things stand out and other things are slowly fading into the background. One of the things that stands out is my involvement with a certain club named The Society for Social Analysis. All of us together were not afraid to criticize each other's work. That is what made the group of us what we were. We voiced our disagreements with each other so that there were no secrets as to how we felt. At times our debates turned into shouting matches but if shouting was a means to get your point across then by all means shout. We soon came to realize that shouting seldom got us anywhere. Most of the time we just agreed to battle it out on paper. Or like Rosemarie and Ann Marie; agree to disagree. As I move forward through life I will always thank God the day I became an active part of The Society. I am not trying to be overly sentimental but when I die and God asks what was my greatest accomplishment, I'll have to say, "My greatest accomplishment is my participation in a club named The Society for Social Analysis for it taught me perseverance, the true meaning of friendship, and my responsibility as a person living in this world" (p. XI).

In a conversation published in *Crossing Swords* (1990), student Nur Jahan Simmons commented on schooling in his essay "Examining the Core: Penny Wise Pound Foolish"

If there is no fear among teenagers, then there must be improved communication if there is going to be a tomorrow. [S]chool [must] no longer be a place only to learn academic subjects but a place were students will learn how to communicate and get along with others (p. 24).

Timothy Gardner, a Hale ninth grader commented on the issue of race:

What is color, but a shade that excites one's curiosity? (p. 77).

Discussing the concept of freedom, Tricia Parris, a senior at Hale, wrote that

Freedom means more than being able to walk around without being bothered. It means to be free from bondage. Freedom is not guaranteed by power but by a burning desire and eternal vigilance (p. 125).

Confronting issues of multicultural concern, these students used critical thinking and writing and framed contemporary situations for analysis and evaluation. Though exceptions to the current educational reality, they provide excellent examples of the contributions all students can make when presented with a worthy educational project. They are reminders of the words of Franz Fanon (1968):

Every generation must, out of relative obscurity, discover its mission, fulfill it, or betray it (p. 128).

In her essay "Meditations on the Legacy of Malcolm X," Angela Davis (1992) asked the following questions, all of which call for critical cultural analysis and could provide the basis for inquiries in a high school social studies class:

> Thus my final set of questions: How do we challenge the police violence inflicted on untold numbers of Black men, such as Rodney King, and at the same time organize against the pervasive sexual violence that continues to be perpetuated by men who claim to be actual or potential revolutionaries? How do we challenge the increasingly intense assault on women's reproductive rights initiated by the Reagan and Bush administrations? How do we bring into our political consciousness feminists' concerns—the corporate destruction of the environment, for example—that have been historically constructed as "white people's issues"? How do we halt the growing tendency for violence perpetrated by African Americans against Asians? How do we reverse established attitudes within the African-American community—and especially in popular youth culture, as nourished by the iconization of Malcolm X—that encourage homophobia, sometimes even to the point of violence, associating such backward positions with the exaltation of the Black man? How do we criticize Magic Johnson's compulsion to distinguish himself as a heterosexual who contracted HIV through heterosexual relations, thereby declaring his own innocence, which effectively condemns gay men with HIV? How can we speak out against racist hate crimes, while simultaneously breaking the silence about anti-gay crimes that occur within the Black community, perpetuated by Black homophobes against Black or Latino or Latina or white gay men or lesbians? (pp. 45–46).

Davis's questions here implicitly recognize the diversity of cultural points of view as well as the necessity for an auto-dialectical cultural critique. Furthermore, the questions themselves present a point of view and thus have a logic that students in the upper grades could critically examine and analyze.

In examining different points of view on cultural issues of social class I am reminded of the story told by Michelle Fine (1989) in her essay "Urban Schooling." Fine described the three social studies lesson of one teacher:

> *Social Studies Teacher*: A few year ago a journalist went through Kissinger's garbage and learned a lot about his life. Let's make believe we are all sanitation workers going through rich people's and poor people's garbage. What would we find in rich people's garbage?
> *Students call out*: Golf club! Polo stick! Empty bottle of Halston! Champagne bottle! Alimony statements! Leftover caviar! Receipts from Saks! Barnies, Bloomies! Old business and love letters! Rarely worn shoes. They love to spend money! Bills from the plastic surgeon for a tummy tuck! Things that are useful that they just throw out cause they don't like it! Rich people got ulcers, so they have lots of medicine bottles!

Teacher: Now the poor man's garbage! What would you find?
Student (1): Not much. We're using it.
Student (2): Holey shoes.
Others: Tuna cans, bread bags!
Student (3): That's right! We eat a lot of bread!
Others: USDA cheese boxes! Empty no-frills cans! Woolworth receipts! Re-used items from rich man's garbage! *The Daily News!*
Student (3): *The Daily News* from the week before!
Others: Old appliances! Rusty toasters!
Student (4): Yeah, we eat lots of burnt toast.
Student (5): You know, poor people aren't unhappy. We like being poor.
Teacher: Let's not get into value judgments now. There are people who are eccentric and don't have these things and poor people who have luxuries, so it is hard to make generalizations.
Student (6): That's why we're poor! (p. 172).

With more experience in the Socratic method, this teacher could have gone on to engage the class in critical thinking about social class, eliciting various points of view. Concentration might have focused on helping students see the logic of their own thinking—the assumptions, inferences, and concepts they harbored about the rich and poor—while at the same time confronting the issue of social justice. Fine's story provides an excellent example of how we can get our students critically to examine issues as well as their own thinking regarding economic and social class if we are, that is, committed to responsible reasoning activities.

Internalized Oppression

Meanwhile, of course, oppression persists, and our students encounter it in their everyday lives. Franz Fanon (1968) recognized some of the ambiguities of oppression:

How could the colonizer look after his workers while periodically gunning down a crowd of the colonized? How could the colonized deny himself so cruelly yet make such excessive demands? How could he hate the colonizers and yet admire them so passionately? I too felt this admiration in spite of myself (p. 128).

Any understanding of the complicated idea of oppression must involve an understanding of both externalized and internalized oppression. This is the logic of the colonized mind as Fanon analyzed it:

The colonized man will first manifest this aggressiveness which has been deposited in his bones against his own people. This is the period when the

Niggers beat each other up, and the police and magistrates do not know which way to turn when faced with the astonishing waves of crime in North Africa. . . . While the settler or the policeman has the right the livelong day to strike the native, to insult him and to make him crawl to them, you will see the native reaching for his knife at the slightest hostile or aggressive glance cast upon him by another native; or the last resort of the native is to defend his personality vis-à-vis his brother (p. 52).

One immediately notices the similarity between this description and the current ethnic fratricide in urban centers throughout America. Also striking in the colonized mentality is the self-deprecation of the oppressed. Subjected to countless images that depict them as lazy, no good, lacking in intelligence, drug addicts, and apt to commit crime, they internalize the message of domination and oppression and become convinced of their own inadequacies. This is why the oppressed must learn the logic of oppression, come to see historical examples of subjugation and resistance, and draw analogies between history and their own psychological and material conditions. They must come to see that the oppressed and the state of oppression are not the logical or inevitable outcome of historical processes but fragile conditions capable of transformation.

For Paulo Freire (1990) this understanding is crucial and formulated a pedagogy for liberation that recognizes internalized oppression as an historical reality:

The central problem is this: How can the oppressed as divided, inauthentic human beings, participate in developing the pedagogy of their liberation? Only as they discover themselves to be "hosts" of the oppressor can they contribute to the midwifery of their liberating pedagogy. As long as they live in the duality in which to be is to be like, and to be like is to be like the oppressor, this contribution is impossible. The pedagogy of the oppressed is the instrument for their critical discovery that both they and their oppressors are manifestations of dehumanization (p. 33).

What internalized oppression calls attention to is the need to examine critically self-hatred, rigidity of thinking, and low self-esteem—all an alienated conformity to the state of subjugation. This task requires a commitment to analyze and deconstruct the dominant structures and institutional arrangements of historical and contemporary society.

The re-evaluation counseling Barbara Love leads at the University of Massachusetts at Amherst addresses this idea of internalized oppression. Love contends that joint economic ties or coalition building among groups of people can be a positive result of stereotyping, bigotry, and self hate. These conditions, largely psycho-socio-cultural in nature, need to be addressed in conjunction with economic points of view when one studies the logic of oppression. Working with Latinos, African Americans, Chinese Americans, Arab Americans, Iranian Americans, and Native American's Love has successfully challenged internalized oppression. Itabari Njeri (1991) described the process:

> A woman came to the front of the room. Love held her hand and asked her to tell the group about herself. "My background is Louisiana-Creole," said the woman with a sigh. She was about fifty and light brown. "In my family I was the darkest one," she said with a shiver. "All my life, my grandmother, my uncle, my Aunts—my everybody—would whisper n____, n____, n____." Then she repeated the hated word as an aspirate hiss. She shivered again and Love embraced her. The woman went on, "When I had my first child he was so beautiful," she said. "A beautiful mahogany-colored boy. . . . And then I had my daughter. Ohhhh," she moaned. "And then I freaked out." There was a long silence and then gently Love asked her, "Why?" "Because . . . she had red hair, blue eyes, and was vanilla-colored." And then the woman began a spiraling scream so primal it seemed to reach back 30,000 years, piercing the room's wall, shaking the leaves and scarring the trees in the woods just a few feet beyond. "And then you freaked out? Why?" asked Love quietly. Sobbing the woman said she spent the last 25 years in mortal fear that her child would hate her and one day leave her because "I'm so black, Oh God, because I am a n____'"' (p. B5).

Promoting peace within our communities means promoting peace within ourselves. This project requires a thorough understanding of the role of oppression and how it has legitimized the wholesale exploitation of one culture by another, creating in the personal and public mind cultural wars and ethnic strife that could easily yield to a recognized common oppression transformed into a common struggle. It also means engaging in a critical inventory—a critical self-examination and critique to banish stereotypes and promote genuine understanding and cultural unity. Teaching how this oppression infects the mind, leaving it distressed, enraged, and irrational should be the goal of any pedagogy of liberation. Such a pedagogy must confront questions like these:

> What assumptions guide the feelings I have about myself or feelings that others have about me? Are they rational, can they be backed by evidence? Where do these assumptions come from? Are they the product of my own thinking or borrowed assumptions I have internalized through a culture of domination? What conclusions can I draw? What are the implications of these conclusions for me, others, and society as a whole? What in contemporary material and psychological reality fuels this type of thinking and why?

We can usually link those who profit from internalized oppression to other social institutions, which prompts the question of who profits from oppression in general. By no means, however, are all oppressed groups irrational, but they all call for us to rethink our acquiescence in the interest of unity and this means discovering those barriers that impede unity. We can begin this course only if we place our present lives in an historical context—if we can, that is, reclaim historical memory.

Cultural Relativism and the Cultural Critique

In 1991, Sandra LeSourd asked her readers to ponder the following question:

> Should a civic culture founded upon a uniform philosophical heritage have a moral right to judge actions inspired by alternative heritages? (p. 52).

She went on to describe two scenarios involving immigrants to the United States. In the first, a Japanese woman was living in California as a dutiful young wife and mother of two. She discovered her husband to be unfaithful and, coupled with a former failed marriage, the discovery was too much for her. She became convinced of her failure as a mother and a wife. In the Japanese tradition, a parent-child suicide is an acceptable reaction to grave family dishonor. The woman attempted to drown herself in the ocean with her children. They were rescued but the children later died and the mother survived.

In the second scenario, in an "entangled conflict of priorities," a Fresno Social Service Agency attempted to force surgery on the clubbed feet of a Hmong family's six-year-old son to prevent total immobility. But a previous operation performed by U.S. doctors in a Thai refugee camp when the boy was one had been unsuccessful, and had been accompanied, as well, by fever and convulsions. The family's next two children were born with cleft palates, and the family associated the son's surgery with these subsequent misfortunes because it had interfered with his natural condition. The misfortunes showed that God was displeased. The agency went to court; the jury that heard the case ruled for the agency; and the agency was eventually upheld in the State Supreme Court (p. 52).

These two scenarios invite an analysis of the idea of ethics and cultural relativism, an important idea for educators, parents, and the community. When private interpretations of a worthy life define reality for some, should they be penalized by the State? Do we have the right to condemn the cultural practices of others simply because we disagree? A still more compelling question is whether all cultures and individuals have the human and moral responsibility to examine and critically analyze their cultural beliefs for the good of humanity in light of their unique historical development. This larger question, in turn, compels us to ask ourselves how we perceive morality and ethics. Do we adopt a relativistic inquiry based on the dominant philosophical way of perceiving the issue? Do we—as universalists or essentialists do—adopt an absolutist approach to morality based on universal principles understood outside the historical arena? Can we really adopt a moral certainty, attempting to locate ethics as some hard fact or as a result of religious absolutism? Or in response to the proselytizing of moralists of the essentialist tradition, do we adopt an anarchic or relativist approach that argues for no morals at all?

In his book *Ethical Dimensions of Marxist Thought*, Cornel West (1991) asked us to understand the particular historical nature of moral and ethical issues. He advocated replacing a philosophic search for moral and ethical understanding with an historical inquiry that adopts critical social theory as its starting point: West argued

> . . . for an historical assessment and political reading of our morality and morale, in order to shed light on how we can make them more contagious to others captive to the prevailing cynicism and nihilism (p. xiii).

This approach both abandons the cynical and destructive banterings of a moral nihilism that argues against the existence of moral truths, and eschews the positivistic notions of essentialism that argues for the universality of moral certitudes or scientific naturalism. Furthermore, West urged us to abandon ethical claims of relativism that argue a particular moral belief may be right for one cultural group and not another. Instead, he sees all moral claims based on "the specific aims, goals, and objectives of particular groups, communities, cultures, or societies" (p. 10).

Understood in the historical context, ascertaining ethics and morality is not simply a free-for-all of moral sensibility or a deterministic project that assumes moral nature to be wholly determined by social forces. Rather it involves an understanding of the historical nature of morality, recognizing that ethics and morality surface in specific manners at particular historical times. Thus, they can be critically interrogated within a critical social theory that seeks to understand them as formed in a particular historical context.

A moral inquiry born from a socio-historical understanding would require us critically to inquire into the nature of the Japanese woman's thinking as it relates to the specific historical aims and goals of her culture. For example, did she come to the conclusion that she was an inadequate mother and wife based on a peculiar patriarchal assumption: that her husband would not have cheated and her first marriage not have failed if she had been adequate? From precisely where did that patriarchal assumption arise? Is it a part of a distinct socio-historical context? Can we understand this assumption outside the confines of a debate that asks us to interrogate critically such historical assumptions and struggle to change contemporary societies and cultures? Does there exist both a personal and social responsibility to examine critically those specific historically derived patriarchal assumptions that guide feelings and those feelings that guide assumptions? Should critical educational counseling have been provided to help this woman examine the assumptions she held, their historical origins, and the socio-political and moral basis for the conclusions she came to? Could this counseling have provided a basis for conscious critical intervention into her own thinking and actions?

In the case of the Hmong family who assumed God was displeased, did they have the right to a conclusion with severe implications for their child simply because they were bound to unexamined self-justifying belief systems? Can we separate from the specific and particular historical circumstances that guided their communities, societies, and thinking, truly understand the assumptions that guided their feelings and actions? The question at issue is really this: Do all cultures share a human responsibility to engage in critical self-reflection and transformative metacognition in the interest of humanity, and if so, can we carry out this critical understanding in purely essentialist or deterministic ways or must we adopt a theory that allows us to illuminate moral and ethical assumptions in light of historical circumstances? If we argue the latter, the position the West adopts and the one in which I concur, then the position bestows upon us responsibilities as members of a community—responsibilities to engage in both socio-historical and personal critiques. LeSourd made an important point when she stated that "future citizens will need to be knowledgeable about the contents of values and beliefs for satisfactory conflict resolution" (p. 52).

True enough, but they must also be capable of understanding that these values and beliefs are socially and historically constructed and require rigorous social and personal examination if they are to inform autonomous decisions. Pluralistic beliefs and values certainly require a willingness to take into account both similar and disparate assumptions about life, to examine critically a multiplicity of viewpoints on any given issue relative to specific historical conditions, and to advocate diversity of thought as a social benefit. Yet to do so critically without falling into the trap of uncritical relativism, deterministic nihilism, and destructive cynicism requires more than just a cognitive ability to examine, analyze, synthesize, compare, and contrast; it requires a willingness to foster the development of values and dispositions that treat difference, ambiguity, and multiple perspectives with intellectual responsibility—with an understanding of their peculiar historical development and the implications for humanity.

Samir Amin (1989) has noted that

> Ignorance and mistrust of others, even chauvinism and xenophobia, testify to nothing more than the limits of the evolution of all societies that have existed until now (p. 104).

All societies are to some degree sociocentric. All societies believe in the inherent superiority of their ways of perceiving the world, their ways of moralizing, and their ways of actualizing existence. For this reason all societies and cultures can profit from a rigorous cultural critique and an enlightened historical sensibility—attempting to sort out the inherently oppressive in their social arrangements, ways of thinking, and ways of treating others.

Kanan Makiya, a Baghdad-born author writing in *The Nation* (p. 629), documented the use of rape to disgrace family honor and thus to wield political power in the patriarchal state of Iraq. The Iraqi state has employed and apparently continues to employ people as official rapists in the service of the government. This government-sponsored "official rape" is, according to Makiya, less the reflective of Saddam Hussein's disposition than part and parcel of an Arab-Islamic cultural identity that assumes the honor of a family is located in the bodies of its women—mainly in their virginity but also in the clothes they wear, and in the modesty they project. The veil acquires its significance precisely because it acts symbolically to protect this honor from public view and thus enhances it. One can understand the idea of the violation of a woman's honor through state-sponsored rape only by first understanding these deep-seated historical assumptions about women.

Makiya went on to depict the cruel operations of these patriarchal assumptions by relating the story of Amal Musairati, a 16-year-old

Palestinian girl from the Israeli-Arab town of Ramleh, who was severely beaten by her brother because he felt shamed by the fact that his sister was romantically involved with a man. Makiya also quoted Tamam Faheela, a 30-year-old Palestinian nurse:

> When a girl is born in an Arab home it is a disaster. The discrimination starts from the moment the girl is born. The message she is impregnated with is that her body is a sin. The prohibitions start in childhood. It is forbidden to play with the boys, forbidden to wear shorts or sit comfortably. She must be modest and quiet so not to arouse anyone sexually. It is a terrible fear (p. 630).

With women's bodies objectified this way as the source of all family honor, female independence obviously threatens traditional cultural values. Yet these values and the cruelty toward women they produce are oppressive and intolerable. Unfortunately, they reflect the unique historical experience of much of Middle Eastern culture, and outside cultures may not impose their own values under the rubric that "might makes right." Only a critique and internal struggle in Arabic communities against a specific socio-historical social development can revise barbarous traditions thereby transforming the personal as well as the political. As more and more Arab women escape, refuse to obey their fathers, insist upon choosing their husbands, join political organizations, do community work, and challenge the basis for cruel cultural assumptions, they critically challenge the historically developed traditional male-dominated Arab culture while simultaneously transforming their own ideas about ethics and morality.

This struggle goes forward as a specific historical project. For those outside or inside of this culture to claim the old ways are simply the ways that Arab-Islamic cultures organize their lives and that they are cultural characteristics beyond critique is to condone historical reification, a cynical and destructive relativism, a brutish patriarchy, and cruel practices against women. It will simply not do for us only to say that Afghanistan performs judicial amputations but Europeans do not; that Iraq sponsors state rape but Greece does not; that in parts of Arabia clitorectomies are performed but in Latin America they are not; and that these are the values of these societies and we should respect them for being diverse cultural values. Such an insidious and cynical relativism capitulates to historical brutality and suppresses humanity. Rather the people of these cultures and throughout the world must understand the unique historical basis for such practices and struggle against them as inhumane and unacceptable. They must critically and historically challenge the hallowed assumptions that perpetuate them. Only in this way can we discard the cultural baggage that burdens humanity.

The 1949 Geneva Convention specifies that "torture or inhuman treatment and willfully causing great suffering or serious injury to body and health" can all be deemed war crimes. Under a 1977 protocol, "inhuman and degrading practices involving outrages upon personal dignity, based on racial discrimination" also became war crimes. Accordingly, the human mind can rationally judge the use of rape by the Iraqi leadership to achieve political ends as inhuman treatment. No room for cultural relativism exists here. The world has pronounced itself on human oppression and prohibits it. Moreover, the protocol makes military commanders with information about such crimes punishable "if they did not take all feasible measures within their power to prevent or suppress" them. These documents clearly enunciate global procedures for assuring that crimes against humanity do not go unpunished.

All cultures suffer from the debilitating effects of homophobia, racism, sociocentricity, and sexism. We must all bring our critical thinking to bear on the historical cultural assumptions that guide many of our actions, questioning the origin of these assumptions, the evidence on which they are based, the implications of their practice, and the interests they serve. By engaging in critical cultural examinations, we can determine what is unjust in our cultural assemblage; we can move toward a more rational appreciation of the limitations of our cultural backgrounds; and we can thus assure that our struggle for human dignity against the forces of oppression succeeds. In this way we avoid becoming the servants of an unquestioned culture, but instead conscious protagonists in the construction of rational and compassionate culture and morality.

A Penultimate Word

The fundamental purpose for providing students with opportunities to reason within diverse points of view is to equip them to make independent and intelligent decisions and engage in a praxis on personal and social issues that go beyond rhetoric, propagandizing, authoritarian manipulation, and socio-centric racist and sexist thinking. To make reflective personal and social decisions, decisions critically examined in light of the evidence advanced in their support requires entering into the logic of contrary, often oppositional points of view. This reconciliation—this need to reconsider one's own thinking in light of the evidence that supports or undermines it—is the key to an autonomous development of democratic decision making and citizenship, the resolution of personal and social problems, and worthwhile social action and public policy. It is a pedagogical promise to make democracy more than simply a cheerful slogan masking unworkable political systems and institutions. Rather it calls for the democratization of thinking and a sense of personal and social ethics and character. John Dewey (1916) understood pedagogy as the need to foster democratic thinking about culture:

> But social efficiency as an educational purpose should mean a cultivation of power to join freely and fully in shared or common activities. This is impossible without culture, while it brings a reward in culture, because one cannot share in intercourse with others without learning— without getting a broader point of view and perceiving things of which one would otherwise be ignorant. And there is perhaps no better definition of culture than it is the capacity for constantly expanding the range and accuracy of one's perception of meaning (p. 145).

Dewey captured precisely what we educators for cultural citizenship desire—that our students begin critically to examine how they create meanings for themselves, how they represent themselves to others and the environment, and how they assemble meaning historically assembled within the discourse of domination. Yet when we ask ourselves how many opportunities students have to study historical figures like Ida B. Wells, whose courage and civic responsibility pushed our legislature to pass anti-lynching laws, or to examine movements of resistance, or to engage issues of domination and unity, the answer discourages. How can students learn to oppose intolerance, racism, discrimination, and inhumanity if they know nothing of the great movements of people who did just that? How can they recognize what it means to struggle socially and personally if they are unaware of social problems? How can they see critical participation in the reconstruction of self and society if they never learn about self relative to society?

I suggested here only a few important historical and contemporary figures and episodes for students and teachers to study. Teachers can easily find much more subject matter to use in the classroom. What teachers and students choose to focus on and how they select activities will reflect both their material and psychological lives. Citizenship education should avoid superficial add-ons in already superficial stuffed curricula; it should be more than a by-product of an already bankrupt social studies curriculum that seeks to establish a veneration for authority and a reverence for dominant modes of self-representation. Rather it should be the backbone of a critical pedagogy that welcomes critical social discourse. It should be an essential ingredient of education, a foundation upon which we build critical thinking.

When we reflect on our own morality and character we should ask ourselves how they were developed. We will come to see they were not handed to us by someone else; they cannot be packaged and sold as commodities. Anything authentic comes through reflection and action, internal and external dialogue, fair-mindedness and empathy, and a conscious entry into opposing points of view. Character is thus something achieved through involvement with reality within a definite historical setting. This objective involvement coupled with subjective thought on the part of the actor, the student, creates character and moral judgment. The more critical the thinking, the more developed the character. If we are to avoid the mistakes and failures of the past and develop critical active participation and reasoned judgment, we must begin to examine history with an eye to what constitutes the common struggle for human decency and what threatens to block human liberation. In short, we must foment intellectual courage in the interest of intellectual action.

Understanding how we and our students make sense of our lives and the lives of others requires us to engage in dialogical activities that expose disparate discourses on cultural issues of contemporary and historical concern for purposes of dialectical thinking and exploration. Understanding the subjective forms of political actualization requires a discourse that critically investigates how people have developed their lives, created histories, accreted literature, and composed and continue to compose their memories and narratives in the search for self-determination, social justice, and human dignity. This critical exploration should comprise the heart and soul of schooling today. In Henry Giroux's (1988) words,

> If we treat the histories, experiences and languages of different cultural groups as particularized forms of production, it becomes less difficult to understand the diverse readings, responses, and behaviors that, let's say, students exhibit to an analysis of a particular classroom text (pp. 105–106).

A cultural pedagogy requires a critical discourse attentive to the histories, dreams, and experiences that diverse students bring to school. By starting with these subjective forms, critical educators can develop a pedagogy that confirms while it engages contradictory forms of cultural experience that constitute how students produce meanings that legitimate and negate particular forms of life. Furthermore, well-structured critical activities can help students gain insights into the affective domain of thinking—that is, learn the importance of independent thought, empathy, and civility while gaining an insight into egocentricity, sociocentricity, racism, sexism, and homophobic thinking and behavior.

Investigating and illuminating the elements of self-production that distinguish individuals of diverse cultures are more than merely sophisticated methods for confirming the experience of students hushed by an ascendant culture; they are also parts of a authentic discourse that interrogates how power, authority, dependent thinking, and social inequality structure the ideologies and practices that sometimes encourage and sometimes restrain a student's critical cognizant development around issues of class, race, sexual preference, and gender. With knowledge, social progress, morality, and values are all bound up together, knowledge becomes the central component of the decision-making process. The acquisition of cultural knowledge-gender, socioeconomic, racial, and sexual knowledge—produces effective democratic thinking and democratic life in a pluralistic democracy. How we acquire this knowledge and whether what we acquire is indeed knowledge—the result of our critical thinking—will characterize our development as human beings and the systems we adopt to advance our social and private agendas.

One rarely gains a knowledge of others through exposure alone. It requires an examination of the logic of the points of view advanced—both a cognitive and affective exploration into self and others. Without the knowledge of diversity, we lose opportunities to know ourselves, a knowledge that could free us from unexamined biases and psychological and material bondage. Lacking significant opportunities to reason from other cultural points of view, both students and teachers lose any chance to redefine their own individuality thorough a critical dismantling of the myths that define them.

Chapter 7

Redefining Knowledge and Vision: The Implications of Critical Multicultural Literacy

> The materialist doctrine that men are products of circumstances and upbring-
> ing, and that, therefore, changed men are products of other circumstances
> and changed upbringing, forgets that it is men that change circumstances and
> that the educator himself needs educating.
>
> —Karl Marx and Frederich Engels,
> *Selected Works*

This book puts forth my vision of a compassionate and just curriculum founded on principles of dialogical and dialectical cultural, economic, and social critique. It presupposes a commitment to both personal and political change; accordingly, it offers implications for
educators willing to labor within its paradigms. It is hardly a complete
treatment of a dauntingly complex and important subject. It is, however, built on the premise that as educators we must create a new
culture and a new contemporary history. It carries my own pledge to
revitalize and embrace the best historical moments of our past in service of a more humane and equitable future for all citizens and all
children. As a result, the ideas expressed here challenge the structures
and routines of current educational theory and practice in the interest
of fashioning a new praxis. They challenge us to turn our exercises
into vigorous intellectual practices, and thus define our role and function as, in Gramsci's (1971) expression, "organic intellectuals." This
transformation is difficult today as humanistic intellectuals find themselves pushed aside in favor of technical intellectuals. Those of us who
labor within such traditional institutions as school districts, community colleges, and multi-versities find ourselves increasingly marginalized
and increasingly supplanted by a rational technical discourse that rein-

forces the class system and the privatization of everyday life. As our vision and work receives less and less credence, we face real demoralization and pain. As we witness the few remaining spheres come of public expression besieged by the forces of marketization and commodification, we can hardly help our melancholy and discouragement. As we observe the devastation done to our children; the decay of our urban centers; increasing drug addiction; the debasement and demoralization of the family; increased racism, sexism, sexual intolerance, and ethical, moral, and economic decay, we find ourselves beyond disheartened, numbed. Yet, as Cornel West (1993) insists, in order to understand the phenomenon of social and personal spiritual decay, we must come to understand the market civilization within which we live and its culture of consumption—a culture that more and more relies on stimulation, and especially sexually and drug-induced stimulation, as a way of defining self.

Rapacious consumerism breeds an individualism separated from community and increasingly dependent on market forces and privatization as more and more sectors of our society surrender to national and multinational corporations. The undermining of commitment and ethics proceeds as commodification, while a rampant consumerism defines a more insidious individualism owing allegiance to self as prosperity and prosperity as self. Those of us who call ourselves humanistic educators and intellectuals increasingly wonder what to do to survive mentally, emotionally, scholastically, and economically within our shrinking confines. No pat answers, no quick fixes exist; yet we can refer to some naked truths.

For one thing, we must build infrastructures to sustain our struggles by developing broad-based coalitions if we are to survive individually while helping to create a more humanistic society. The control and exercise of power is so centralized and vast that only united coalitions can redefine and create new forms of personal endurance, educational equity, economic justice, and political democracy. These coalitions must be diverse, reflecting the pluralism of our society. If they grow and strengthen these coalitions will reflect our willingness to confront and overcome sexism, homophobia, and racism, now so heavily ingrained in the American system and way of life.

We will not, I submit, be able to rely on multinational corporations to change the plight of the underclass and provide educational leadership and equity for our children. Their agenda is clear: the accumulation of greater profits in an era of global depression and economic downsizing. Nor will the dwindling middle class attend to the plight of the homeless, the poor, and the disenfranchised. To begin with, we lack evidence that the middle class has the desire, let alone the political, intellectual, or economic means, to set an agenda and carry it out. The answer lies in the public sphere, and we see this sphere attacked daily by the forces of reaction.

The task before educators is to embrace a sense of historical certitude and engage our students in critical social and personal discourse around issues of power, authority, sexism, racism, homophobia, and social class. This task is particularly compelling for those of us who work in the elementary and middle grades, for in these grades children often learn uncritically to internalize the dominant culture of social reality. Yet if we are to embrace even some of the ideas I put forth here, we must recognize the far-reaching implications both for ourselves as intellectuals, and for the institution of education in general. For example, can we use the current designs built as they are around fragmented and skill-driven disciplines? Or should we struggle for their abandonment and seek pedagogical redefinition? David Purple (1989) perceptively characterized the current design of schooling this way:

> The major difficulty with the basic design resides exactly in its hegemonic character and its sense of inevitability and permanence. The design has been with us so intimately that we find it difficult to imagine any way of organizing educational experiences other than through the medium of courses in disciplines and subjects. Indeed, as I have tried to show, these disciplines have led some of us to an idolatrous posture in which we are prepared to devote our lives to their preservation and continuing existence. Just as it is difficult for us to think about education apart from schools, it is equally difficult for us to think about curriculum without regard to subjects. This, as I have indicated, amounts to another dimension of our technological orientation in that our rhetoric speaks to an educational system focused on the study of techniques and forms (p. 152).

Although most progressive educators agree on the inadequacy of current educational designs, we are often at odds over a praxis designed to redefine and restructure them. Some, like Paul, promote the infusion of thinking activities within the current educational design arguing with some merit that all teachers must work with lesson plans within the current structure and that these plans can be remodeled to promote thinking in any discipline. Others, like Ivan Illich and Howard Gardner, claim that abandoning the current curriculum constructs for promising alternatives would lead to authentic designs aimed at appreciation of humanity and the human condition. They would reject the notion that we can institutionalize critical discourse within current educational configurations. At best, they believe, critical thinking under these conditions amounts to mere clandestine activity within the parameters of the existing structure. The current commodification of critical thinking activities by educational companies marketing their wares confirms the enormous capacity of capitalism for absorbing its own critique.

I advocate centering a curriculum on questions, issues, and moral claims as opposed to rigid disciplines that fragment and isolate thinking. Centering a curriculum on issues of historical and contemporary concerns demands a critical sense of reading, writing, speaking, listening, and role playing about issues of multilogical and monological concerns. Students in the early grades can learn reading and writing skills within a body of thinking activities built around relevant questions at issue, rather than reasoning activities built around trivial pursuits. A curriculum built around questions at issue invites teachers and students to adjust their thinking as they acquire knowledge. Such a curriculum unifies and consults the other disciplines, according to the question at issue, and it presents reality as interdisciplinary and holistic.

Whether we argue for infusion or abandonment as educational redefinition, at the very least, we can point to some requisites to nourish if we are to organize a curriculum around morality, social justice, critical questions, dilemmas, and issues.

The Orientation of Disciplines

A curriculum organized around questions at issue concerned with critical discourse and collaborative problem solving requires lengthy teacher discussions with children and opportunities for the children to engage in collaborative Socratic activities among and between themselves. Current educational designs oriented around disciplines and time constraints preclude anything more than superficial discussion—forcing both the teacher and students to bend to the pedagogical clock. Rarely, if ever, do students and teachers receive enough time to engage in critical examination, insightful analysis and exploration, and well-reasoned argumentation before they hurtle headlong into the next subject. Interdisciplinary understanding and structural and curricular redesign must take their places in any meaningful educational endeavor if students are to have the time to engage in critical thinking, see the connections between disciplines, and perceive the artificiality of their persistent fragmentation, especially in the elementary grades where teachers must separate and teach up to a dozen subjects each day.

Curriculum Planning

Teachers must be granted paid time to plan lessons that create a critical discourse focused on questions or problems. As constituted, the structures fail to give elementary teachers any preparation time to construct lessons. Until they have the reimbursed time to reflect on the nature of their educational mission and construct critical activities for their students, they will either continue to rely on inadequate texts and discipline-centered activities, or labor on their own time at home or after school—a commitment few teachers can currently afford.

Teacher Training

I have already discussed the overall lack of adequate teacher training. Yet before we can expect teachers to actualize themselves as intellectuals, we must establish critical and compassionate teacher training programs that offer opportunities for teachers to reflect on their vocation and help them develop problem-centered activities in concert with other teachers and students. Teachers must come to understand principles and strategies of critical thinking within a curriculum focused on disenfranchised narratives, historical and contemporary questions, and social critique—a curriculum where students learn to reason within various culturally informed points of view on issues of authority, power, injustice, racism, sexism, homophobia, social class, and particular historical and contemporary struggles against oppression. Teachers should come to see their role as political, and sound teacher training programs should erase the idea that teachers are neutral disseminators and their curricula are politically detached and fragmented into false domains. Current teacher training programs are so antiquated and so morally and intellectually bankrupt, that many new teachers graduate without having even been exposed to many of the seminal works cited in this book. Without an intellectual culture and environment where teachers can work collaboratively through critical issues of importance to both themselves and the students they serve, we can hardly expect them to sustain effective discourse and activities within their classrooms.

Texts and Other Resources

This book thoroughly discussed the failures of contemporary texts. With multinational corporations responsible for the content, manufacturing and distribution of these texts, teachers can be sure that the ascendant curriculum will dominate the discourse and that disenfranchised voices and memories will remain intentionally excluded. Teachers committed to a critical multicultural literacy find little use for textual representations that mimic the dominant culture. Any serious curriculum aimed at achieving justice, compassion, and liberation has no use for the current texts. We must find new texts that engage personal and moral dilemmas and critical questions and issues, and do so by embracing multiple perspective. Because the current texts perpetuate and disseminate the hidden curriculum of authority and power, teachers wanting to promote a critical multicultural literacy will require resources that reflect the issues I have emphasized. Currently, few resources are "question-at-issue based," and those that exist are usually the by-product of private market concerns with little interest in critical thinking or unmasking dominant discourse. Teachers will need a commitment to new resources if they expect to engage in an educational endeavor devoted to liberation. Too many teachers find themselves creating their own resources, often devoting the off-time hours searching for critical and developmentally appropriate literature and audiovisual resources, or in many cases, creating these resources from scratch. A commitment to a liberation education requires a pledge on behalf of educators to the development and availability of new educational tools.

Teacher Organizations

The teachers' unions in this country have, by and large, developed a vested interest in a system that does not serve the interests of teachers, students, or the community in general. I recognize the need for strong teacher organizations; however, I also see the need to reconstitute and resuscitate teacher unions in the service of those they are designed to serve. They must rededicate themselves to the bread-and-butter issues of raising teachers' salaries and protecting their benefits, yet of equal importance are the problems I discuss throughout this work. Furthermore, if teachers hope to engage in controversial discussions with students and to challenge traditional impressions of knowledge, they must have the support of their unions as they proceed. Many teachers, especially probationary employees, feel intimidated. They fear losing their jobs and as a result avoid engaging student thoughts on controversial issues. Union leadership must reflect an understanding of the importance of challenging the hidden curriculum and support teachers who engage their students in critical controversial discourse. Without union commitment and protection, few teachers will encourage the critical thinking of their students and instead will find economic security and comfort within the prevailing system.

Community Organizing

Together with redefining the nature of teachers' unions, I see a need to involve the community in the struggle for educational equity and curriculum redefinition and redesign. Educational equity cannot be realized within an inequitable social system; thus, we must struggle within our unions, collectives, and community organizations to develop broad coalitions that challenge unjust and inequitable structures of domination and power. Without effective community organizing that involves parents and the community at large, educational reform will proceed in traditional, comfortable ways. The movement beyond reform must embrace parents as accomplices in the educational struggle, forging a partnership that transcends existing parameters.

The Need to Resist Privatization

If we hope to maintain and strengthen the Jeffersonian vision of the "common school" available to all citizens, we must resist the beguiling movement to privatize schooling. Teacher unions and community coalitions must brace themselves to launch an all-out offensive against the pernicious destruction of public education by privatization and the so-called voucher system. The agenda, goals, and claims of the privatizing hucksters devoted to the elimination of public schools must be objects of critical scrutiny for purposes of public dissemination.

Epilogue

As citizens of this country, some of us have somehow fallen beyond the protection of liberty and others of us have never really enjoyed that protection. We have in many ways become ruthless protagonists in a social drama of economic and ethical decline. Yet we are more than simply economic units or human capital; we are human beings. If the Statue of Liberty, the icon of our country, is to remain the embodiment of lived reality for all citizens, if democracy is to be more than simply cynical rhetoric, we must have the courage and intellectual commitment to illuminate threats to freedom and struggle together to assure liberty's survival. Only concerted efforts grounded in prophetic hope can resurrect an idea that has recently degenerated into self-serving individuality and a battered ethic. The concept of hope is paramount here, for idealism breeds vision, and with vision comes possibility. On the other hand, despair and a lack of idealism breed personal and social myopia and a capitulation to despondency and demoralization leading to oppression or worse, authoritarianism. Hope is often elusive and difficult to sustain. Yet we must understand our struggle as historical, a struggle linked to larger, earlier commitments to the sustenance and preservation of human liberty, social and economic justice, and personal freedom. As Karl Marx said, "Up to now philosophers have only interpreted the world, our goal is to change it."

For the sake of society's children and for the sake of ourselves and future generations, we must remember these words as we move forward toward a liberation pedagogy.

References

Part One

Introduction

Adorno, T. W., Horkheimer, M. (1972). *The Dialectic of Enlightenment*. trans. John Cumming. New York. Seabury Press.

Amin, S. (1989). *Eurocentrism*. New York. Monthly Review Press. pp. 6, 7.

Baldwin, J. (1988). *A Talk to Teachers*. The Graywolf Annual Five: Multicultural Literacy. St. Paul. Graywolf Press. p. 28.

Banks, J. (Winter 1991) *Multicultural Education for Freedom's Sake*. Educational Leadership. pp. 32–35.

Birnbaum, N. (1993). *What Rough Beast Is Reborn? The Nation*, April 5, 1993. p. 441.

Freire, P. (1985). *The Politics of Education: Culture, Power, and Liberation*. South Hadley, MA. Bergin & Garvey. pp. 11, 54.

Giroux, H. A. (1988). *Teachers as Intellectuals: Toward a Critical Pedagogy of Learning*. South Hadley, MA. Bergin & Garvey. p. 132.

Giroux, H. A. (1985). *Theory and Resistance in Education*. South Hadley, MA. Bergin & Garvey. p. 163.

Green, M. (1988). *The Dialectic of Freedom*. New York. Teachers College Press. p. 89.

Lawday, D., Marks, J., Stille, A., Stanglin, D., Fisher, J. (1991). *No Immigrants Need Apply*. New York. *U.S. News and World Report*, December 9, 1991. pp. 46, 49.

Milgram, Stanley (1974). *Obedience to Authority: An Experimental View*. New York. Harper and Row.

Parekh, B. (1986). *The Concept of Multicultural Education: The Interminable Debate*. eds. S. Modgil, G. K. Verma, K. Mallick, and C. Modgil. PA. The Farmer Press. pp. 19–31.

Reich, W. (1946). *The Mass Psychology of Fascism.* Farrar, Straus, and Giroux.

Chapter One

D'Souza, D. (1991). *Illiberal Education: The Politics of Race and Sex on Campus.* New York. The Free Press. pp. 232–233.

Giroux, H. A. (1988). *Teachers as Intellectuals: Toward a Critical Pedagogy of Learning.* South Hadley, MA. Bergin & Garvey.

Giroux, H. A. (1985). *Theory and Resistance in Education.* South Hadley, MA. Bergin & Garvey.

Greene, M. (1988). *The Dialectic of Freedom.* New York. Teachers College Press.

Paul, R. (1990). *Critical Thinking: What Every Person Needs to Survive in a Rapidly Changing World.* The Center for Critical Thinking and Moral Critique, Sonoma State University. p. 320.

Stent, M., Hazard, W., & Rivlin, H. (Eds.). (1973). *Cultural Pluralism in Education: A Mandate for Change.* New York. Appleton-Century Crofts. p. 73.

Chapter Two

Amin, S. (1989). *Eurocentrism.* New York. Monthly Review Press. p. 72.

Costa, A. (1993). *How World Class Standards Will Change Us.* Alexandria, VA. Educational Leadership, February 1983. pp. 50, 51.

Feinberg, W. (1989). *Fixing the Schools.* in *Critical Pedagogy, the State, and Cultural Power.* eds. Henry Giroux and Peter McClaren Albany New York. State University of New York Press. p. 74

Freire, P. (1990). *Pedagogy of the Oppressed.* New York. Continuum Press. pp. 44, 54.

Freire, P. (1985). *The Politics of Education: Culture, Power, and Liberation.* South Hadley, MA. Bergin & Garvey. pp. 63, 105, 170.

Giroux, H. A. (1989). *Critical Pedagogy, the State, and Cultural Struggle.* Albany New York. State University of New York Press. pp. 130, 136, 143.

Gordon, L. (1991). *Helping Young Children Take the Offensive Against Offensive Toys.* ReThinking Schools. Milwaukee, WI. Vol. 6, No. 1. p. 19.

Greene, M. (1972). *And It Still Is News.* New York. Social Policy Magazine. pp. 135–136.

Guevara, C. (1968). *The Complete Bolivia Diaries of Che Guevara.*

Marcuse, H. (1941). *Reason and Revolution: Hegel and the Rise of Social Theory.* Boston. Beacon Press. pp. viii, xiii.

Marx, K. (1932). *Capital*. Chicago. Charles H. Kerr. pp. 102, 198.

National Commission on Excellence in Education. (1983). *A Nation at Risk*. Washington D.C. U.S. Government Printing Office.

Nin, A. (1983). *The Early Diary of Anais Nin*. pp. 138.

ReThinking Schools. (1992). *ReThinking Schools*. Milwaukee, WI. pp. 2, 6.

Weil, D. (1992). *Critical Thinking as a Developmental Necessity*. Think Magazine, April 1992. San Antonio, TX. pp. 12–16.

Chapter Three

Amin, S. (1989). *Eurocentrism*. New York. Monthly Review Press. p. 103

Austin, A. (1993). *Union Maid*. New York. Monthly Review Press. February 11 '93. Vol. 44. pp. 40–44.

Collins, P. (1992). *Learning to Think for Ourselves: Malcolm X's Black Nationalism Reconsidered*. in *Malcolm X: In Our Own Image*. Joe Wood, ed. New York. St. Martin's Press. pp. 59, 61.

Dewey, J. (1916). *Democracy and Education*. New York. Macmillan. pp. 16, 192.

Educators for Social Responsibility (1992). *Dealing With Differences: Conflict Resolution in Our Schools*. Cambridge, MA. p. 5.

Freire, P. (1990). *Pedagogy of the Oppressed*. New York. Continuum Press. pp. 57, 58, 62, 81, 118.

Freire, P. (1985). *The Politics of Education: Culture, Power, and Liberation*. South Hadley, MA. Bergin & Garvey. pp. 2, 3, 17, 22, 47, 53, 57.

Gardner, H. (1991). *The Unschooled Mind*. Basic Books. p. 48.

Giroux, H. A. (1988). *Teachers as Intellectuals: Toward a Critical Pedagogy of Learning*. South Hadley, MA. Bergin & Garvey. pp. 103, 104.

Giroux, H. A. (1985) *Theory and Resistance in Education*. South Hadley, MA. Bergin & Garvey. p. 42.

Grambs, J. (1972). *The Negro Self-Concept Reappraised*. In *Black-Self Concept*. New York. McGraw Hill Book Co. pp. 185.

Hegel, G. W. F. (1900). *Philosophy of History*. New York. Cooperative Publication Society. p. 65.

Hentoff, N. (1966). *Our Children Are Dying*. New York. Viking Press. p. 33.

Hunter, E. (1991). *Focus on Critical Thinking Skills Across the Curriculum*. NASSP-Bulletin. Vol. 75, 532. pp. 72–76.

Lipman, M. (1988). *Critical Thinking-What Can It Be?* Educational Leadership. September 1988. pp. 38–43.

Malcolm X., Haley, A. (1964). *The Autobiography of Malcolm X.* New York. Ballantine Books. p. 333.

Marx, K. *The Collected Works of Karl Marx and Fredrich Eagels.* International Publishers. New York. pp. 102, 198.

Paul, R. (1990). *Critical Thinking: What Every Person Needs to Survive in a Rapidly Changing Global World.* Center for Critical Thinking and Moral Critique. Sonoma State University Rohnert Park. pp. xvi, 2, 3, 9, 34, 35, 194, 196, 203, 270, 320, 362, 370, 391, 392.

Reich, W. (1948). *Listen Little Man.* Canada. Noonday Press. Farrar, Straus, & Giroux. pp. 30, 31.

Strom, M., Parsons, W. (1982). *Facing History and Ourselves: Holocaust and Human Behavior.* Watertown, MA. Intentional Educations, Inc. p. 4.

Sweezy, P. (1992). *The Theory of Capitalist Development.* Monthly Review. December, New York. pp. 15, 16.

Tavris, C. (1991). *Who Took the Grit Out of Self-Esteem.* The Los Angeles Times. September 16, 1991. p. 85.

Welch, S. (1985). in *The Principle of Hope, III.* ed Ernst Bloch. Cambridge, MA. MIT Press, 1985. pp. 1366–1367.

West, C. (1993). *Beyond Eurocentrism and Multiculturalism: Prophetic Thought in Post Modern Times.* Monroe, ME. p. 6.

Chapter Four

American Association of University Women. (June 1992). *Creating a Gender-Fair Multicultural Curriculum.* Washington D.C. pp. 2.

American Association of University Women. (1992). *The AAUW Report: How Schools Shortchange Girls.* Washington D.C. pp. 3, 5.

Amin, S. (1989). *Eurocentrism.* New York. Monthly Review Press. pp. vii, 73, 90, 108.

Asanti, M. (1991). *Multiculturalism: An Exchange.* The American Scholar. Summer, 1991. p. 270.

Beneke, T. (1992). *The Empire Strikes Back.* Berkeley, CA. Express Magazine. pp. 16–24.

Bowers, C. G. (1932). *Beveridge and the Progressive Era.* pp. 68–76

Byrnes, D. (Spring 1988). *Children and Prejudice.* Social Education, pp. 267–271.

CTA (1992). *California Teacher's Association Action.* November 1992. CA.

D'Aulaire, I. (1955). *Columbus.* New York. Doubleday. p. 16.

D'Souza, D. (1991). *Illiberal Education: The Politics of Race and Sex on Campus.* New York.The Free Press. pp. 230, 255, 256.

Fordham, S., Ogbu. J. (1986). *Black Students' School Success: Coping with the Burden of 'Acting White.'* The Urban Review. 18(3). pp. 1–31.

Gates, L. (April 1991). *Multicultural Education.* Time magazine. p. 16.

Hofstadter, R. (1948). *The American Political Tradition.* pp. 212, 213.

Homestead. (1982). Lakeside, CA. The Interact Company. pp. 2, 4, 7, 13, 14, 74.

Lifetouch Inc. (1992). *Multicultural Lesson Plans: Teacher's Guide.* Minneapolis, MN. pp. 14, 15.

Karp, S. (1991). *African American Immersion Schools.* Milwaukee, WI. ReThinking Schools. Vol. 5, No. 4. May/June 1991. p. 18.

Martinez, E. (Winter 1992–1993). *When Slavery is a "Lifestyle." What Happens to Mexicans?: How California Texts Portray Latinos.* Milwaukee, WI. ReThinking Schools. pp. 10, 11.

Mercer, J. (1990). *Multiethnic Education: Practices and Promises.* Phi Delta Kappa Bloomington, IN. Educational Foundation. pp. 13, 14, 25, 32.

Moody, J. (1910) *The Railroad Builders.* p. 188.

Murrell, P. (1993). *Afrocentric Immersion.* as published in *Freedom's Plow.* ed. Theresa Perry and James Fraser. New York. Routledge Press. pp. 233, 237.

Oakland Unified School District (1990). *Africa: A Culture Kit.* Oakland, CA. p. 2.

Osborne, M. P. (1987). *The Story of Christopher Columbus: Admiral of the Ocean Sea.* New York. Dell. p. 3.

Perry, I. (1993). *I Am Still Thirsty: A Theorization on the Authority and Cultural Location of Afrocentrism.* as published in *Freedom's Plough.* ed. Theresa Perry and James Fraser. New York. Routledge Press. p. 268.

Roosevelt, T. (1916). *Fear God and Take Your Own Part.* pp. 56–57.

Roosevelt, T. (1905). *The Winning of the West.* pp. 1–4.

Sharing Our Diversity. (1976). *The Mexican American: Level 2.* Sacramento City Unified School District, Sacramento, CA. pp. 189, 252.

Scherer, M. (1991,1992). *School Snapshot: Focus on African-American Culture.* Educational Leadership. December 1991/January 1992. p. 17.

Tawney, R. H. (l954). *Religion and the Rise of Capitalism.* p. 99.

Taylor, J. (1991). *Down With PC.* Utne Reader, July/August 1991. p. 50.

Time Magazine. (April 22, 1992) p. 16.

Wasserman, H. (1972). *Harvey Wasserman's History of the United States*. New York. Harper & Row. pp. 43, 47, 55, 70, 71.

Part Two

Introduction

West, C. (1993). *Beyond Eurocentrism and Multiculturalism: Prophetic Thought in PostModern Times*. Monroe, ME. Common Courage Press. pp. 4, 5, 8.

Chapter Five

American Association of University Women (June 1992). *Creating a Gender-Fair Multicultural Curriculum*. Washington D.C. pp. 1, 2.

American Teacher (1992,1993). *Pulling the Pin on School Violence. Learning to Teach in the Inner City*. Washington D.C. December 1992/January 1993 Volume 77, No. 4. pp. 6, 8, 14.

American Teacher (1993). Washington, D.C. May/June 1993. p. 14.

Arnez, N. (l972). *Enhancing the Black Self-Concept Through Literature*. in *Black Self-Concept*. ed. James A. Banks. New York. McGraw Hill Book Co. 102, 110.

Banks, J. A. (1990). *Citizen Education for a Pluralistic Democratic Society*. Social Studies, Vol. 81. pp. 210–214.

Bond, Horace Mann (1934) *The Education of the Negro in the American Social Order*. New York. Octagon Books. pp. 12, 13, 490.

Boyer, E. L. (1983). *High School: A Report on Secondary Education in America*. New York. Carnegie Foundation on the Advancement of Teaching. pp. 143.

California Association of Bilingual Educators (Spring 1992). *Meeting the Challenge of Language Diversity*. CABE Post-conference Newsletter. pp. 19–22.

California Teachers Association (1992) ACTION. December, 1992.

California Tomorrow (1992). *Teacher's Voices from California Classrooms. Embracing Diversity*. San Francisco, CA. pp. 1–13.

Charters, W. W. (l933) *Curriculum Construction*. New York. The Macmillan Company. p. 9.

Dewey, J. (1916) *Democracy and Education*. New York Macmillan. pp. 13, 80.

Economic and Budget Outlook (1992). Office of Management and Budget. Washington, D.C. 94–98.

Educational Leadership (December 1992/January 1993). B. R. Wager, p. 35.

Feinberg, W. (1989). *Fixing the Schools*. in *Critical Pedagogy the State and Cultural Struggle*. eds. Henry Giroux and Peter McLaren. New York. State University of New York Press. p. 75.

Fine, M. (1989). *Silencing and Nurturing Voice in an Improbable Context: Urban Adolescents in Public School*. in *Critical Pedagogy, the State, and Cultural Power*. eds. Henry Giroux and Peter McLaren. State University of New York Press. pp. 158, 163, 164, 165, 169.

Freire, P. (1985). *The Politics of Education: Culture, Power, and Liberation*. South Hadley, MA. Bergin & Garvey. pp. 22, 23.

Gabelko, N. (1981). *Reducing Adolescent Prejudice*. New York. Teachers College Press.

Gintis, H. (1973). *Toward a Political Economy of Education: A Radical Critique of Ivan Illich's DeSchooling Society*. in *After DeSchooling What?* ed. Alan Gartner, Colin Greer, and Frank Riessman. New York. Harper and Row. pp. 69.

Giroux, H. A. (1988). *Teachers as Intellectuals: Toward a Critical Pedagogy of Learning*. South Hadley, MA. Bergin and Garvey Publishers. pp. 4, 9, 102, 103, 126.

Giroux, H. A. (1989). *Critical Pedagogy, the State, and Cultural Power*. State University of New York Press. p. 243.

Grambs, J. (1972). *The Negro Self-Concept Reappraised*. in *Black-Self Concept*. ed. James A. Banks. New York. McGraw Hill Book Co. p. 207.

Harty, S. (1981). *Hucksters in the Classroom*. Social Policy. Vol. 12, No. 2, pp. 38–39.

Hentoff, N. (1966). *Our Children Are Dying*. New York. Viking Press. pp. 13, 14, 30, 46, 47, 50, 117, 132.

Illich, I. (1970). *DeSchooling Society*. New York. Harper and Row. pp. 23, 24, 45.

Kozol, J. (1991). *Savage Inequalities*. New York. Harper Collins. pp. 5, 17, 21, 55, 58, 59, 63.

Krashen, S. (1988). *On Course: Bilingual Education's Success in California*. The California Association of Bilingual Education.

Lovin, R. (1988). *The School and the Articulation of Values*. The American Journal of Education. February. pp. 143–161.

Lowe, R. (1992). *The Hollow Promise of School Vouchers. ReThinking Schools: False Choices*. Milwaukee, WI. pp. 3, 27.

Moe, T., Chubb, J. (1990). *Politics, Markets, and America's Schools*. The Brookings Institute. Washington, D.C.

Moore, A. (1970). *The Inner City High School, Instructional and Community Roles.* in *Reaching the Disadvantaged Learner.* ed. Harry Passow. New York. Teachers College. pp. 203, 225.

National Association for the Education of Young Children (1992). *Teaching Young Children to Resist Bias: What Parents Can Do.* Washington D.C., p. 1.

National Commission on Excellence in Education. (1983). *A Nation at Risk.* Washington D.C. U.S. Government Printing Office.

Parsons, T. (1972). *The Black Revolution and Education.* in *Black Self-Concept.* ed. James A. Banks. New York. McGraw Hill Book Co. p. 46.

Reich, R. (Autumn 1992). *Business Talks Big, Does Little.* Milwaukee, WI. Rethinking Schools. p. 6.

ReThinking Schools. (1992). Milwaukee, WI. p. 7.

Romanish, B. (1992). *Empowering Teachers: Restructuring Schools for the 21st. Century.* University Press of America. p. 27.

Smith, D. (1972). *The Black Revolution and Education.* In *Black Self-Concept.* ed. James A. Banks. New York. McGraw Hill Book Co. p. 46.

Tanzer, M. (1992). *After Rio.* November. Monthly Review. pp. 9, 10.

Wall Street Journal. (1993). May, 5. New York. p. B2.

Welch, S. (1985). in *The Principle of Hope, III.* ed. Ernst Bloch. Cambridge, MA. MIT Press. pp. 1366–1367.

Wigginton, E.. (1985). *Sometimes a Shining Moment.* New York. Anchor Press. Doubleday. pp. 72, 35.

Chapter Six

Adamic, L. (1958). *Dynamite: The Story of Class Violence in America.* p. 126.

Amin, S. (1989). *Eurocentrism.* New York. Monthly Review Press. p. 104.

Bales, C. A. (1972). *Kevin Cloud: Chippewa in the City.* Chicago. Reilly and Lee Books.

Banks, J. A. (1991). *Teaching Strategies for Ethnic Studies.* New York. Allyn & Bacon. pp. 32, 86, 87, 160, 161, 212, 216, 258, 261, 271.

Banks, J. A. (1990). *Citizen Education for a Pluralistic Democratic Society.* Social Studies, 81. pp. 210–214.

Bean, Benneth, R. (1932). *The Races of Man: Differentiation and Disposition of Man.* New York. University Society. pp. 94–95.

Bennet, L. (1967). *Black Power: The Human Side of Reconstruction.* p. 40.

Bigelow, B. (1992). *Two Myths Are Not Better than One.* Monthly Review. p. 28.

Bonacich, E. (1991). Los Angeles Times. November, 1991. B5.

Bruce, P. (B. (1905). *The Rise of the New South*. p. 427.

Buckmaster, H. (1966). *The Seminole Wars*. New York. Collier.

California Tomorrow. (1992). *Teacher's Voices from California Classrooms*. Embracing Diversity. Santa Cruz pp. 1–13.

Christensen, L. (May\June 1991). *Unlearning the Myths that Bind Us*. Milwaukee, WI. Rethinking Schools. p. 15.

Cochran, T. C., Miller, W. (1961). *The Age of Enterprise*. p. 264.

Coleman, M. (1930). *Eugene V. Debs: A Man Unafraid*. p. 249.

Costa, A. (February 1993). *How World Class Standards Will Change Us*. Alexandria, VA. Educational Leadership. pp. 50, 51.

Crossing Swords. (1988, 1990). Sarah J. Hale High School. New York. pp. 77, 125.

Davis, A. (1992). *Meditations on the Legacy of Malcolm X*. in *Malcom X in Our Own Image*. ed. Joe Wood. New York. St. Martin's Press. pp. 45–46.

Dewey, J. (1916). *Democracy and Education*. New York. Macmillan. p. 145.

DuBois, W.E.B. (1924). *Diuturni Silenti*. in *The Education of Black People*. pp. 50–54.

Fanon, F. (1968). *The Wretched of the Earth*. New York. Monthly Review Press. pp. 52, 128.

Fine, M. (1992). *Facing History and Ourselves: Portrait of a Classroom*. Educational Leadership. December/January 1992. pp. 46, 47, 48.

Fine, M. (1989). *Silencing and Nurturing Voice in an Improbable Context: Urban Adolescents in Public School*. in *Critical Pedagogy, the State, and Cultural Power*. ed. H. Giroux. State University of New York Press. p. 172.

Fish, B. (1971). *Eskimo Boy Today*. Anchorage, Alaska: Alaska Northwest Publishing Co.

Freire, P. (1990). *Pedagogy of the Oppressed*. New York. Continuum Press. pp. 27, 32, 33.

Fromm, E. (1966). *The Heart of Man*. New York. p. 41.

Garaty, J. (1966). *The American Nation*. in *H. Wasserman's History of the United States*. New York. Harper Colophon. p. 484

Garcia, M. (1987). *The Adventures of Connie and Diego*. San Francisco, CA. Children's Book Press.

Giroux, H. A. (1988). *Teachers as Intellectuals: Toward a Critical Pedagogy of Learning*. South Hadley, MA. Bergin & Garvey. pp. 105, 106.

Kadetsky, E. (April 19, 1993). *High-Tech's Dirty Little Secret.* New York. The Nation. Vol. 256, No. 215. pp. 517–520.

Kim, E. C. (September 1993). *Toward a Cord of Solidarity: Progressive Social Change in the 1990's.* New York. Monthly Review. pp. 54–55.

Law and a Free Society. (1986). *Authority.* Calabasas, CA. p. 15.

LeSourd, S. J. (1991) *Integrating Pluralistic Values for Reconstructing Society.* Social Education. Vol. 55, January 1991. pp. 52–54.

Loewen, J. (November 1992). *The Truth About the First Thanksgiving.* New York. Monthly Review. pp. 21, 22.

Makiya, K. (May 10, 1993). *Rape in Service of the State.* New York: The Nation, pp. 628–630.

Moment. (1992). *Reframing Resistance: Images and Stories of Hope.* Ontario, Canada.

Nash, G.B., Weiss, R. (1970). *The Great Fear.* p. 115.

The Nation magazine (May 10, 1993) New York. p. 629.

Njeri, I. (Nov. 29, 91). *Perspective on Race Relations: Power Elite Turns Out a Bitter Brew.* The Los Angeles Times. pp. B5.

Platt, A.M. (1990). *Racism in Academia: Lessons from the Life of E. Franklin Frazier.* New York. Monthly Review. September 1990. p. 45.

Riis, J. (1957). *How the Other Half Lives.* p. 35.

Sleeper, M, Stern, M., Zabierek, H. (November 1990) *Facing History and Ourselves.* Educational Leadership. Vol. 48, No. 3. pp. 2.

Stoskopf, A. (Fall 1991). *Examining Historical Roots to Racism and Anti-Semitism: A Profile of Facing History's Research. Facing History and Ourselves News.* Brookline, MA. p. 14.

Tran-Khanh-Tuyet (1987). *The Little Weaver of Thai-Yen Village.* Children's Book Press. San Francisco, CA.

Wasserman, H. (1972). *The History of the United States.* New York. Harper Colophon Books. pp. 71, 79, 81, 85, 89, 91, 106, 107, 113, 152.

West, C. (1993). *Beyond Eurocentrism and Multiculturalism: Prohetic Thought in Postmodern Times.* Monroe, ME. Common Courage Press. p. 20.

West, C. (1991). *Ethical Dimensions of Marxist Thought.* New York: Monthly Review Press. pp. xiii, 10.

Woodward, C.V. (1951). *Origins of the New South.* p. 270.

Yashima, T. (1955). *Crow Boy.* New York. Puffin Books.

Chapter Seven

Gramsci, A. (1971). *Selections from the Prison Notebooks*. New York. International Publishers. p. 3

Marx, K. *The Collected Works of Karl Marx and Fredrich Engels*. New York International Publishers. p. 85

Purple, D. (1989). *The Moral and Spiritual Crisis in Education*. New York. Bergin & Garvey. p. 152.

West, C. (1993). *Beyond Eurocentrism and Multiculturalism: Prophetic Thought in PostModern Times*. Monroe, MN. Common Courage Press. p. 148.

Studies in the Postmodern Theory of Education

General Editors
Joe L. Kincheloe & Shirley R. Steinberg

Counterpoints publishes the most compelling and imaginative books being written in education today. Grounded on the theoretical advances in criticalism, feminism and postmodernism in the last two decades of the twentieth century, Counterpoints engages the meaning of these innovations in various forms of educational expression. Committed to the proposition that theoretical literature should be accessible to a variety of audiences, the series insists that its authors avoid esoteric and jargonistic languages that transform educational scholarship into an elite discourse for the initiated. Scholarly work matters only to the degree it affects consciousness and practice at multiple sites. Counterpoints' editorial policy is based on these principles and the ability of scholars to break new ground, to open new conversations, to go where educators have never gone before.

For additional information about this series or for the submission of manuscripts, please contact:

Joe L. Kincheloe & Shirley R. Steinberg
637 West Foster Avenue
State College, PA 16801